LIVING THE LIFE

A COMPANION BOOK

WRITTEN BY
JULES WILLIAMS

First edition published in 2012 by Backdoor Production and Management Ltd.
Pinewood Studios
Pinewood Road, Iver Heath
Buckinghamshire
England SL0 0NH

Written by Jules Williams

Creative Director Rosemary Reed

Published by Backdoor Production and Management Ltd.

Butler Tanner & Dennis
Caxton Road, Frome
Somerset, BA11 1NF

Distributed by Tesco Entertainment

A catalogue record for this book is available from the British Library

ISBN 978-0-9571170-0-6

DEDICATION

Helloooo. I was initially approached to participate as a contributor in 'Living the Life' and yet, very quickly found myself immersed in a producer's role for what I consider truly wonderful television.

It has been a long time since I have felt so passionately about a project. I have been fortunate to have enjoyed a sustained and varied career, yet from the day I filmed the pilot episode with Robin (Gibb), something about the intention and overall 'feel' of the show moved me deeply, and I knew it was something I really wanted to be a part of.

It has been a pleasure to have been on set as our multifarious contributors shared intimately and honestly about their lives. The simple premise of omitting an interviewer may sound of little consequence, yet the many resulting nuances have reaped rich conversational rewards.

I wish to thank all the Back Door Production team, the numerous crew that were employed throughout the series and of course our contributors, many of whom are long standing friends and others who have become so. Finally a heartfelt thank you to those of you who have followed the series and have enjoyed it enough to open this book, you have made an old (ish) man very happy.

Leslie Phillips

Director/Producer Jules Williams (left) with Joanna Lumley

WELCOME

Welcome to this companion book for the Television series 'Living the Life.' A labour of love, this book will guide you through all 14 filmed episodes of the show, and offer intriguing insights into each pairing's behind the scenes day of filming...the introductions, the venue, the bits left on the cutting room floor, and also the common ground, coincidences and patterns that emerged over the whole series.

The book includes never before seen photographs of the well known personalities on set and also complements many of the anecdotes described between the pages.

Having directed the shows, and endured extensive hours in the editing suite, I have still not tired of the episodes. I feel that being able to stand up to repeated viewing speaks volumes for the lasting quality of 'Living the Life.'

Companion as a label for this book says it all – *A mate or match; assisting in the capacity of a helpful friend.*

Echoing Leslie's sentiments about the production team and crew, particularly our Technical Producers (Guillem Santapau & Meryem Mehmet) and Co-Producer Caroline de Wolfe, whose specialised assistance and creative passion helped make the project possible, and of course Executive Producer Rosemary Reed, an amazing 'tour de force' who worked tirelessly in achieving the (almost) impossible in bringing the whole series to fruition.

I would also like personally to thank the contributors who were all 'stand out' professionals and very giving of their hearts and their time. With such esteemed individuals with such rich and bounteous lives, it made my job a lot easier to remain in the background with limited interference.

We hope you enjoy reading about the series as much as we enjoyed making it.

CONTENTS

1

INTRODUCTION

THE BIRTH OF LIVING THE LIFE – Rosemary Reed, the Executive Producer of the series, had long felt disenchanted when watching so called celebrity (more on that word later in the book) interviews. Of late, they seemed to fall into two categories; the standard televised 'sound byte' that was driven by the latest book/album/movie promotion or personality interviewers, with a need to self-publicise or hijack proceedings in the name of entertainment.

What was missing, and excited Rosemary and co-producer Caroline de Wolfe, was to bring together two legendary characters and gently guide them to share about their personal and professional lives, with no product to sell and no interviewer's ego hampering 'the stories.' Rosemary was also keenly aware that this approach would deliver a more heartfelt, revelatory and emotionally intelligent show than the other approaches.

Rosemary and her director Jules Williams set about bringing together the contributors in the right pairings and also the right environment. The pairings for our first series – which you may have already seen televised or on DVD, were not just random couplings but guided by our sensitivity to the nature of the show – which was a non-salacious, intelligent sharing by both personalities in a safe and trusted environment.

For example, on the surface Stephen Fry might look a slightly skewed match with Bill Wyman, but Stephen is, in fact, an avid Rolling Stones fan and both of them love their cricket. More importantly Stephen, renowned for his intellectual prowess, illuminated the viewer to the similar capacity for facts that Bill has. Bill is a remarkable archivist and can pin point times, dates and events at an amazing rate of instant recall. Hence a show is born and a template formed.

Each of the following chapters of this book will revisit the day's filming – how the pair came together, what it was like before filming began, what ended up on the cutting room floor and the miscellany that ties it all together.

Co-producer Caroline de Wolfe, Director/Producer, Jules Williams and Executive Producer Rosemary Reed

STEPHEN FRY

Stephen Fry is one of our best-loved and most interesting personalities, known for his quick wit and extraordinarily diverse range of talents. Having been part of early comedy classics like 'Blackadder' and 'Jeeves and Wooster,' he was also acclaimed early in his career for his writing skills, penning the story for 'Me and My Girl,' and going on to write numerous novels and non-fiction books.

Bill Wyman is the legendary musical impresario who found fame as the bass player in what is considered to be the greatest rock band of all time, 'The Rolling Stones.' He has recorded and toured with Bill Wyman's 'Rhythm Kings,' produced and scored for Television and Film, and is a successful restaurateur, not to mention the accidental inventor of the fretless bass.

BILL WYMAN

One of the early nuances of the show was to bring the two celebrities together in a fun – albeit slightly contrived – way, that allowed each of them time to record their feelings about meeting up with the other. A time to share any anecdotes of their previous meetings and what they were hoping to learn about them, with the time to actually just sit down and engage in conversation.

Although the pair of each episode had maybe met before, often this had been at 'celebrity' (honestly more of this word later) events, sit down meals, charity auctions and such like where the conversations were snatched, polite or within a large group. Yes, some of our pairings were actually friends, but again it's not often you get the luxury to relax into conversations covering a timeline of each other's life.

For Stephen and Bill we chose the Gore Hotel, in Kensington, (which was so relaxing and luxurious that we revisited it many times to film more of our shows at later dates) which is around the corner from the Royal Albert Hall where both Messrs Fry and Wyman had performed. Bill filmed his musings for the introduction at a private room in the hotel and then strolled around to the Albert Hall...simultaneously Stephen, who is renowned for travelling around London in his own black cab, had the camera crew in the taxi with him filming his introduction, which ended neatly with him spotting Bill (with an outstretched hitch-hiker's thumb) and pulling over to pick him up.

Stephen Fry and Bill Wyman introduction scene

As with all the personalities involved with each episode, this sense of fun and professionalism made it possible for us to film our quirky intros for the series – we saved these exclusively for the DVD, because the televised shows themselves needed graphics and a voice-over that would have diminished the 'bringing together' introductions.

Stephen had recently returned from a trip abroad and was twittering away on his smart-phone, managing to be polite and professional with the crew and also entertain the outside world at the same time. (More on twittering on page 274) Bill was taking the morning's preparation in his stride as the crew set up, and was happy settling down with a cup of tea. He likes to bring his own regular standard brand with him (builder's tea) and is very particular how he likes it...

SHOW-TIME

A Strange Couple – Stephen starts their 'Living the Life' conversation off by referring to the fact that people must think they are a strange couple, as their lives couldn't have been more different in some ways. Bill agrees he grew up in some poverty in, South London – Lower Sydenham, near the gasworks where his Granddad and Uncle worked (Bill also mentions that his father had been a bricklayer since the age of 14).

Stephen immediately draws factoids from the back of his mind, remembering that as a child he used to listen to records of radio comedians and remembers Jack Warner's *Letters From My Brother Sid*, where the comedian said, 'We've just moved in next to the gasworks and there's always a horrible smell from your brother Sid...' They both chuckle at what Stephen calls a stupid joke but asks seriously if, having grown up in that era, Bill remembers the Blitz.

Bill: 'Once we got caught, me and this boy called Dennis Dutley, suddenly the air raid went so we ran, we got to Franklyn Road just at the top of our road and there was a German plane coming up the street, about fifty, sixty feet off the ground, machine gunning...

And we ran. Luckily those houses we lived in, they were a bit like *Coronation Street* except you came straight onto the pavement and there was a little coping wall and we just ran behind one of them and ducked down the very first one and he came roaring up the street machine gunning, he went right past us. Then we ran because I was halfway down this side and he was the bottom of the other side, so we tore down and I raced up the stairs and my Gran was waiting and she grabbed me, and we saw him go zooming past again and then we went down to the shelter and we were okay.

I found out much later that it was the plane that dropped the bombs on the Lewisham School and killed, like sixty kids, and four teachers at lunch.'

One of the important decisions we made for the show very early on was the use of archive material. One of our maxims was akin to Aristotle's quote that '*When storytelling goes bad (in society) decadence is the result.*' We felt that every episode was so rich in the 'storytelling' that it was often a difficult edit to simply reduce the footage of the pairings conversation down to a broadcastable 50 minutes.

Saying this though, once we had a final edit for conversational content, there were a few core dramatic pieces that were complimented by footage to tell the story. For example, a few that come instantly to mind were the sporting feats of Lord Sebastian Coe and Sir Ian Botham – we all benefit from seeing as well as hearing. Also on a more nuanced level, when Britt is talking about Peter Sellers and the emotional isolation she felt dealing with his silences and depression. The archived photograph we used of them on the yacht captured the emotion and reminded the viewers of who Peter was.

In Bill's case, to have lived through a German bomber gunning down your street as you dive behind the coping wall was accentuated with the sinister black and white clip of a swooping German warplane, and also the imagery of the destroyed buildings served as a remembrance for those that died in the Lewisham bombing, where the archive added gravitas.

Another interesting confirmation for us concerning the intention of the show was highlighted very early on, namely the connection and empathy of each pairing. Throughout Bill's telling of his childhood Blitz story, it was peppered with empathetic exclamations from Stephen and full engagement with the retelling leaving very little to be said. In traditional interviews such confessions can usually present an awkward moment for the interviewer to suddenly move on to what may seem a flippant or out of context question. Stephen though, having been drawn into Bill's story, is genuinely involved and shares that it is exactly the kind of world he used to read about in Blitzkrieg novels as a child, and not only that, it then gives Bill a natural balance to ask Stephen about where he grew up and his childhood experiences.

Stephen states how he was born in Hampstead but grew up in Norfolk in a big country house with gardeners and the like and how he felt he was ridiculously lucky. At age 7 he shares how he was sent away to board at a prep school 200 miles away in Gloucestershire, although Stephen's natural self-effacement and 'Englishness' comes out as he plays down the event.

'So I was a seven year old boy and I was sent away. If you tell that to people now they go, oh how cruel, how awful, how monstrous, but the school was full of boys to whom the same thing had happened and they sort of overlook that. If it had been only me, if I'd been singled out, it would have been weird and if you were the only child who had been sent off...'

Bill, warming to the point, intercedes – like Churchill – and then the conversation reverts back to more 'triggered' memories for Bill about the war years. This again was what we as a production team felt was a quality of the show. Often, if you trawl old memories back to the forefront of your mind through conversation, it is like a tap that will keep trickling associated feelings and thoughts after the initial memory has been expressed.

So rather than the cut and 'move on' thrust of an interview, Bill remembers how as a child he used to go onto the bomb sites and pick dandelion leaves to wash and put in bread as a sandwich. He also used to go to the market and get the rotten cabbages and vegetables to cut out the salvageable parts to eat too. When Stephen asks if it was because Bill was always hungry, it surfaces memories for Bill about the hardship and how that related to his father.

Bill Wyman (right), childhood family photograph

'If it was bad weather my dad didn't work. My dad had a horrendous life, it was like reading Dickens, it really was. One of ten, the stories I've heard about the way they were brought up, you know, and the hardships he suffered. He didn't treat us good but it was ten times better than him so he thought he was being good to us...

Oh he'd hit you all the time, everything like that.'

Despite the difficulty of Bill's upbringing and his relationship with his father, it is emotionally poignant that Bill expresses that he wishes he had had more time with him.

'There was once he took me, I don't know why it happened, but he took me to a church in Beckenham and he said look at this church, look at that entrance, and there was this magnificent doorway with decorated brickwork and all that, masses, you know. I said "yeah?" He said, "I did that"...he said, "Come on, let's go home." He just took me there to show me this thing...but that was probably the closest thing that we ever did together and I really regret not being any closer to him.'

Elsie Carlisle – The conversation finds a natural pause and Stephen asks about music and if it was part of Bill's life right from the beginning. Bill describes – with some delight – how as a child his aunts used to sit around and play records on an old wind up gramophone, animatedly dancing around. He felt it was probably influences from the likes of Sinatra and Bing Crosby, but also reveals that later in life he heard a female artist from that era and was immediately transported back to that nostalgic part of his childhood. So much so that he found out that the singer was called 'Elsie Carlisle' and he now collects all her stuff, stating that playing her music still fills him with nostalgia and feelings of having met her before.

An Absolute Duffer – Bill swings the conversation back to Stephen and asks him if music was part of his childhood. Stephen explains how music was a passion in terms of listening to it but in terms of performing was 'an absolute duffer, completely hopeless.'(Described beautifully Blackadderesque)

'My father was very musical, he'd been a chorister at St Paul's Cathedral and he was evacuated out to Truro, the whole St Paul's choir went out to Cornwall and so he sang beautifully and he played the piano magnificently and I was always listening to Chopin, Brahms and Beethoven being played.'

Astutely, Bill picks up on Stephen's relationship with his father, asking if maybe that was why Stephen avoided pursuing music, and went against type trying not to copy, to which Stephen concurs.

'Exactly, we go against and I had a very troubled relationship with my father. At the age of seven I was sent away to school as I say and I was beaten a lot, I was a bad boy.'

Stephen, with his usual honesty and frankness, describes how he was in trouble at school, caned on numerous occasions but also how his real passion – as it is today – was language, words, reading, thinking about words. 'I could do words in a way I couldn't do music. I couldn't sing.' Stephen then shares a relevant anecdote of how he and Hugh Laurie, for one of their earlier comedy incarnations on Saturday Live, were preparing for a skit they were doing which required Stephen to sing. He explains how he started to get incredibly nervous and sweaty as the Saturday approached so Hugh recommended a hypnotist, something that Stephen had never considered but was certainly open to.

Congregational Practice – This part of the show highlighted many of the much loved skills and characteristics that Stephen Fry is known for. He regaled Bill with his visit to the aforementioned hypnotist complete with Hungarian accent, describing how he had to explain he wasn't there for smoking or sex addiction but the ingrained nerves of having to sing live on television. Bringing to life how the hypnotist took Stephen into his subconscious, Bill interjects how he can feel the pull of the trance too. Stephen then goes on to describe how he was suddenly transported back to a suppressed memory of childhood humiliation.

'I can remember it but I was completely out as it were. And this was the weird thing; he said "Why do you think you can't sing? What makes you think this?" and I had, and I know it sounds weird, I had a memory that I had never, ever consciously recalled before which was back at prep school, aged seven, there used to be a thing called Con Prac which stood for Congregational Practice.

Anyway, it was my third or fourth week at school, a seven year old, slightly nervous and a prefect is patrolling and he suddenly shouts out "Listen everybody, Fry's singing flat" and the music master who was playing went "Fry, on your own" and I sang on my own and everybody went "Ha-ha-ha-ha" like that and I was so humiliated and that completely closed me down and I had never ever been able to sing again and I'd forgotten that and this came out.

So then I remembered this hypnotist was saying "Now we have identified the source of your fear, tell me, when do you have to sing?" and I said "It's on Saturday and it's going to be in the evening." He said, "What is the word you use for the trigger for you to do something?" "It's the cue." "Yes, what is the cue for you to start singing?" And I said "My colleague says hit it bitch." "All right, when you hear the words hit it bitch you will be relaxed, there's no one listening, everything will be fine, you will have confidence and you will be able to sing with joy. Now I pull you up from the darkness." And so on and then I wake up. So I'm thinking, "great." So on Saturday I said to Hugh "If you get the cue wrong and don't say hit it bitch, we're in real trouble." He said "It's okay, it's okay,

I'll say it!" and he said it and I got through it and everyone said "That was great, what was the problem?" but I now realise that if ever I want to sing I have to have Hugh by my side saying "hit it bitch!" '

Foaming Shrimps – After such an enthralling retelling by Stephen of what was actually an emotional trauma from his past, we had to include the clip of Stephen singing on *Saturday Live*. That was the thing though, Stephen is renowned for talking openly about his past and challenges with his bi-polar disorder, but has his own inimitable style of mixing humility with humour to express his past experiences candidly and engagingly. This had also warmed Stephen to the topic and he expanded on what he saw as an addiction in childhood triggering a chain of traumatic events.

'It sounds silly but it started when I was very young, I was the first generation almost to have sweets and breakfast cereals and things like that sort of aimed at us. I remember Sugar Puffs, I was absolutely addicted, I'd get through three or four packets a week easily of Sugar Puffs, eat them from the box, pour them. We had the groceries delivered to our house and my mother would say "Do we really need more Sugar Puffs?" and I'd go "Er...umm..." and sweets.

There was a tuck shop at school and I would spend all the money, the pocket money my parents sent me would go into this book and the master would say, "Oh you've used it up" and so I would steal just to buy sweets. This pattern of just...and it was sherbet fountains and things like that...the flying saucers with the rice paper and the foaming shrimps and all these kind of things and this...desire for sweets and things. It became then a...I was just always outside. I am obviously younger than you; I was born in '57 so 21 years after you.'

As is the way with conversations, Bill couldn't help but comment on the age reference, saying that he was doing his military service when Stephen was born, and tying in his earlier description of how his aunts introduced him to music he quantifies his military service by the music he was exposed to. He was in Germany in the RAF, when he first heard the beginnings of Rock' n 'Roll on the American Forces Network. Bill shares how they used to go to the American Zone and buy the early Elvis records like *That's Alright Mamma* and *Mystery Train*, animating the fact they were all the early Sun Records, Bill breaks into a little riff singing another early Elvis song, *I've Left That's Right She's Gone.* '

The Fretless Bass – Bill then drops a massive musical bombshell.

'Unbeknownst to me, I invented the fretless bass without knowing it. It has only been the last five years it's been acclaimed that I actually...'

Stephen: 'You were the one?'

Bill: 'I was six years ahead of when they first made a fretless bass.'

Although Bill is obviously renowned for his musical genius, the 'fretless bass' story he shares on 'Living the Life' highlights the attention to detail Bill has and his practicality and intelligence. Bill quite matter-of-factly describes something which is, in fact, ground breaking in musical terms. He regales how upon hearing what a bass sounded like in his early days back in South London, he realised what his band was missing, and canvassed for someone to go about learning and playing one. Naturally this ended up being Bill himself, and he brings to life how he bought an old Bass guitar from some mate for eight quid and set about destroying it.

'I took all the electrics out, I took the strings off, I took all the frets off because they were all rattling, I took all them off. I got the body, I turned it over, I looked at pictures of Little Richard's band and...'

Stephen: 'You based it on the pictures!'

Bill: '...and I redrew it on the back like it had two little horns down, just a little body like that and kept everything else the same. I went down the road to a guy who had a fretwork machine and I said "cut that out will you." He cut it out and I rubbed it all down and painted it, did it again, painted it again and then I put new electrics in it, I put new tuning things in it, I put a Baldwin pick up, the original pick up, I put all new electrics in it, I found flat wound strings instead of those ones that go [Bill does a great impression of the musical differences between the basses] that most bass players use because they go "dong-dong-dong" but I don't, I play "du-de-du" like a double bass.

...And so I had a fretless bass. So I bought an eighteen inch speaker, a Goodman speaker which everybody else was playing with six inch or eight inch but I had this eighteen inch speaker and I built this big cabinet with the help of a friend and put this eighteen inch speaker in it, it was like a little wardrobe and then it was so big that it used to lie on its side when I used to play with the Stones, when I first joined and I used to sit on it on the back and play.'

Nerd – Stephen is impressed, joking how Bill was in fact a bit of a nerd, leading onto asking how Bill moved from his band in South London to the Stones, wondering if he auditioned for them. In fact Bill's drummer was playing for them and Dick Taylor who later played with the Pretty Things was the bassist who had had enough and left the Stones to go back to college. Bill's drummer relayed the information and asked the band about giving Bill an audition. Bill recalls the date in an understated way, although giving us a glimpse of his passion for archiving and retention of detail...'It was 8th December 1962.' Bill explains it in such a way that he wowed them not just with his guitar skills but also with all the kit he had.

'I had all my amplifiers. I came in and said "here's a Fox A230, you can borrow that, plug in that." I had a little Watkinson's Westminster amp with tremolo on it and echo, so you could do the Bo Diddley [Bill does another sound effect impression] with the tremolo going and I said "and this cabinet's mine, this is mine." They were all gobsmacked with shock. They only had little amps.'

Stephen Fry (left). Bill Wyman (right) gesturing playing bass

What a Tosser – Onto the next chapter of the show, Bill casually asks Stephen where he went to university, to which Stephen's reply of 'Cambridge, but that was after prison,' Shows the naturalness of genuine surprise as Bill's voice raises a few octaves with an exclamation of 'prison.'

'Yes, yes, I'm afraid I had a very troubled adolescence – lots of sturm und drang as the Germans say, lots of storm and stress. I was always an outsider. I was bright, I won't deny it, I could pass exams and things, maybe that was the problem. You see I took my O Levels when I was 13 and 14 because in those days they encouraged you to, then I got expelled, then I got expelled from another school and ran away from another one. It was credit cards; I was eventually caught up by the police in Swindon of all places. I pleaded guilty; I was in this place called Pucklechurch which was rather hard, and has since been closed. They would occasionally have riots.

It made me realise what a tosser I was, I had all these advantages, extraordinary advantages, expensive education, I had the curiosity, I grew up in a house full of books and both my parents were university educated, deeply intelligent...and I loved it and here I was pissing my life away, it was inexcusably wrong of me.'

Emotional Intelligence – As a production team we speak in terms of 'emotional intelligence' in relation to our programming and by association, 'Living the Life' Given the time, both Stephen and Bill relax into a time-lined conversation of their lives, (rather than focussing on isolated publically documented experiences) the show (as with all episodes) gives the viewer the freedom to put together certain pieces of the jigsaw that has shaped a contributor's life, albeit subjectively.

The viewer has the opportunity to join Stephen on his journey of being sent away to boarding school, through being ridiculed in front of class mates, falling into an addiction to the sweeter things in life, played out as stealing small change to buy confectionary as a child, to maturing into an adult adept at credit card fraud and material purchases of a mature palette. It also shows how Stephen has sought to recognise his discordances in life and delve more deeply into the nature of his bipolar disorder. This same emotionally intelligent timeline can equally be applied to Bill describing his relationship with women and love from childhood to fatherhood.

Stephen describes how, after leaving prison, (aged 18) his parents hadn't given up on him, but were seriously concerned for the direction his life was taking. Concerned himself, Stephen explains how he knew that Norwich College had 2 days of registration for A-Levels and was drawing to a close as he joined the end of the second day's queue. He picks up the story...

Starter for Ten: – 'There was a queue and I was at the end of it. I finally got there and there was a little man with silver hair and a smiley beaming face, his name was Peter Butler, I'll never forget. I said "I'd like to register to do A-Levels" – they did a one year course of A-Levels – "I'd like to do English, French and History of Art."

He said "Oh, I'm afraid they've all gone, all the places have gone." I stared at him and said, "No, no, I have to do this." I said "If you let me do these I will get 'A' grades in all of them and I will get a scholarship to Cambridge." He said. "What?" I said, "I promise you, that is what will happen." He looked at me, he folded his arms and put his head on one side and I wasn't to know but...

...but this was the hinge on which my whole future life was to turn and he stood there, just like that, for what seemed an eternity and then he went, "oh all right then!" He signed the piece of paper and fortunately I was as good as my word.'

There is a lovely response part way through Stephen's recounting of the story where Bill finds out Stephen is only 18 and proclaims how confident he was for stating such a direct promise. We included in the show an archived clip from University Challenge which we felt summed up not only Stephen's recognised intellect, love of language and even early foray into television, but also as a natural visual to prove he was in fact as good as his word. Bamber Gascoigne's opening gambit of 'Queen's, Fry' complements the story giving us a glimpse of the exuberant Stephen Fry representing Queens College, Cambridge in the intellectually grandiose University Challenge.

Stephen still recognises his acceptance to do A-Levels at Norwich as one of the pivotal moments of his life, a decision upon which his future rested. Bill completely resonated with such moments in life, and shared how in a 'sliding door' moment of his actual existence, his father in the thirties had gone out on a double date with a friend of his and two women. Comfortable with both ladies, the men had privately flipped a coin to see who dated who – the pivotal moment where the heads and tails decided Bill's father's future wife and hence a genetic gateway of DNA for the procreation of Bill himself (was it coincidence or predetermined?) – This segment was reluctantly cut from the final edit but was a gripping retelling by Bill.

Continuing on with the theme of defining moments in their lives, Stephen asked Bill whether or not the explosion of Rock n Roll made him greedy for money. In what is astonishing in today's perception of rock royalty – and royalties, Bill counters that he never really made any money in the sixties.

Everybody was Filching – 'We never got it, we never got it in the 60s, we weren't rich. You didn't have merchandising, you didn't have all that sponsorship or any of that stuff that later came to everybody, other bands. Mick and Keith wrote all the songs so they got some writing and publishing, you didn't get that. There wasn't a lot of money around and of course, with the managers we had, everybody was filching stuff off and you'd end up with next to nothing.

The Rolling Stones, Bill Wyman (centre)

It is fascinating that after six years of being the top band in the world Bill only had £1000 in the bank, not as a result of profligacy but because of corruption and poor management. It is also a theme that became apparent throughout the whole series of 'Living the Life', that so many of the contributors did it the hard way. Although they all allude to luck playing a part in their success, they all grafted, worked hard at their talent and were completely immersed in their creative passion.

Leslie Phillips worked every single job in theatre, from call boy, to stage hand, director, producer and actor. Robin Gibb and his brothers ate, slept and breathed singing. Ian Botham used to skip over the barriers at the tube station to get to cricket matches, he made so little money. Des O'Connor worked as a *Butlin's Redcoat* and bluffed his way onto stage manufacturing the chance of securing an agent.

All of them make reference to the modern day zeitgeist of 'celebrity' and the urge for recognition or recompense over and above talent and graft. A malaise that can be applied to the modern footballer (even English rugby player circa 2011 World Cup,) the reality 'pop' star, the wannabe actress, glamour model or inept blogger. Jeremy Clarkson, when filming the pre-show introduction alludes to Nick Mason, a rock legend with Pink Floyd compared to 'quote' 'some breathy little monster' singing 'wannabe'. Without labouring the point, it was apparent throughout filming the series that there was a genuine disdain for the blurred edges of what constitutes celebrity now – talent or profile, and for what drives creativity – the passion or the profit.

The Wobbly – Empathising, Stephen recalled his publicly wobbly period in 1995, where he had a breakdown of sorts and left the play 'Cellmates' early into its run.

'I had a strangely wobbly period, in '95 I was doing a play, it wasn't exactly stage fright, I mean you can call it stage fright but it was fear of failure I suppose. I was in a kind of weird frame of mind, I have a mood disorder anyway so I get kind of ups and downs and it seemed to coincide with a very bad period for me when I was doing this play, Cellmates it was called, with Rik Mayall.

One Sunday I was sitting in a terrible state thinking "I never want to go on stage again, I never want to be in England again, I never want to face the public again," and I pictured – God knows why, I don't think I'd actually even been there – I pictured myself somewhere on the north-east coast of Denmark in a huge white pullover with a pipe stuck in my mouth writing strange poetry and maybe getting a job teaching English, that's all I could imagine! But being completely anonymous.

It was a ludicrous fantasy. I did actually consider suicide, I went into my garage, a lock up garage, I lived in a flat in St James's but I couldn't bear the idea of my parents, you know all that sort of thing. So it was pretty horrible, not a nice time at all for me.'

Bill: 'How did you get out of it?'

Stephen: 'I drove to Dover, got on a ferry, got to Hanover which is northern Germany as you know and thinking maybe I would then get up to Denmark. I imagined at the time there might be some little column in the arts section of the newspaper saying "Strange, Stephen Fry seems not to be in his play" kind of thing and there was my face on the front. There was a picture of police on the roof of my house in Norfolk, I have a country house, looking obviously for a body or something and I suddenly realised this thing had got wildly…I mean I don't know why I'm laughing, it's awful. And I was in a complete state.

Another positive aspect of the show is the reality that two friends/peers/mutual achievers, open up more candidly about their experiences. There is the trust that the other person can not only relate to what you have been through but has also probably experienced it in some shape or form themselves. This in part contributed to one of the most telling and poignant chapters of the episode. When Stephen relayed in a full and frank manner his experiences of being besieged by nerves and doubt with *Cellmates*, Bill confided that he once went to a professional to talk through his problems, both validating Stephen's childhood repressed memories and also an understanding of the *Cellmates* affair.

Penny Violets – Bill explained how during his sessions with the professional, a memory also surfaced of suppressed childhood trauma.

'My mother had had a sixth child and he was born, he was called David, it was just after the war and he was born with yellow jaundice and something else and so was in hospital most of the time and he died after about five months. There was a little funeral at the house and me being the eldest child, I went to the market round the back and bought a little bouquet of…I think they were violets or something, just a little one like for a penny or something.

I bought them round and when I got round there they were bringing the little coffin out of the house and my mum and dad were there, us other kids and all that and there were some flowers on it and I gave them to my mum and said "Put them on there" and she just grabbed them and threw them away.'

Stephen: 'Oh no!'

Bill: 'She threw them away and I had completely forgotten about it'.

Stephen: 'That's the cruellest thing…'

Bill: 'But she just took them and dumped them behind the coping wall, you know, slung them. We didn't go to the funeral and it was an unmarked grave and all that, I hardly saw the child so I never really…'

Stephen: 'Said goodbye.'

Bill: 'Exactly.'

It was an emotional confession for Bill and offered an insight into Bill's relationship with women and his search for love and approval that was discarded that day of the funeral. He refers back to a similar piece of his emotional jigsaw when describing later in the episode how his parents never hugged or expressed their love to the children.

Eye-Popping Sums of Money – Stephen professed to one of the luckiest things that ever happened to him being when his agent, Richard Armitage, gave him a script of a show that his father had written the music for.

'The father, Reginald Armitage, rejoiced in the name, his nom de guerre was Noel Gay and he had written this musical called *Me and My Girl* and it had the song *The Lambeth Walk* in it as well as *Me and My Girl*. He asked if I would rewrite the book of it, the story of it, for a new production and I was able to add other songs by Noel Gay, *Leaning on a Lamppost*, *The Sun Has Got His Hat* on which he also wrote, great songs and we did the show in Leicester and it moved to the West End and then it moved to Broadway and it ran for years and years and years and years and having just left university, I was finding these cheques landing on my doorstep for what I considered eye-popping sums of money.

I bought a house in the country myself, went mad on cars and credit cards. You know that sheriff in the Bond movies who opens his wallet and a concertina falls out, that was like me. Partly, I suppose because I'd been to prison for credit card fraud, I wanted to prove to myself that I now had the right to have these things so I was guilty of conspicuous consumption, I think is probably the phrase. I had eleven cars I think – Aston Martin, Austin–Healey, Wolseleys – all British classic cars, very weird, this is in the 80s I'm talking about. It took me a long time to calm down and realise. I was very fortunate, I think anybody listening to my story will probably want to punch me because it seems like I never really had to suffer with the wolf at the door in the way that so many people do.'

Botham & Jagger – A huge passion of Bill's is cricket. One of the most animated sections of filming was the way he lit up when he talked about playing charity cricket and getting to bat and bowl with the likes of David Gower, Michael Holding, Wayne Daniels, Viv Richards and Ian Botham. It was an engaging exchange, Bill talking passionately about his cricket and Stephen sharing stories about the matches he loved being present at. A clip that didn't make our final edit gave us a glimpse of how maybe 'well known' personalities have their own heroes and passions outside their expertise. Stephen talked about being at one of the popular test matches at Lords in a hospitality room with Mick Jagger (Bill qualified that Mick liked to watch whilst he liked to play) and Ian Botham. Ian wanted to talk to Mick about the Stones and Rock n Roll while Mick wanted to know why there wasn't a fielder at long off...neither wanted to talk shop but had seriously interesting lives to the other.

Love at first sight –

'I was very lucky in a professional and personal way. When I was at Cambridge I had a very good friend, Emma Thompson...we used to do plays together, we were both in the same year doing English and in my last year she took me to meet a friend of hers who was Hugh Laurie and he was in his room – he was at Selwyn, another college – and I'll never forget it.

His girlfriend, Katie, opened the door and said "Hi, Hugh's really pleased; he wants to meet you," because I'd written this play the year before as an undergraduate. It was a comedy and Hugh had taken over the Footlights, which was the comedy club at Cambridge, and he wanted someone to write with. So he asked Emma if he could meet me so that's why she brought me round. So there's Hugh, sitting on the bed, he's got a guitar and he's written this comic song and he plays it and I said, "That's brilliant" and he then says what he's writing at the time and I join in and it was an exact version of love at first sight, which is a professional love at first sight, a comedy love at first sight. We instantly had this extraordinary, and it was like a chemical thing, those sort of friends you have to hug yourself that you can have someone that you are that close to.'

Bill understood the value of such a close friendship, saying that he didn't have a lot of friends, and that when he was in the Stones he had a huge address book which reduced dramatically once he left. The fair weather friends fell by the wayside when he had a few problems in the 90's, leaving him knowing exactly who his 'few and far between' friends were.

Making the link to the Rock n Roll lifestyle, Stephen confirmed with Bill that he had been married three times, which he felt was 'not excessive in your game.' Bill replied very similarly to Peter Stringfellow, in that in those days you married just to get out of home, marrying the girl next door so to speak, just to get away. He also said that he divorced in '68 and got custody of his son, which was mostly unprecedented in those days too, explaining how he brought him up.

Sexuality – This episode of 'Living the Life' with Stephen and Bill was refreshing in its honesty and nowhere more so than when the subject of sex and sexuality raised its head. Being a wordsmith Stephen actually used the word uxorious with Bill (didn't make the final edit) in terms of a much married man, a loose interpretation of a word defined as someone who is overly devoted to his wife, although derived from uxorial relating to wife and wives (plural) we could see the connection – more on words at the end of this chapter.

Returning to the theme, Stephen thought it was fair to say, without delving too much into Bill's private life, that he had quite a reputation for being a ladies man 'You love women, no one is ever going to say you're gay are they, let's be honest, you are well heterosexual.'

Bill took it all in good jest reaffirming he was, 'well, very well.' (Heterosexual)

Sex Addict – Stephen continued: 'They say that you've had 2000 women or something, you weren't a sex addict though were you, or maybe you were? Do you think that would now be how you would be described?'

Without belabouring the point, the essence of 'Living the Life' is the two famous people sharing what they feel comfortable with. Honesty shared by one, very often in the series became reciprocated by another. A crass intrusion by an interviewer with no revelation of their own or inability to empathise can quite rightly put the interviewee on the defensive and metaphorically speaking pull the shutters down.

'Living the Life' was, from the very outset, clearly guided sensitively towards the contributors, they shared what they chose to, had a say in the final edit and were there to be nurtured by the production, not pilloried.

What was a moving and heartfelt chapter to the show was Bill being given the opportunity to explain that, over time, he recognised his relationships with women as an addiction and also, in a subconscious way, he was searching for love. The emotionally intelligent jigsaw we talked about earlier created a much broader picture than a one off salacious sound bite.

'I think it was an addiction. Maybe I was looking for love or something. My mother and father never hugged us or kissed us or said they loved us and it all came out in the open on their 50th anniversary when they all got to my house with all the family. We were celebrating their 50th anniversary and they said something about we've been a great family and all that and my sister said "Yes but mum, you never told me you loved me."

Bill Wyman and his family

And she said, "Of course I did" and my brother said, "No you didn't, you never told me either and you never cuddled us."

Suzanne has taught me to show my emotions so much, she's been brilliant like that. I used to find it hard to say "I love you" to her because when it's not said to you, you find it very difficult to say it to other people so she has taught me all that and of course the three girls, from when they were little, "love you Daddy," and give you hugs, you know "love you." It's very easy for me to show my emotions to them now but it was very difficult in the first place.'

I Love my People – Stephen, (not dissimilarly to talking about their early contrasts with wealth and poverty) explained that he was the complete opposite of Bill (homosexual and celibate) saying that from the time he left university right up until 1996/97 he was celibate.

'I don't trust my explanations any more than anybody else's but part of it is fear of rejection. I have always found the gay world very threatening, particularly in the early 80s. I left university in 1981, as it so happens around the same time the HIV virus arrived in the world although I wasn't to know it until a few years later as friends started to tumble but it was at a time when there was an enormous confidence, a new confidence in clubs and things and I moved in to Chelsea and just round the corner from a gay bar and I absolutely loathed these places. I loathed going into them and seeing eyes raking you up and down and I felt undesirable and undesired and all I was interested in was talking and chatting to people, I don't want to dance and pump away and stare at people and wear strange leather things and all these peculiarities.

I know, I know, I love my people and I am very proud of the work that I've done for gay rights, the small amounts I have done and I am very pleased that things are better now and there are civil partnerships and all the rest of it but in those days there was this kind of physical body fascism almost amongst some elements of the gay scene as it was called that I found completely off-putting.

Plus I had this passion for the new world I had thrown myself into, this comedy and television and writing and journalism and plays and films and radio and stage. I filled every unforgiving minute with 120 minutes worth of distance run and I was completely obsessed with work and excitement and the idea of having to wake up next to somebody and talk to them and make tea and coffee and have breakfast – I couldn't see the point of it. It sounds terrible now but that's how I was.'

Abandoning the Casanova – Talking of relationships or in Stephens' case, lack of them, Bill regales his conversational partner with how he met and subsequently married Suzanne. The couple had initially met in Paris in 1979, thirteen years before they actually married. Bill was in the city recording with the Stones and Suzanne was modelling. It was in 1992 when Bill decided that he had to choose a woman to settle down with for the rest of his life, because 'this fooling around, philandering as (Stephen) called it is not on'. He admitted that he had to be serious about the rest of his life and settle down with one person – 'who can I choose?'

When Stephen asked is that really how Bill went about it, Bill confided that he had this massive address book because he used to have girlfriends in every town of the world; 'six or eight in London'. The black book as Stephen called it. Bill continued.

'...and three in Paris and so on, and I came down with Suzanne's name. I thought "yes, I think I could live with her for the rest of my life." So I phoned her up in LA, we had a chat, I said "do you want to come over for ten days?" and she said "Are you going to change your ways?" '

Stephen: 'Very tactfully put! Abandon the Casanova.'

Bill: 'Because she knew what I was like so I said "Yes, I will." She came over for ten days, a spark was still there, it was magic and I said "will you marry me?" She said "I'll think about it," and she went back to LA and after about a week she said "Yes" and it's the best thing I ever did in my life.'

Stephen: 'And you've been a one girl man ever since?'

Bill: 'Yes, of course.'

Stephen: 'That's fantastic.'

Living The LIE (Life) – The original title for the series was initially 'Living The Lie', one that we as a production team were very happy with and also understanding of the intention. All contributors are not only very high achievers in their field, unique and gifted personalities they also by the nature of their success are high profile targets for the media.

The essence of 'Living The Lie' was to allow the contributors to offer a deeper insight for the viewers than the perpetuating cycle of media caricature that usually accompanied their press and hence public perception.

The Lie, was the Lie itself of what stories, realities, events and expectations contributed to how the 'well known' personalities were perceived, how much they self-perpetuated any myths or even how much the continued labelling shaped the way they lived their life or presented themselves to the public.

That was the nature of 'Living The Lie'. However we understood that many contributors – because of such a perception – were cautious of the word 'lie' being misconstrued and the honesty and integrity that they (OK, most) strove very hard to incorporate into their lives would be weakened. The compromise was 'Living the Life' – a change only in title, all the original direction and production values for the show were kept exactly the same.

Stephen and Bill's was the second show filmed for our series, still operating under the working title 'Living the Lie' which I mention here because the topic of media, media intrusion and media 'spin doctoring' became a passionate discourse by the pair for the final chapter of the show.

Stephen revealed that he never reads the papers, having never taken one for twelve years and literally doesn't read them and was passionately scathing about the likes of David Aaronovitch, Melanie Phillips and Julie Burchill declaring no interest in what they had to say.

'Why the fuck should I give a toss about what they think of anybody? Why should I listen to them? Hideous.'

Bill completely agreed, wondering why anyone should be interested and that Britain was 'a small village gossip centre'.

Stephen agreed and felt that the victory was just never to read it, and Bill felt that a lot of it was envy, of not being like them. Stephen continued.

Fry Lashes Out – 'I don't know, it may well be or it may be genuine dislike. I am perfectly prepared to accept that people will look at me on screen and think "what a twat", especially if you're like me and you shoot your mouth off a lot. I did the BAFTA TV lecture the other week, it's an annual thing when they get someone to do a discourse on television and in the opening remarks I said of course one of the problems with this gig is that I could spend an hour saying how great the BBC is, how much I worship it, how much I value it, how fantastic it is but if I just spent ten seconds saying that, I don't know, "Junior Apprentice isn't very good" – not that I've seen Junior Apprentice, for all I know it's brilliant – then the headline would be "Fry Lashes Out at Reality Television! In an astonishing scene at BAFTA, television insiders were reeling in their designer seats as Stephen personally assaulted the..." and sure enough it happened. I spent the time saying how great the BBC was and then in the question and answer session afterward I muttered something about infantilism and that was all the story was.

There is a part of one that says "actually I don't need this shit," I can live a life now where I no longer have to make any statement in public, I don't have to be interviewed, I don't have to go on a TV show as myself, I don't have to go on Twitter or Facebook, I can completely retreat so that I will never be misquoted or misunderstood and I will not be part of this world. As I say, I am tempted to do that. I think I won't because I enjoy too much the interacting with people that you get social networking and things like that, I actually enjoy that and I just have to put up with it as the price that is paid for the fact that one will get hammered occasionally.'

Endings and Goodbyes: – With the media rant off his chest Stephen settled into a natural calm and timely conclusion to the show, telling Bill that when it was suggested that they had 'this chat together' he wasn't sure what to expect, except that he had met Bill and obviously admired him for his 'walking bass' and all the rest of it and noticed the fact that there would be people who would say Bill has led the perfect life in some ways.

'You've had the adventure and risk of being a Blitz kid, a war baby, all that thrill of seeing German bombers and...'

Bill: 'And the beginnings of 'Rock n Roll.'

Stephen: 'Being there at the beginning of Rock n Roll, having the pick of the girls throughout the heady days of excess (Bill chimes in with an 'All Nations') and now being a country gentleman with your beautiful manor house that you've had for forty years or whatever and the love of your life. You've just kind of had it all haven't you, Bill Wyman, you bastard! No, it's fantastic and although we seem on the surface to have so little in common, we have a huge amount I think.'

Bill: 'Well I'm not highly intellectual like you so I was a bit concerned because you know everything about books and plays and famous people and all that but you've opened my eyes to some things and I've really enjoyed it too.'

Stephen Fry (right) and Bill Wyman (left) leaving The Gore Hotel

The pair agreed to do it more often and maybe next time over dinner at the *Sticky Fingers* restaurant. They shake hands on what was an intimate, honest and revealing conversation.

For all the shows in the series we wanted to wrap the conversational feel together neatly and although all the contributors naturally end with a hand shake or final comment, we filmed all the pairs leaving the venue and going their separate ways. They had come together in anticipation, had shared a relaxed and yet intense conversation for a couple of hours and would be seen leaving, then separating, an ending of a special sharing of how they live and have lived their lives.

LORD MELVYN BRAGG

Lord Melvyn Bragg was born in Carlisle and is a well known television and radio broadcaster, novelist, writer of non-fiction and screenwriter. He collaborated with the late Ken Russell on several occasions, and is known largely for his phenomenally successful work on the 'South Bank Show.' He has been awarded numerous honorary doctrines for his works on Law and Literature.

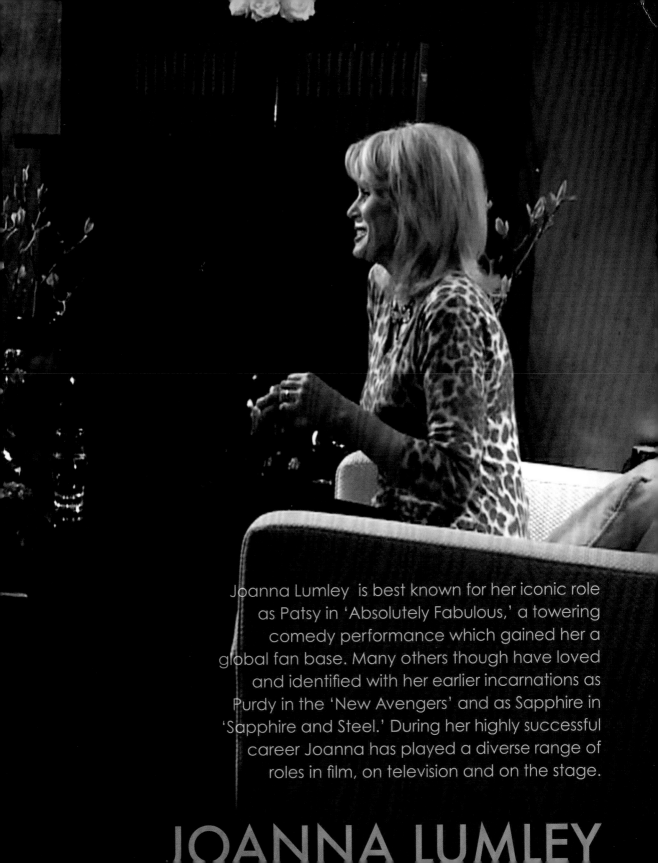

Joanna Lumley is best known for her iconic role as Patsy in 'Absolutely Fabulous,' a towering comedy performance which gained her a global fan base. Many others though have loved and identified with her earlier incarnations as Purdy in the 'New Avengers' and as Sapphire in 'Sapphire and Steel.' During her highly successful career Joanna has played a diverse range of roles in film, on television and on the stage.

JOANNA LUMLEY

3

LORD MELVYN BRAGG & JOANNA LUMLEY

The second episode of the series included our first Lord and, with sensitivity to the working schedule of Lord Bragg's professional life that also had to accommodate sessions at the House of Lords, we upped sticks and located to a plush suite at the Baglioni Hotel, near Hyde Park, a short taxi ride from the Houses of Parliament. The pairing of Melvyn and Joanna was one of our favourites and although to the outsider, a slightly strange mix, they turned out to be the perfect complement for each other.

When filming the introductions for each episode (saved for the special extras on the DVD) we were cautious of not 'hamming' them up, needing to outdo the previous effort or becoming too elaborate with the set up and distracting our contributors from the main focus – the quality conversation. It worked well with Stephen and Bill to use not just Stephen's taxi, but the Royal Albert Hall where they had both performed. The same way it worked to have car enthusiast Nick Mason pulling up to Top Gear's Jeremy Clarkson's house in his top of the range Audi. The subtlety of Joanna and Melvyn was for us as a production team, on task, in that Melvyn – who later shared openly on the show how nervous he gets before filming or recording anything – could record his piece to camera in the comfort of his hotel room, with minimal disturbance before 'show time' and Joanna, who was filmed slightly off the main set, demonstrated a wonderful example of her acting and comedic talents.

I try to ask the minimum of questions off camera to our contributors just to (a) settle them in: Have they met the other contributor before? What are they looking forward to finding out about them? And also (b) to remind those viewers who may not be as au fait with the contributor – What is 'x' known for and perceived as being by the public?

With these simple questions and absolutely no direction from myself other than to "look down the barrel of the lens and incorporate my off camera questions into the answer", Joanna was first take word perfect and off the cuff made a play about their ages and that she may be in luck with Melvyn, with a coy flick of the hair and a pretend 'ooh here he is...just kidding.' To so naturally be able to captivate with just the right tone impressed the whole crew, and set up an ability to relax others that carried over throughout the whole episode.

Lord Melvyn Bragg and Joanna Lumley in their pre-interviews

The Impresarios – A natural introduction that had already been alluded to by Melvyn in his filmed piece to camera kicked off the show. Joanna asked where they first met, to which Melvyn responded.

'Well you don't remember, in the 1960s I did a series for BBC2 called The Impresarios... and one of them was Lucy Clayton of the Lucy Clayton School. The director was Gavin Millar and I made a film with Gavin at university and he directed it. He and I made a film together and we acted together in a play, The Tempest, but you were in that film, you must have been 19 or 20.'

Joanna: 'Because I'd been to Lucy Clayton, the programme was focusing on modelling I think of some kind and even though I was just an ordinary run-of-the-mill model, it was the most thrilling thing. I lived on the fourth floor of a shared flat in Earls Court, just behind the station and the camera crew came round to my house, to my flat, a two bedroom flat, four girls sharing, and they used a clip of it just last year in a film about Duffy, it was so extraordinary to see yourself moving and speaking, not as an actress but just as a person. That was in 1966 or something, 1967.'

Joanna confirmed that she had come to London because for her it was the 'Mecca' and knowing that Melvyn was a Cumbrian man, wondered if he came for the same reasons. Melvyn journeyed to London because he got a traineeship at the BBC. At university he felt that if he had wanted to do anything it was to go to the WA or to teach, but all he really wanted to do was write. He had started writing at university for the university paper and then started writing fiction. Realising he had to have a job (he was married in his third year at university) he applied to the BBC for something called a general traineeship and got it.

Joanna Lumley at the begining of her modeling career

Melvyn Bragg starting out as a trainee at the BBC

'I started in the *World Service* and went up to Newcastle into the Third Programme, I went in television – I thought it was the life of Riley to be honest. I never met anybody or had been anywhere near anybody who could do this and get paid at the end of the week for it, it was just amazing.'

It was apparent very early on in the show that both contributors were highly intellectual and verbose. Joanna very quickly piecing together the snippets she was hearing from Melvyn and pushing forward the train of thought. She probed Melvyn as to whether or not his ability to study and throw himself into something wholeheartedly was due to being an only child 'was it an only child thing?' and presumably he had friends.

A Room to Yourself – Melvyn agreed he had numerous friends but with what he debated was either an advantage or disadvantage, he didn't know anything else. What he did divulge was that having been born at the start of the Second World War that his father was not really around until 1946/47, but that one of the advantages of being an only child was that you could get a 'room to yourself.'

'...that was massive so you could get uninterrupted time reading and I got into the habit of it and I still like it. I sometimes think it is a bit of a toss-up – am I alone to write or do I write in order to be on my own, I don't quite know. I like being on my own.'

Many of our contributors would clarify an event in their childhood, as 'just what you got used to' like Melvyn being on his own, Stephen being sent away to boarding school, Bill contending with the Blitz, and Joanna (below) being a nomadic child of the British Empire. Growing up in a pub though (in Wigton, Cumbria) Melvyn felt he found the balance of both social worlds. Living above the pub...

'There was noise and sometimes at weekends we had a singing room so there was masses of noise and sometimes there were fights and that sort of thing but mainly it was a very jolly, decent, extremely well run pub. There were darts, a singing room, a kitchen and a bar so there was all that downstairs and I liked to go down there and serve behind the bar and help and meet all the people and then upstairs you were on your own. I liked that two layers and funnily enough that has been the way that my life's fallen out, as it were. I am on my own to write and I work with a gang of people in television.'

It served as apt imagery for the show, the isolation and the social, reflecting Melvyn's current professional life.

The Franconia – Joanna was then asked if she grew up at the end of the Empire – she did in 1946, born in Kashmir, the year before Indian Independence.

'Yes and I wasn't quite one year old when we went down to Bombay and caught the Franconia because everybody British left India, everybody had to leave and so although I don't remember that time, I know that both my parents were brought up in India because my mother's father was a diplomat, my father's father was a banker in Lahore which is now in Pakistan, but India was all one in those days. It was a shock for them because this was their home really. They had come back to boarding school in England, which is the way that things were in those days if you were living overseas, but Melvyn, I didn't have a kind of root because on both sides of my family there was a sense of travelling or living from where you weren't, if you know what I mean. So we never had a home town or a house that was our own, so we moved and moved and moved like gypsies really, packing up and moving on, packing up and moving on. It was like a tribe and that tribe I think is almost gone now.'

Melvyn: 'The British Empire military tribe, yes.'

Joanna: 'It is difficult to put into today's terms, because now soldiers or anybody in the services are flown to and fro. In my childhood we went by ship so it took a month to get out to Singapore, it took five weeks to get to Hong Kong, where I spent two years of my long life and these were long journeys, you know, and for a little child it was a different world.'

Melvyn: 'You see, I was brought up in a place of 5000 people who had been there since the 8th century and I got the old directories and there were 12 places of worship in this place, it was set like that and I sort of didn't really move out of it until I was 18. Your life seems fantastically romantic, this great Imperial nomad drifting across oceans in massive ships and going to places like Malaya.'

Joanna: 'But when you are a child, whatever you do as a child is completely normal, it's never glamorous, it's exactly normal so no matter what your life is like, it seems completely normal to be packing up every two or three years.'

Joanna describes the moving so animatedly that Melvyn refers to her seeming rather wistful when she talks about it, rooted in moving around as he put it. Joanna wholeheartedly agreed, confiding that still to this day at the age of 65 she always keeps suitcases in the rooms and hallways of wherever she is living. Although she uses most of them for storing things, she knows that in the back of her mind it is the feeling that she can always move on – not a running away in a sense but ability to move on. The pair of them then joked that some of the cases stored the Christmas decorations so as Melvyn so humorously put it, if Joanna did move on quickly at least she would have a decorated tree...and some reading books.

Deeply Decent Parents – Joanna then asked Melvyn to describe his parents.

'I had deeply decent parents, very fine people indeed, I still have, my mother is still alive. For instance my father, and we all talk sentimentally about our parents, but he was a seriously clever man and there were all sorts of things, it doesn't matter but...'

Joanna: 'It does matter, it does matter.'

Melvyn: 'Well it would take too long, it is burdensome in a way, but he passed a major scholarship when he was about eleven and another when he was twelve from a little parish school, a parish of what, about 110 people, whatever it was but he couldn't take advantage of them. He was the oldest of nine children, he left when he was 14 and went to work, so he was thwarted in that sense but he was never bitter. More importantly, he had no ambitions for me that he revealed, so he never said "you've got to do your homework" and he never said, "how are you getting on at school?" and he never said, "your report wasn't very good", he never said that once. Looking back, I thought that was extraordinary self-restraint because he clearly, now I know, wanted me to do well...'

Joanna: 'An extraordinary man.'

Melvyn: 'Yes, yes, very.'

Joanna wanted to know if Melvyn's father had lived to 'see him fly' which Melvyn said that he did – he died in 1996/97, but he didn't see Melvyn becoming ennobled.

Body language is an interesting and often subliminal aspect of human nature but there were times during the filming of the 'Living the Life' series where the contributor's body language really validated the narrative of what was being said. Stephen's tics when talking about leaving Cellmates, Dylan Jones getting hot under the collar with an early interrogation from George especially in reference to an out of context word, (druid). Melvyn, who remained humble throughout the show, physically squirmed in his seat when Joanna directed questions about his entering the House of Lords and whether he felt his father would have been proud of his ennoblement.

Lord Melvyn Bragg's body language

Melvyn, of course, is the consummate interviewer. Very few people have held interviews with such an esteemed list as he has, which makes it slightly more understandable to physically exhibit discomfort when put back under the scrutiny and focus as opposed to driving the questions.

The Bucket of Brimming Mercury – Melvyn offered his interpretation as to why he was ennobled.

'The fact is that in the late 90s the Labour Party wanted to do things in the arts and they didn't have people in the Lords who were speaking to it and they said would I go in. I was nervous about it, I did it and it was like walking around town with a bucket of brimming mercury on your head for about six months or so, it was really curious as to how do you conduct yourself when this thing's happened to you. Then you profoundly realise it didn't matter, there was a job to do and you got on with it.'

It was at this point of the show when Melvyn revealed how nervous he gets before filming or recording 'absolutely everything'. Not just a few quiet nerves but a genuine unease, he Melvyn explained he tries to be alone, and locks himself away in the bathroom or dressing room to try and relax. Even before the episode of 'Living the Life' he had become very anxious, saying "you'd think it would go away at 71 years of age".

Joanna gave her interpretation of the professional paradox for Melvyn.

'But you see you're extraordinary because writers I would have thought, I mean I know many writers and it doesn't mean to say that they are necessarily introverted people but on the other hand very few people have married a writing career, which yours is, with a broadcasting and communicating side, I mean this seems to me, you seem to be two men tied into one, do you feel that sometimes?'

Melvyn: 'Sometimes less tied than others! Loosening, disassembled.'

I Hove into your Ken – Joanna reminisced about her own father, who was in the Indian Army – he was with the Ghurkhas – the regiment that Joanna has fought selflessly for with the Justice Campaign to guarantee UK settlement rights from the British Government. She also revealed that she had to pay the British Government to become a British subject, around the time she was modelling.

We mentioned it earlier and also when referring to Stephen Fry's well documented label of intellect, that Joanna was as verbose as any of the contributors in the series. She had a wonderful turn of phrase that was a delight for the crew during filming, not only for the ease with which she expressed herself but also the immediacy that a seasoned broadcaster such as Melvyn clarified the meaning for a wider audience. Joanna referred to the time she was modelling as around the time 'I hove into your Ken.' To which Melvyn instantly retorted – 'we made a film, and you were one of the stars in it when you were modelling – yes.'

Without missing a beat the conversation rolled on with Joanna explaining that she had to travel abroad at that time, possibly to America, and they (the Home Office) said 'But you aren't a British citizen'. She explained how she overcame the obstacle and also her recollections of her father.

'So I paid £4.17.6d to become a British citizen, isn't that odd? And I was born to an Army member, but born abroad and my father having been born abroad – daddy was born in Lahore – and so two generations born abroad and you were treated as outside.'

Melvyn: 'What was your father like?'

Joanna: 'A darling, he was a bookish man, a great historian, terribly funny. He was one of four children of which he was the only boy. They were sent back to school, he was sent back to school from far away when he was seven, he didn't see his parents for four years, it was rather like that Baa-Baa Black Sheep, Kipling's Baa-Baa Black Sheep, where the children were just sent home and they never saw their parents because it was expensive, their parents were working out in wherever it was, the Far East or India, there were no real schools for them to be sent to so they were sent back and also disease was pretty rife in those days, but four years is a long time away and he had to sleep in his sister's boarding school in the holidays, they had no holiday homes to go to.

I love pretty much everything, I have been born without a critical nature, I love everything until it's really vile and then I hate it. So I'm nothing, I'm as shallow as a puddle actually.'

Issued in Brusque Commands – Melvyn assumed that one of the qualities that Joanna gained from her father was discipline and she explains with much warmth how her father wasn't like that at all. Although he was a Major in the Army, and although it would be easy to make associations of other children from military families her father never brought his Army persona home.

Joanna continues with a delightful story about when she was performing in a play in the West End with Glenn Close. Glenn had revealed that when she was cast for the role of Cruella de Ville in *101 Dalmatians* she wanted to base her voice on Joanna's, and the English voice coach said, 'Oh that's because Joanna grew up in an Army family where everything is issued in brusque commands'.

'...that made me laugh so much. I love the idea that somehow your father continues being a military man at home. It is absolute rubbish. He loved reading books and roaring with laughter and he loved the garden. He was quite solitary, he quite loved being on his own and as time went on he preferred more and more his own company, he became almost reclusive, he never went to Army reunions or anything like that. He

As children both Melvyn and Joanna experienced time separated from their fathers because of the war and or military commitments abroad. Joanna described her separation poignantly, when asked how she returned to England. It was also a section of the show where Joanna shared a self-analytical insight into how a nomadic childhood existence and periods of loneliness had shaped her ability to get along with others, to be liked.

'...both of them (her parents) having hated being sent away from home, their home which was India, determined that my sister and I wouldn't have that so we came back and I went to boarding school when my father had to go back to Malaya and my mother stayed on. The longest I didn't see my mother was six months which was when she went out to Malaya to stay with daddy for a bit and the longest I didn't see my father was a year and a half, which was awful. I used to have dreams that I went down to Southampton docks to meet daddy and in my dream I'd go down to meet him and the great gangplank would come down and I didn't know what he looked like. Now this is rubbish because in real life of course I knew what he looked like in waking life, but in dream life I'd stand there and think he wouldn't know what I looked like either. It was awful. Separation from parents is awful, I was terribly homesick.

I get over everything because I'm an easy little tick, I make friends with people, I'm oily, fit in, say yes when I don't really mean it, I can chum up to anybody. I would have been a good spy, I would have. I sometimes think if I had actually been in the Second World War I would have liked to have joined the Resistance, I've worked out all sorts of ways I would have worked my way round into getting close to Hitler and then with my grandmother's favourite weapon, a hatpin, I could have sorted him out. You see, I wanted to be an actress, I wouldn't have done it, I just wanted to act it!'

The Hitler Effect – There was a section in the footage of Stephen Fry and Bill Wyman's episode of 'Living the Life' (which didn't make the final edit) where Stephen talks about the third novel he wrote (Making History) where a permanent male contraceptive pill is sent back in time to a well that Hitler's father drinks from and becomes infertile and consequently Hitler is never conceived. The plot then imagines an even worse reality where someone even more ruthless but more cautious accedes to forefront of the Nazis and ends up with world domination.

Joanna also relayed her imagination creating fantasies of how her character would have been well suited to the Second World War resistance and her own fanciful plotting of Hitler's demise (using her grandmother's favourite hat pin) – two intellects, independently imagining a parallel universe of a changed history concerning Hitler.

The Grim Reaper – If there was one recurring theme throughout the whole series it was that of death. Death was mentioned by pretty much every contributor of the series. The conversations may not have all made the final edits but death was certainly discussed by them. In essence, if anyone is given the luxury of sitting down with a 'like-minded soul' and openly discussing their 'journey of life' death is bound to, in some way or another, rear its topical head. Jeremy Clarkson confessed to thinking about it all the time and the importance of dying in an anecdote. Robin Gibb emotionally shared the trauma of having lost his brothers, and Joanna, by talking about it in her own inimitable way, revealed a very spiritual persona and somebody who had not only thought about the subject a great deal, but was also at peace with what she felt the reality would be like for her.

As in the majority of philosophies around the world, death is a major lesson to confront, understand and reconcile with yourself in some way, akin to the Zen quote, 'Once you understand death, then you can truly live.' However high your public profile, the beauty of the show is an insight into the emotional challenges everyone faces irrespective of fame.

Melvyn suggested to Joanna that maybe she wouldn't remember anything because she would be dead, but she revealed her belief.

'I think I will. But just for that fortnight or so that we linger around after we've gone tidying up...this is the saddest thing, I realise that what I'm going to miss when I die is this, (Joanna holds her hands up) because this is the useful little body that has walked about doing all these things for all these years, teeth too big, do you know what I mean, nose too short to do Shakespeare, rather ratty hair, over dyed, quite tall, broad shoulders, all these, this dear little car I've got used to will disappear...

I don't believe we just go 'bong'. The taxi stops, we can't comprehend how it will be and yet we all know people who've died and they've gone and we go, "oh they've gone". But because we don't know what it is, I'm fascinated, I think about death all the time with the greatest interest. That J.M. Barrie thing, the last great adventure, and you think "what is it like?" I have a feeling we are just going to go, oh I get it, as we go through, oh I get it. Like a riddle, so little, so nothing, so tiny.

Melvyn: 'I hope I'm not frightened of dying but I think I am very, very, very nervous of the way it will happen. The idea of being unable to talk or think or just to vegetate there, that's a thing I think I really don't want to go there. I just want to keep…unlike you, that can fall off and a knee can go wonky but it's inside my head, if it's not 'clearish' and I can communicate in a way, if that stops happening, that would be exit stage left as fast as possible.'

Since the successful broadcast of the series on television we have received so much positive feedback about the show and also validation about what we felt to be its unique selling point – there is no interviewer. Before it was screened or people had seen rushes, they would offer comments comparing the series to other televised conversation/interview shows. Following any episode being viewed either independently or as part of the series, it becomes clear though that there is a significant and obvious difference to other shows that employ an interviewer.

Even if the interviewer is deemed a minor celebrity in their own right, they are there to ask questions of the guest/celebrity. They may have their own entertaining quirks or patter, but categorically they are not there as a person of equal interest and are not there to share their own anecdotes and experiences.

This was probably never more apparent than during the following section of the show where Joanna is keen to understanding more about Melvyn's documented nervous breakdown. It would be both intrusive and out of context for an interviewer to suddenly pounce a similar question. It could also be deemed to be rude and shut down the guest from responding.

With Joanna and Melvyn they had both already shared fairly weighty themes including spirituality and death and Joanna without being prompted felt by her own volition that the nature of their previous topics led naturally to her in the natural direction of asking Melvyn to expand on such a difficult part of his life. As an aside, Joanna was certainly the only person in the room who could so naturally and good naturedly tick Melvyn off for his shoe tapping...but in doing so there was a very natural lead into the question and following section of the show, that epitomised 'Living the Life' being a conversation between the two 'well known' personalities...not a scripted/fishing/salacious or publicity junket interview. There is a very real and distinct difference.

Joanna: 'Just stop for a second. For a famous broadcaster you are extraordinary with your feet, you've got to keep your feet still.'

Melvyn: 'Have I? Am I disturbing you?'

Joanna: 'No, no, you're just doing it like this because you are a very jittery person.'

Melvyn: 'Yes. Jittery is a good word isn't it?'

Joanna: 'But go on, go on, go on. I want to know why you had a nervous breakdown.'

Melvyn: 'Well I'd quite like to know as well...the first one was when I was about 13, 12½, 13 to about 14½ so about a year and a half.'

Joanna: 'So a little boy.'

Melvyn: 'Yes. That was just, I don't know how it crept up on me...it manifested itself in… it was...well it started in bed, I had this little bedroom, a very nice little bedroom, a bit narrow, like a narrow cell and what happened was something that was in my head, inside my head, left my head and drifted across the room and was in the top right hand corner of the room. It was something like a light but I knew that that was me and I didn't know what this was. Now I am being very comparatively clear about it, but I was a teenager, I didn't know what to do except wait for it to come back. I didn't know how to get it back and so I was frozen. Meanwhile downstairs in the pub, it was a Saturday night and people would be singing and I just was waiting for it. That became acute so that was one thing that happened.

The second thing that happened was it was impossible for me to...what you were saying earlier, to look at myself in a mirror or catch myself in a shop window as I walked to school, because I thought that...I suppose I thought that that would stay there and when I went away that would be me, but what went away wouldn't be, so it was this split thing quite badly. Anyway, it got to be chronic and my school results plunged and I got really physically frightened.

The third problem was that there was absolutely nobody on earth I could even intimate, I couldn't tell anybody but I couldn't even hint it to anybody because I couldn't...I'm finding it hard enough to talk about now but I couldn't express it. Who did I tell? I couldn't tell my parents because in those days you didn't, you got on with it. How could I go to a doctor? I couldn't tell my teachers. Looking back, I think two things happened that were really important. One was work, I just got lost in work, school work, History, English, other stuff and I would work at home, just work. I played rugby for the school, that was something you did in those days, I sang in choirs, all that stuff and I fell in love when I was about 15.

Joanna: 'So this lasted and lasted and lasted.'

Melvyn: 'Yes and it came back in my 20s, early 30s, with a sort of vengeance for about a year and I thought I'd had it then. It was almost the same thing but had shifted in a certain way.'

Joanna: 'Was it the same idea, the same light, did that light ever come back to you?'

Melvyn: 'No, no, that didn't, no.'

Joanna: 'Has it come back yet?'

Melvyn: 'No, and actually I...really want to stress something because it was as a result of that that I got interested in MIND and I have been President of MIND for many years now, but I got through it and that is really important to tell people. I got through it and for the last forty years I've felt nervy now and then but nothing's happened and I've done a lot of work and I've made friends and I've brought up a family and I've done this, that and the other. I've got through a lot of stuff so you can get through it and I think those were particular clusters of circumstances that I haven't worked out yet and I don't know whether I want to. I tried to in the second one in a novel I wrote but you can get through these things, you can get through these things.'

Joanna: 'So this is very frightening.

Melvyn: 'Yes. Not now, I've been very steady, especially since I met Cate, so it's been fine.'

It was very honest, brave and open of Melvyn to try and explain so succinctly how he felt and what he went through. It was also important that he reminded the audience how he not only got through it, but has enjoyed a very successful and fulfilling life since.

The Mind Presidents –

One of the reasons Melvyn attributes to getting through his breakdown was his involvement with Mind. He has been an active champion of the leading mental health charity in England and Wales and has also served as the Charity's president. For someone of Melvyn's stature and achievements to talk so candidly about his own experiences whilst living and demonstrating his successful management of mental health is a real and valid motivation to others who can relate to his experiences.

In a quirk common to the 'six degrees of separation' of the 'Living the Life' series, Stephen Fry has recently become the new president now Melvyn's tenure has finished. The charity has certainly been blessed with two champions of the mind for MIND. To find out more about the charity visit www.mind.org.

Joanna instantly related to Melvyn's description of his experiences and shared her own story of having suffered extreme anxiety.

The Wobbler – 'I had a bit of a wobbler once. I was on stage, I was doing a play at the time, I had Jamie, my son who I was bringing up on my own because I was unmarried, I was getting no money from the play I was in. The au pair girl, which sounds very grand but they were just sweet girls who came and lived in the box room I had where I shared a flat on half a top floor in west London, had just bolted. I had been hallucinating about people in the stalls because there was a man who was a flasher who used to come and buy a ticket in the front row and…. I complained to the management and they said "no, he pays for his seat so we can't throw him out".

Then I began to see people levelling guns at me out of the boxes, I'd see the glint of a rifle, I'd see it levelling down and I used to work out how I could throw myself in front of this actor so I could protect them but also bring us both down to the ground. So my mind was not…I was completely skewed off and one morning, a Saturday morning, I woke up and we had two shows that day, it was at the Garrick Theatre and I woke up with the clearest sense in my mind, I thought "oh I won't go to the theatre, that's the end of it, I'll never go back to the theatre again".

So I got on to a train and I went down to Kent to my parents. They said, "what are you doing, what are you doing?" I said, "I'm not going back to the theatre". Now this is what later Stephen Fry had and I've since been...because I've been hypnotised you know.'

Melvyn: 'Did you go back to the theatre?'

Joanna: 'Not that play, not that play. I went away for six months but what I mean is by then I was on the brink that was the beginning of what was then huge. I couldn't cross the road, I didn't dare go into shops, I had to concentrate – I'm sure you've done this – on breathing in and breathing out to keep breathing.'

Melvyn: 'Panic attacks'.

Joanna: 'Its panic attacks and you are on the brink of utter insanity. I was in my mid-20s I suppose and I thought "I will never go there again". I set up a series of tests for myself. What would be the very worst you could do? Okay, you can't go into the supermarket, why? Why can't you go in? Because there will be people there and what might happen. Well what might happen? I kept on pushing myself – what if? What if I fall over? Yes, then what happens? Kind people will come up. What if I fall over, break things, cut myself and I'm not wearing any pants and I've stolen something? I'd run that one in and out would come the same answer, kind people will help you. People will pull your skirt down over your no pants, they will bandage up your cut wrists from whatever has happened, they will take the stolen thing out of your basket and put it back so you don't have to pay for it and they will put you on your way.

So I began to push myself forward to what if, what if, what if, what if. I thought I must never, ever get to this stage again so like you, when I can feel the thing, I worked out ways of getting round it because I thought I must never go this near to the edge of the precipice again because otherwise I will go mad.'

Melvyn: 'I think it is worth saying, honestly, because a lot of people, since I've been with MIND a lot of people have...I mean you do get through it. You have lived, you said this was in your mid-20's, you said earlier you were nearly 65 so for 40 years, and it is about the same for me, you have lived a terrifically busy life, life has gone on and, as it were, the waters have closed over enough.'

Single Motherhood – Melvyn picked up on Joanna having mentioned three or four times that she was an unmarried mother and wondered if that was a strain, especially considering the stigma at that particular time.

'No, I think I was lucky. I was born into this darling family who couldn't have loved me more and I was born into this darling profession, however, I hadn't any money. I had a darling family who also didn't have any money. We might have had presents from the 13th Dalai Lama but we didn't have any money!

The difficulties of being a solitary parent, which is the same for divorced parents, widowed parents, is being the one person who has to get the money in and look after the child as well and trying to split those two is the difficult thing because you'd much rather be reading them a bedtime story than going off to the theatre to earn £40 a week. So those were the difficulties but there was no 'snootery' or snobbery because modelling didn't give a jot about those things, acting couldn't give a toss about those things. If I was in a steadier profession and maybe in a smaller town with a more bigoted family, I may have had to give up the baby, have him adopted or ben thrown out of the family completely.'

Joanna Lumley and her first child James

Fay Weldon an her first son Nicholas

Birgitte Nielsen and her children Killan, Douglas and Raoul

Caitlin Moran with her two daughters Dora and Eavie

Both Joanna, Fay Weldon and to some extent Brigitte Nielsen all contended with having a child early in life and also bringing up the child on their own in a more judgemental social climate. All of them too exhibited a strength in character to believe in themselves, and their path in their careers and life that they actually attracted very little judgement or ostracism for their choices.

Interested in this early life that Joanna had experienced, Melvyn asked her if she had enjoyed being a model in the 60's with all that went with it. Joanna had the crew stifling laughs on set as she described in mock 'Patsy' character fashion the 'feel' of that era.

'It was terrific, it was sensational! It was just when everything was starting. Give me a hippy headband darling and a few beads and I'm there but in the end, a very few died which was awful, they were fools. None of us were rich enough to have a lot of dope – don't Bogart that joint my friend, you'd watch it like a hawk, would it come back to you, no it had finished there so you'd only have one puff. So this idea of getting stoned out of your mind was for the rich or for the very carefree, anyway I wasn't one of those. So I loved it. I never had any dope, someone else would bring some along, so it wasn't really a drug culture, I had no money for drink so you didn't drink. Well you had the odd G&T at the end of an evening, ice and a slice thank you! So cool. But you just got on. '

Spent Like a Kicking Horse – Melvyn followed on from Joanna's retelling of her early modelling days, intrigued as to how she had progressed into acting, and then an actual career in acting. Joanna couldn't pinpoint the time but it was interesting to see that she was in two iconic productions very early in her career – Coronation Street and a Bond movie – which Melvyn thought genuinely amazing, and Joanna described in humorous detail.

'Even now, even now people queue outside the theatre holding a picture of my Bond girl person who is 21 to sign. Being a Bond girl you get some tattoo in your soul, "Bond Girl." My part was so small, I was only called "The English Girl", I didn't even have a name but by golly gee, it was at the time when the Bond films were at their biggest and brightest and they spent like a kicking horse and it was glamorous beyond measure and it was thrilling. It was two years of my life and we got £100 a week.'

Two Bond Girls for 'Living the Life' –

A natural coincidence for the series of 'Living the Life' was our inclusion of two Bond Girls as contributors. Both Joanna and Britt have starred alongside fiction's most charismatic secret agent.

Joanna Lumley as 'The English Girl' in On Her Majestys Secret Service

Britt Ekland in The Man with the Golden Gun

Luck and Guilt – Two oft quoted words from the series. Everyone agreed to the hand of 'Lady Luck' stroking a career into existence. Melvyn stated once again that he felt he had been fantastically lucky, unbelievably so,and asks Joanna if she felt the same. She wholeheartedly agreed – 'more than lucky...completely blessed...' and then by way of steering the show to a close she added that she wasn't that enamoured with the statue on the table either.

As a production team we felt after such deep and honest sharing about huge themes of their lives, it was a nice way to gently draw the curtains on what had been a wonderful meeting of minds and emotions. (The statue in question was of a ballerina which Joanna shared a little story about her childhood ballet experiences, describing the statues balletic position and how her fledgling passion ended early with a change of teacher. With a self-mocking 'what am I good for', both Melvyn and Joanna wrapped the show.

'I love talking to you, we never get this do we, even at dinner parties and things, you never get the chance to talk. There may be a few people watching – "Hi". Joanna acknowledges the 'future' viewers, and they both drink from their glasses of water, with a beautiful little 'Patsyesque' exit.

'Wow, this is strong' (the water doubling for Patsy's vodka).

Lord Melvyn Bragg and Joanna Lumley saying their goodbyes

LESLIE PHILLIPS

Leslie Phillips is the legendary British actor with an incomparable 75 years of performing. During his career Leslie has acted, directed and produced for the stage, television and film. Although he is still well known and well loved for his performances in some of the best-loved comedies of all time including the 'Carry On' films and 'Doctor' series, he has acted in a huge range of parts from playing Falstaff at the RSC to memorably bringing to life the Sorting Hat in the 'Harry Potter' franchise. He has become a Hollywood heavyweight with films such as 'Venus' and 'Empire of the Sun.'

Robin Gibb makes up one third of one of the most successful groups of all time – the Bee Gees. Known across the world for their distinctive sound and harmonies, they became living legends with the release of their soundtrack to 'Saturday Night Fever.' Along with his brothers the group have sold upwards of 100 million albums, cementing their status in pop history.

ROBIN GIBB

Setting in – In essence, Leslie and Robin's conversation was the pilot for the 'Living the Life' series. Leslie has a vast career that has encompassed 75 years of directing, producing and above all delivering a huge array of comedic and serious acting performances for television, theatre and the silver screen. It is not often that someone in their late eighties with such a history behind them is still eloquent and precise about the life that they have lived.

Leslie is much loved and endeared to the public for certain memorable roles and catchphrases (more on those later) but we felt as a production and management team that a chance to showcase a more human side to Leslie's life and career was a story worth telling. Robin Gibb, of course, is the legendary Bee Gee and phenomenally successful singer and songwriter who, unbeknownst to many, is an avid fan of the old British comedies and had followed all of Leslie's filmic career – a template pairing for a 'Living the Life' conversation was born.

Location – During the initial discussions for the series, there were certain qualities that were givens' from the very inception of the show: A comfortable environment, time for the contributors to reminisce and relax into deeper conversations and minimal distraction and intrusion from the team. For the first (pilot) episode the place where we felt our contributors may feel most comfortable and relaxed was at one or others home. We were very fortunate that Robin and his family are such genial hosts and that their beautiful 12th century Oxfordshire manor house had an array of quiet areas in which to film.

Consequently, one crisp autumn morning we arrived at Robin and his wife's Dwina's house and set about preparing an area for the filming. For those who have viewed the series, you will probably have noticed slight differences with camera angles, lighting and background in Leslie and Robin's episode compared with the rest of the series. That was us finding our feet, the obvious main focus on managing the time and gentle directional prompts to allow both contributors to open up with each other.

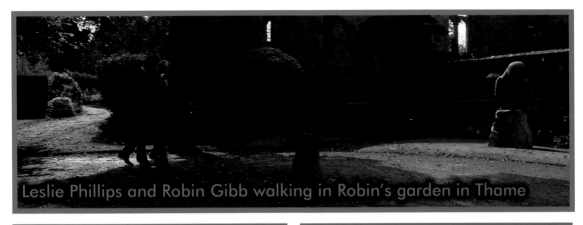
Leslie Phillips and Robin Gibb walking in Robin's garden in Thame

Child Labour – Robin fell naturally into conversation very quickly with Leslie, itching to trace the actor's career right back to its inception all those years ago.

'After your father died in 1934, do you see that as a principal starting point in pursuing a career or was it being a big brother and head of the family?'

Leslie: 'Yes, it was really the whole point because we weren't a well off family and my father had always been very seriously ill all though his life and when he died, I had a brother and sister, they looked at me and said "We're all going to get some work, we've got to get some work."'

Leslie Phillips with his older Sister Doris

Robin: 'The family were not in show business, the same as mine.'

Leslie: 'No, no, neither was I. I mean I did at school like all the other ghastly children, you know, so that was it. My mother, strangely enough, wrote a letter having seen an advert in the paper wanting children for a Christmas show and she got a reply. Italia Conti, the dear lady who I remember so well, she asked me up to meet her and that's the story, I met her.'

Robin: 'Up till this point it was really about making sure the family survives and being the breadwinner?'

Leslie: 'It led to money, that was the reason, it was money. We were looking for some money. It's still about the money.'

It was a frank confession for the start of a show and subtly, many times during the filming Leslie alludes to money, earning money, needing money and also the responsibility of looking after the women in his life, as a result of taking financial responsibility for his mother from the earliest of ages after his father died. It is an ingrained subconscious response to always be sure he is safe financially.

The Male Bronte – Robin shared that he grew up with his two brothers, Maurice and Barry, and that they had each other to turn to in good times and bad. Leslie also picked up on the fact that it is quite unnatural to go through such a large part of your life, so intricately linked with your brothers. Robin explained:

'I don't remember having many relatives when we were kids, we were very isolated. We weren't that well off, we didn't have any presents at Christmas and such like and we were copying what was on the radio and pretending, at eight years old we were imagining writing songs for their next single, we'd pretend to write their next single –

Young Gibb borthers, Maurice (left), Barry (centred and Robin (right)

we're still pretending – and in a way I think we were a bit like a male Brontes.

We never had any friends, we were very isolated, it was a very windy part of Manchester! But our friends didn't share the same fascination for music as we did, organically, they'd rather be outside kicking a football or doing evil deeds, messing around. They couldn't really relate to us, pretending to write songs is something they just couldn't connect with so by the nature of us, we had each other.'

The Dodgy Teacher – Reminiscing about their childhoods, Robin asked Leslie what in his estimation was the most traumatic period of that time, or the event that stood out, to which Leslie shockingly revealed the following childhood experience.

'Oh God, yes, well I can think of one quite incredible thing that has literally leapt into my mind. When I was about twelve I think, I was at school, I was at an elementary school in Chingford, Essex and we had a slightly dodgy teacher. It became quite common knowledge in the school, he used to get hold of the boys and sort of chat them up and try and be a bit naughty with them. He used to get these kids and he used to hold them quite tight right up against and then he encouraged them to put their hands behind and feel him up, absolutely. All the boys knew but they kept it secret. It was a big scandal, it went right round Essex that did. I bet those kids, none of them will forget that.'

Leslie asked Robin if he had a trauma from his childhood that had stuck with him and he described a horrendous car crash he was involved in at about 13 years of age.

'Mine involves actually a very bad car crash where the three of us rolled eight times just outside Sydney, probably about the time you were there. It stands out because

Leslie Phillips (blonde boy, front row) school photograph

nobody usually came out of that road alive, there were no other cars involved, it rolled eight times and the three of us, me, Barry and Maurice, and my father was driving, with one kidney, and I remember the car coming to a halt on its roof and the minute it came to a halt I saw my dad's hand going to the ignition to turn it off. I think back to the presence of mind that he had of doing that, because he thought it could catch on fire.'

Leslie was aghast at Robin's childhood experience of the car crash and lightened the mood by joking about how thankful the nation was that he'd made it out alive to bring such joy through his music, and brought up 'Saturday Night Fever.'

Saturday Night Fever album cover

'You know everybody loves you for that wonderful…

Robin: 'Oh that Fever film, the one with the pointing finger.'

Leslie: '*Staying Alive* wasn't it?'

Robin: 'It is one of the aspects of this business, you start out hoping to create that kind of thing…we were very cautious

58

about it because it wasn't the thing for music and film together because nobody was actually singing in the film, thankfully. The fact is we didn't see the film at all until it came out...on paper a lot of people would like to have something that marries music and story together and this one just did it in the right place at the right time. It was totally unexpected, just off the radar...it is still the biggest selling soundtrack in history.

Robin Gibb mimicking the iconic Saturday Night Fever dance move

Catchphrases, everybody when they think of a certain actor or even a musician, always something stands out.'

Leslie: 'They go with you.'

Robin wholeheartedly agreed and enjoyed the opportunity to quiz Leslie about his catchphrases, or at least the iconic ones that are forever associated with him. Leslie agreed that audiences loved them, which was why as Robin explained they latch onto them, as they do with musicians' lyrics. Robin continued, asking Leslie how it felt that people always automatically associate him with the phrase 'Hello' and 'Ding Dong'.

The Twitterati Anecdote No1–

During the final editing of the whole series, Leslie Phillips was encouraged by the Macmillan cancer charity and by his agent and Executive Producer, Rosemary Reed, to start 'Twittering.'

He has since confided in us that it has really perked up his days, but more relevantly to the above topic of conversation, his most common tweets are from those asking for a Ding Dong...almost as an incarnation for a birthday or event, for joyful news, as a pick me up from depressing news and all round 'gong' for positivity. To witness such love and association for the phrase reunited Leslie's affection for it.

Robin: 'Does it bother you?'

Leslie: 'No, it doesn't really. I mean it depends who it is and where it is and whether they're taking the piss out of you or whether they love you. It's a punishment in a way for playing parts and using a kind of catchphrase.'

Robin: 'It's also proof that you've connected, you have actually reached people.'

Leslie: 'Yes, they are reaching you and they've seen you on the telly or in the theatre or something and I have enjoyed myself with hello "Hello", yes, "Hello", I breathe it out you see. I have played many serious roles, I have been to Stratford-upon-Avon, played Falstaff, Shakespeare and often the audiences come round and just watch me as Falstaff and then they come up to me and say "Hello". So it doesn't hinder you.'

Leslie Phillips playing the Shakespearian role of Falstaff

Famous Friends – One of the interesting 'sidelines' that surfaced throughout filming the 'Living the Life' series was the incidental anecdotes about other famous people. It is obvious that our contributors move in and socialise in circles of other 'well known' people, but the way in which a story about someone else would just 'pop into' the conversation was riveting.

Leslie had great fun describing Kenneth Williams' interaction with the public.

'Actually Kenneth Williams, he didn't like being interfered with...I don't mean interfered with but he didn't like people interrupting him when he was out...and he was, I mean he was a great character, bless his heart, but my God did he go, he really used to tear people apart. "Will you go away, I'm not going to be wasting my time talking to you, darling, piss off, go on", all that went on and he used to love those occasions, it was part of his joy, but it can go either way.'

There were also repeat offenders throughout the series – Keith Moon throwing the cat at his girlfriend Annette and then popping up when Peter Blake wondered how Ken Russell handled him when directing *Tommy*. Cilla shared her early career anecdotes of hanging out with the Beatles and Peter Stringfellow recalled the experience of booking them as his first major band at *The Black Cat Club*. Both Sebastian Coe and Gary Newbon were friends of Brian Clough and even royalty were included in some stories.

Casual Sex – With two highly charismatic men, it wasn't long before the conversation turned to sex. Robin threw out the opening gambit of 'sexual relationships' and there followed a little 'toing and froing' of who was renowned most for their exploits including a wry joke that was almost lost with both of them talking over each other when Robin

Leslie Phillips surrounded by show-girls

deadpanned that 'there was no such thing as casual sex, as it has always been hard work.' He then suggested that women can sometimes spoil men's careers, but Leslie was still in playful mode, admitting, 'Women never spoil my life at all because I really like women.' Robin persisted, asking if Leslie always put his career first.

'The thing is, fame attracts much more than normal people, the bounty as it were. Most of your films, many of your films, have been involved with women and sexy ladies, wonderful roles and great parts to play where you were the charmer, the Casanova, the roving eye. Has it been allowed to creep into your private life? Or has it done it unwittingly?'

Leslie: 'Well yes. You see these women are very necessary aren't they? That's what everybody wants to see, the lovely girl in the film. I'm no woman hater, I can assure you, I adore women and I find it a nice way to spend your time. I'd pay them if I couldn't get it any other way. No, I think it makes the audience very conscious of the fact that, oh you lucky devil.'

Robin: 'It's the nature of the beast, isn't it?'

Leslie: 'I get that in the street and in restaurants; "oh you're a lucky devil aren't you?" I do occasionally get left a couple of phone numbers I must admit. I don't always ring them but I occasionally do, just for company. I think you know that, I think everybody understands that.'

Robin: 'You're quite right, it's always different, a lot more…'

Leslie: 'It's disgusting, but I love it!'

It was a difficult edit for the final cut because of the three competing trains of thought in that one short and snappy exchange between Leslie and Robin. Firstly, Robin was attempting to ask seriously how Leslie's relationships had affected his career. Secondly, Leslie remained throughout the whole exchange on a witty monologue about his love of women which, although 'tongue-in-cheek' and an entertaining play for the viewer, was actually, (thirdly) old school sexism in action – 'I adore women and find them a nice way to spend your time.' That is the nature of the show, and because the theme of relationships was revisited later on in the episode I chose to leave the opening gambit in.

The Six-Week Celebrity – Both Robin and Leslie, like most of the other contributors, became very animated when discussing what constituted a definition of the word celebrity. Robin began with:

'The fact that television could produce celebrity in six weeks of constant television... so advanced technology has actually created the fifteen minute celebrity from reality television shows but what I have to say is, I don't see the kind of celebrity of your stature coming through by that, it is turning more to celebrity scandal and all of that kind of rubbish. It's more about ratings than quality.

In the record business technology allows people who would never have been signed up to make records thirty years ago, they can make records at home and they don't even have to sing the record, they can just sing one line and have the voice tuned. The artist can actually be a model that the record company sign up, as long as they are a good looking model and they go on telly and mime the record, that's fine, the producers can do the rest. So in a way it has become a very...a business certainly for manufacturing, a reason for not paying an artist, for creating one that they don't have to pay because they are getting the same results.'

Leslie: But you couldn't do that years ago, you couldn't do that, you had to have a career but now you can be a star, come off the pavement, come off the television, one night and you're a star.'

Robin: 'Well somebody tells me someone's a star but I've never heard of them. They are a star? I'm supposed to know who they are, you know...it's not lasting celebrity.'

Leslie: 'Our work is real, it's not a joke, it's not being silly, it's talent and using it in such a way that you make the audience enjoy themselves. I did play every part, every job; I mean every job in the business. I was a call boy, I worked in the box office, I did all those sorts of things as well, moved scenery and I've also been a star, I've been a director, I've been a producer and I've been a writer. I've covered the whole gamut, it's a long career if you are going to be loved and it's a difficult career if you are sensitive or over sensitive, that is for sure.'

Reminiscing about the trials and tribulations of their industry, Leslie shared what he felt was one of the main pitfalls.

Pissed out of their mind – 'One thing I've noticed, the one solid thing right through from a kid to now, which is a long time, it's over 70 years, the biggest killer that brings trouble is drink. That comes into this business in many ways and even out of this business, but drink is a mistake.'

Robin: 'I know, I've seen, I've lived through a lot of people from early on in our career, people like Jimi Hendrix and all those people who couldn't see the wood for the trees, there's a lot of casualties there, casualties of first fame from the late 60s.'

Leslie: 'I'm lucky, I'm not a drinker, I just have never been a drinker but I've lived with people and I've been with people that come on the stage pissed out of their mind and it is really hell.'

Robin: 'It's a hard job when you're working with them.'

Leslie: 'It is tough for those people particularly. I could tell you so many stories but I'd like to forget them because none of them are here anymore apart from anything else.'

Leslie paused for comic effect here as he looked heavenwards to where the departed drinking 'thesps' had returned to spirit. As a natural ending to the train of that conversation Leslie swung the emphasis back to Robin, urging him to share some of his stories. Robin quite matter-of-factly described an amazing incident where he was made to sing live at gunpoint, before following the retelling up very quickly with a train crash tragedy he was involved in.

'There was one show that we did in Jakarta, 60,000 people, and the Governor said that the Army would take care of us if we didn't go on in the middle of a thunderstorm which was happening at the time. We didn't want to go on because the live mics might strike...be struck by lightning and kill us. He said "if it's not that it's going to be the Army, take your choice!" So the Governor said "we'll strike a balance, if the supporting cast go on and they live, will you go on?" So the supporting cast went on, that was the deal and then when we went on we had the Army pointing at us to make sure we didn't leave the stage because one particular act was shot on the stage the year before.'

Leslie: 'That's one you'll never forget.'

Robin: 'I was also in a train crash in London, nearly 100 people were killed in that one, Lewisham, just outside Charing Cross, that's something…and they didn't have counsellors in those days to get you through, they just got people out of it. It was in black and white and you kept away. By coincidence we had our first UK number one, it was the night, November 5th 1967 and I was in that train crash. That's how I celebrated that number one record.

It was like a Spielberg movie, you could see the fireworks and you could see the blue lights because the train was on its side and silhouettes of all the carriages in different positions on the embankment and people screaming and shouting. There was about eighty people killed and God knows how many were left with severe injuries.'

It was a poignant memory for Robin of both traumatic incidents, and following on from the lightness of the preceding conversation, Leslie was really moved and a little subdued in his responses as he absorbed the gravitas of the experiences Robin had gone through. With the Hither Green rail crash, we were fortunate to have access to the original news footage (Movietone) and arranged it with Robin's first Number One (the song Massachusetts) that tried, in some way, to give a little impression of what Robin had gone through.

Leslie Phillips (left) with Michael Caine (right)

Slaughtered – Sometimes, however diplomatic 'well known' personalities are about their work and more especially about the people they work with, every now and again an experience occurs that changes the shape of their usual reserve. For Leslie, this was undoubtedly his experience of witnessing the finished film 'Is Anybody There'. Despite Robin guiding the conversation towards mentions of a vast 75 year career, almost immediately, Leslie chose to get something off his chest. The full dialogue is below.

'It was an experience that is an actor's worst possibility because we shot the film and it was great fun doing it, it really was, and it was an interesting film and some marvellous elderly people because it was taking place in an old people's home, and yet it was a comedy. I was invited to the premiere in London, okay, I turned up for the premiere, everybody was very happy, Michael Caine was the star, undisputedly the star of the film.

He got up and made a speech and invited all the character actors, it was superb for character actors in that film, really superb. In fact a lot of them were so old, and one of them actually died just before the opening and that was very sad. Anyway, I walked in, saw the director who I adored, a wonderful young director (John Crowley) and Michael made a speech and in his speech, we all stood round – we weren't invited to speak ourselves, but he introduced us as his crew, you know, in the film and we were actually going to watch this film now.

So he said, "I would like to say", he got up to the audience and said "I would like to say that it's not really a film about an old people's home really, that comes into it but it's got other factors" and that was true but it was strongly a thing about the old people's home and I was quite surprised when he said that. And he went on saying that it is still this and that and something else but none of us were invited to say anything, there were about six or seven of us standing there, all famous character actors, okay.

The film started, I sat down and as soon as it started I thought, "My God, it wasn't like that was it? We shot that in another way". Before I knew where I was, and there were some nice little bits that came up, I realised that they'd **slaughtered** the film, they'd **slaughtered** the characters in the film and made it much more a story about Michael Caine and the little boy that was the son of the mother and father who ran the home. All the other parts disappeared, they were less interesting and the press picked it up later.

When I saw the director, I just couldn't believe that they'd **slaughtered** everybody, it was all diminished. I think Michael was worried about him being in a film that was about an old people's home, simple as that, so they minimised all that. I heard him going on about it at the party after and in fact some of the character actors wouldn't go to the party because they were upset, very understandably really. I was upset and I've never, ever had that happen to me before. I have made 120 odd films throughout my life and that's what happened. I don't know who was responsible. I said to the director "why, why would you do that?" And he said, "the film just didn't stand up", he said, those were his exact words. I said, "well I don't know about that" but I never did any more to help the film because I think we were all rather hurt.'

We know Leslie very well and he is a friend as well as a working colleague, and even now a couple of years later, he still gets upset when he talks about the film *Is Anybody There*. During a break in filming, Leslie expanded on certain facts that made it such a difficult experience for him. He said that obviously, parts that he really resonates with come up much more infrequently now and with his experience (and he is on firm ground talking of experience) he felt the script and the delivering of the character actors as a whole had a great feel for a finished movie.

Consequently, not only did he feel the supporting cast, including himself, were disrespected but that also the strength of the movie was diminished. These days it may be a more common occurrence or maybe Leslie has been lucky, but to be faced with a diminished role from the one that was intended, and also to witness a finished product diminished from the one intended, was a career sting for Leslie that hurt maybe all the more for coming at such a late stage in his career.

Robin, empathising with his experience, asked Leslie about other regrets he may have in his life.

'I think of only one person really, straight away – my mother. My mother was a very unusual woman, when my father died she never looked at another man, never, and

Leslie Phillips (left) on a beach outing with his sister (centre) and mother (right)

she lived to be 92, she never looked at one. She gave her life to me, my brother, my sister and she never changed. She never was a theatrical mother, she never followed me around, she was so fantastic but my mother remained absolutely amazing and sadly came to a ghastly end, a really ghastly end. She was mugged, she was mugged in the street and three kids tried to get her handbag and she fought them off and she was badly injured and she died.'

Robin: 'That is absolutely dreadful.'

Death was, (as previously mentioned) a powerful theme that surfaced time and again throughout filming the series. For Leslie, who had suffered the loss of his father at such a young age, to lose his mother who he had taken care of and who had been his lone parent for most of his life was painful, but to lose her in such a tragic and senseless way has also shaped a sadness that Leslie will take to his grave. Robin could empathise unequivocally with Leslie too, having already suffered the loss of his younger brother Andy years earlier; Robin describes the cumulative effect of losing his twin brother.

The Bee Gees, Maurice (left), Robin (centre) and Barry (right)

'For myself, losing Maurice, my twin brother, very, very unexpectedly is something I still haven't accepted, there's no closure for me because I still imagine he is out there somewhere and I'll bump into him one day but for me that is the single most event that he's not here and that's a life sentence. It was so sudden. I am supposed to accept it after three days?

We're not built like that, we're not made like that and going to a funeral for me was worse than actually being told he'd died because it was actually seeing that he'd died.'

Robin kept with the theme of regrets, and continued asking Leslie if he had any regrets about something his work had prevented him from doing.

'Really in relation to my first wife. I wasn't married, we parted, we'd divorced and it was very sad, mainly because of the children, of course. I was in Australia with a play which was a big success, I was contracted, I'd signed my contract and we were packing the halls. As you know, it's big money isn't it...I suddenly got this communication that she'd died and...'

Leslie Phillips with his first wife, Penelope Bartley

Robin: 'You didn't make the funeral?

Leslie: 'I couldn't go, I am under contract. Obviously I asked but they said...we didn't have understudies, you were employed for your name, they can't put Joe Doe in. I mean I questioned it but I couldn't let the whole play fall on the ground so I had to say look, I can't be there for the funeral and I was never forgiven for that, never, not even by my children.'

Robin: 'Do you feel guilty about that?'

Leslie: 'Yes, I do, yes. I do sometimes.'

Homosexuality – There are certain people in life, probably because of their esteem and because of their age, where an offering of an insight is truly fresh, or at least differently expressed from the common consensus, and although the conversation still had nuances of both contributors attitudes, and experiences, Leslie unravelled a train of thought that ended up describing one of the biggest changes to the industry and the social scene – homosexuality.

'But I've not altered in my attitude since I was a boy to being a young man, being in the Army and getting older and my attitude is I've always liked women, I'm very straightforward. Very early on I met this kind of atmosphere that you're a pretty little boy, you have got blond hair and you're really sweet and you're going to be an actor, and so you have got to be a bit careful who you talk to and who you take sweets from. I think they were really trying to wise me up against homosexuality and that was very in the market at that point, until eventually I realised what it meant. Nothing has changed more since then to now than homosexuality or sex. I mean it's completely altered.'

Robin: 'Heterosexual or homosexual don't exist, it's just sexual.'

Leslie: 'It was against the law; people were arrested for things like that.'

Robin: 'When I arrived back in England in 1967 it was still illegal, people were going to prison, it was still the days of Oscar Wilde, it was incredible.'

Leslie: 'It doesn't bear analysis, the changes that have taken place. People have suffered so badly and now it has become even more of a kind of a luvvie thing to be, being cool and get what you want, eh? And nobody minds. I've always liked women and I've never been worried or even tasted anything that's called odd, I'm very straightforward and I've never had a problem, not a serious problem, but I've had a very great life where I found that area of my life very interesting.'

The Peter Sellers Factor – Peter Sellers was another 'non-contributor' who managed to inveigle his way into many of the episodes from beyond the grave. Britt shared candidly about her experiences of being married to him, Des O'Connor talked about his disappointment of being passed over (in favour of Sellers) right at the last minute for the role of introducing Frank Sinatra at the Royal Variety Performance and Robin cited a conversation he had had with Sellers regarding identity, and the blurred edges of professional and personal expression.

Robin: 'I asked Peter Sellers once who he thought he was and he didn't know who he was. He said "that's why I like to play, that's why I'm an actor, because I don't really like being alone with me". Do you feel that you've missed out?'

Leslie: 'You know, you've got your family with you at your work, I didn't have that at all, I didn't have any family. In fact, in a way I kind of lost some of my family because

I didn't have time to see them or I was away abroad doing a movie or something but you have to pick up again.'

Robin: 'But that's always been the case with you, hasn't it? Obviously you had to go away and make films, the same way I had to go away and make albums and do tours. You do spend great vasts of time away, I don't know if I can separate my professional self because, like yourself I've been doing it for so long it's almost like an escape valve, but I think there is a side of us that when you are in front of a camera, on the stage, you become a different person that you probably wouldn't be.'

Robin Gibb (second left) in a recording with The Bee Gees

Robin and Leslie were the contributors for the pilot episode of 'Living the Life' when we still had a working title of 'Living The Lie' and that subtext drove their final talking point.

Leslie: 'I suppose being an actor is living a lie. It's a thing that is natural to us, isn't it, and we are intentionally living a lie but you have to succeed with that lie because if you don't succeed and make the lie the truth to the public, you've missed out.'

Robin: 'We actually concentrate on writing for other artists whereas we don't have to be out there bearing the brunt or fronting the record, we write for people like Barbra Streisand and people like that and I have done Diana Ross and Dolly Parton and all that so when they do songs like *Islands in the Stream, Chain Reaction* and Dionne Warwick and Beyoncé doing *Emotion*, you are able to enlarge on what you're doing without having to go out there and do it yourself.

Let them record the song and in the same way you feel you are just a part of it except you are not performing it, they are but you are still the composer which is kind of a good feeling really. Being an actor of your standing, surely the fulfilment of the position of being able to be in the trade with so many people, right up to the present day, it is given to so very few.'

Leslie: 'It is becoming a good character actor really and not letting it hurt your private life. Keep your private life going and the people you meet, the people that come to see you, the people that like you, they probably like you even more if your lie is so truthful.'

Robin: 'The fact is when you act, you don't seem to be acting. The characters and the people that you have portrayed have always been very honest and believable people; they weren't the dark underbelly of society.'

Leslie: 'I managed to get a great difference into my career as I got older. I took chances and made the lies even greater. I think the dangers of it, in terms of a life, is that if it overspills into your private life and turns you into something that you're not as nice as you would be without that lie.'

Robin: 'I think you have to be grounded to a degree in your private life.'

Leslie: 'It can be quite dangerous keeping up some level of understanding of what you're doing so that when the curtain comes down you don't do something bloody silly, you know? If you think you're something you're not. Come back to normal, leave the lie alone. Do it tomorrow.'

And Robin and Leslie left the 'Lie' alone. It had been a wonderful conversation, a rollercoaster of emotions and revelations, and their genuine regard for each other was summed up in the final exchange.

Robin: 'You are an international treasure and I'm honoured to have this conversation with you and as far as I'm concerned you are living a truth because it is to millions of people exactly that.'

Leslie: 'You are a really smashing bloke, thank you.'

Leslie Phillips and Robin Gibb walking away together after the show

This was the one show where we decided these two 'chums' should be seen walking off into the distance, not as a separation, but as a continuance of what still exists today as an enriching, mutual friendship.

DYLAN JONES

Dylan Jones broke the mould of a military family, moving to London aged seventeen to immerse himself in 70's youth culture. After running nightclubs for two years, Dylan turned his attention to journalism and became editor of 'i-D' magazine in 1984. He subsequently worked in various editorial positions for a number of magazines and newspapers such as 'Arena,' 'The Face,' 'The Observer,' 'The Sunday Times' and 'GQ.'

George Lamb developed a love for the limelight after helping out on set with his father, actor Larry Lamb. George had long been interested in the nightclub scene, and having left school, he headed south to the shores of Ibiza where he worked as a music agent and helped launch the careers of both Lily Allen and 'Audio Bullies.' He is now a successful television presenter and fashion designer.

GEORGE LAMB

5

DYLAN JONES & GEORGE LAMB

It was a return to the Gore Hotel to film these doyens of journalism, fashion and media – the hip young TV presenter, fledgling fashion designer, sitting down and chatting with the father of men's journalism. Although Dylan and George had met at a few charity functions and media events, and had crossed paths through mutual friends and related work, this was the first time Dylan and George had had the opportunity to face each other with undivided attention for a couple of hours.

Welshness – With all the episodes, there is often a little verbal dancing around each other, or light banter to break the ice. It is all really just about beginnings. When editing some of the episodes I started the televised final cut some three minutes or so into the filmed footage. This was in order to find a naturalness of introduction and a point when the contributors had settled into their conversations. You could use the analogy of a sword fight; sometimes the protagonists skip around each other feigning a few thrusts to weigh up the opponent and at other times they charge in and are instantly engaged in the fight.

With George and Dylan, it was George with the cut and thrust of ancestry that kicked it off. He began by inquiring how deeply the 'Welshness' ran through Dylan, considering his name was Welsh. Dylan agreed that yes it was a Welsh name (he was named after the poet Dylan Thomas) but he was technically speaking not Welsh, he was born in Cambridgeshire and being an 'Air Force brat' travelled the country and Europe (Cyprus and Malta) depending where his father was stationed, including a stint in Anglesey.

George, warming to his theme and definitely with a hint of mischief about him, pushed the Welsh angle again, getting Dylan to confirm that Anglesey was indeed in Wales and 'wasn't that where the druids came from.'

We talked earlier in the book of the physical 'tells' contributors often give away under the line of fire of awkward conversation, and for Dylan the word druid prompted a bit of heat under his collar, an uncomfortable scratch and tacit 'if you wish' answer to move it along.

It may sometimes go unnoticed to the viewer, but already the two had proved they were very comfortable with each other; George was hyper-relaxed and as the show progressed this relaxed demeanour would rub off on Dylan for a more candid sharing of their respective journey's. Back on more comfortable footing Dylan directed the question back to George, asking him if he grew up in London. Quite quickly in George's answer he had clarified where, and also managed to give an insight into his father – well known actor Larry Lamb.

Picking up women –

George Lamb with his parents, Larry and Linda

'I was brought up in London. I was born in Hammersmith, my mum's from Scotland; she's from Broughty Ferry on the east coast of Scotland, which is famous for journalism actually, for D.C. Thomson – jute, jam and journalism. She was a buyer for Mackay's which was a fashion house, a high street fashion house and she came to London on a buying trip for fashion week and my dad met her in the Copthorne Tara Hotel or something like that...'

Dylan: 'What was he doing in the hotel?'

George: 'He was just hanging out...trying to pick up ladies who were there for fashion week I guess.'

Dylan: 'Was your father famous at the time?'

Larry Lamb as Matt Taylor in Triangle

George: 'No...just as I was being born he was starting to crack it and so he had a show that ran for about six years called *Triangle* which was a terrible show that actually won on TV Hell.'

Dylan: 'So when you were growing up he was beginning to be famous then.'

George: 'Very much so and he did a bunch of other films towards the late 80s and then he hit a really rough patch around 50, you know.'

Something that became apparent early on was George's honesty. Honesty was an integral aspect to what we wanted to achieve with the series but obviously wasn't something we could force. We could set the environment up to facilitate it, but the chemistry with the other contributor and how relaxed they felt were all important. George, throughout the whole show, told it how it was with a delightful mix of endearment, humility and humour.

Dylan's nature, having been an editor for so long would probably err on the side of succinctness, being clinical and incisive with questions and not one for frippery – (director's judgement) but the magic of George and Dylan together, certainly seemed to bring more revealing honesty out of Dylan, and also more cohesion out of George.

Another noticeable thing from Dylan was his speed with humour – the instant witty retort – for example, mid-sentence as George is explaining his father's role on *Triangle* as the 'one under the captain', Dylan replies without breaking stride 'literally?'

George went on to explain his own fairly unorthodox schooling and living with the highs and lows of a father in the acting industry. Picking up the conversation from when his father struggled at age 50, when George was 16.

Dylan: 'Your father had money by this time didn't he?'

George: 'Well actors have money, "oh I've got loads of money, let's go and spend it

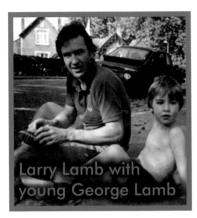

Larry Lamb with young George Lamb

all" and then "oh I don't have any money again" and so…I think also there was a bit of, if you get sent off to a school that is something that dad has to pay for and it's tangible and there can't be any "Oh I haven't got any money this month" or whatever...'

I was there (school) until the age of 16 and then I came back, went to live with dad, he was having a bit of a bad one at that period, him and my step-mum were breaking up and so it was a weird time and it is a weird time as well that time when you come back from…coming back from school when you're 16 and it's weird now when you look at 16 year olds, I see them as little boys but I thought I was a man, I was responsible for me and then you get back and there are these people telling you you've got to do this and you've got to do that and you're like, "what? Give me a break...", that's probably why I wanted to go and live with dad when I came back from school because I knew he wouldn't give me as much a hard a time as my mum would give me. I left home at 17.'

The conversation took a natural swing back in Dylan's direction as George asked him if he had gone to boarding school, because in George's school there were numerous children that boarded because they were from a Forces family and didn't want to be uprooted every twelve months. Dylan however was from the 'uprooted every twelve months school of thought' as he explains below. Interestingly – and as a 'heart warming' emotional anecdote – Dylan (very similarly to Joanna Lumley) may have had a 'serving' father but that didn't detract from a caring, human relationship with him.

'It was very odd, I remember my father having a conversation with me and actually asking me at the age of eleven I think whether or not I wanted to go to boarding school and for some reason I was dead set against going to it and he sort of accepted that which I thought was odd because he might take my opinion on board but it was odd, to base a course of education on an eleven year olds opinion I thought was really strange...so anyway, we would move every year, every two years, we'd move all over the place. It toughens you up if you move around a lot.'

George: 'Absolutely. You find your role.'

Dylan: 'You become very chameleon like actually.'

The Black Sheep – As is the way with surfacing memories, Dylan returned to his earlier thoughts on growing up, how his brother had gone into the Air Force too, and how by not following type he let his passions in life (art and fashion) shape his destiny.

'I've got one brother who is also in the Air Force; I mean I was the black sheep! I was meant to go in and I was always, I suppose at that age, early teens, I was always obsessed with that...for me it was mythical but it was obviously very real...that Andy Warhol, Americana, kitsch, night clubs, music, the world...'

Dylan Jones (right) with his father and brother, both RAF servicemen

George: 'Which is about as far away from RAF Leuchars or whatever it is...'

Dylan: 'It is, it's a different planet and when you are 12 years old it is a very different planet.'

George: 'So 12 was when you started to look at counter culture and subversive...'

Dylan: 'For me and for a lot of boys, men of my generation, it was David Bowie, *Top of the Pops*, *Starman*, that was the button and...'

George: 'That was the link, so David Bowie being on television and you were like, "Dad, do you know what, I'm probably not going to be in the RAF." '

Dylan: 'Yes.'

George: 'Wow, and that was age 12? How do you, as a young boy living on an RAF base, how do you find out a little bit more about David Bowie?'

Dylan: 'Well that's the thing. When you're that age, then, glamour, the life, going to London, going to a town, going to London, going to New York, doing this, consuming this and then meeting those people, the line from that is just exponential. It's not exponential but you would never be able to achieve what you wanted to and I suppose what I wanted to do, I wanted that life. I'm not sure that I wanted that life but I wanted to see it.'

George: 'Study wise, were you naturally leaning more towards the arty end of things?'

Dylan: 'Yes, from the age of 12 all I wanted to do was go to art school.'

George: 'Did your mum and dad encourage you, when you said "look, I don't want to go in the RAF?"'

Dylan: 'Yes, as soon as I could, in the summer of 1977 I came to London and it was gratuitous that that was the earliest I could escape, you couldn't enrol on a course if you were 16, you had to be 17 and so I came to London, to Chelsea, in the middle of 1977 when punk was just sort of going vertical and it was just extraordinary.'

There was a funny interlude at this point where George asked Dylan what he was wearing at this point when he travelled down to London, to which Dylan replied he was dressed like a Ramone, asking George if he remembered the Ramones. 'Of course' says George, 'Jerry Ramone'...(humorous pause as we realize he doesn't know the others) before he laughs himself and says 'and the rest of the Ramones.'

Dylan: 'Then I cut my hair and I immersed myself, I got into the rock scene, that was my life, that's what I did and all my whole being was consumed. I went to gigs seven nights a week; I don't know how we afforded to in those days...did a foundation course Bagley's Lane every day. I did that for a year and then I went to St Martin's. I basically followed a girl to St Martin's and I knew that it wasn't the best college but it was one that you couldn't get more central than St Martin's. It was on the Charing Cross Road, all the clubs were around there...the epicentre of Swinging London in the 70s.'

Dylan Jones dressed like one of the Ramones (1977)

George: 'So were you soaping your hair up and all of that stuff?'

Dylan: 'Oh yes, all of it, I mean total immersion. Then I went through a period which lots of...I'm sure you've been through this, where that's all you are.'

George: 'You're consumed by it, yes.'

Dylan: 'That's all you are, you're not really interested in anything else apart from that world, the scene, the people, the clothes, the music, the clubs. I think for me that's where my love of journalism and magazines and newspapers came from because everything that you bought – you know this probably more than I do, that everything you buy has to be the right thing. And it's the right shirt and it's the right pair of trousers and it's the right magazine...so actually when you decided to buy something it became very important, it became like an artefact.'

George: 'What was the period between you seeing *iD* and *Face* come out and thinking "That's where I'm going, I want to get involved in that?" '

Dylan: 'What was happening is that because that world started to be mediated, because people started to take notice of it, it became very competitive. You'd pick up a magazine or see a television programme and there'd be someone you knew on it and this hadn't happened before, it didn't happen when you were 16. So suddenly your world was getting bigger and so you were like, hold on, they're in a magazine, why aren't I? So that ambition, that drive, was sort of accelerated.'

George: 'So there was an element of narcissism in there that was "I want you to know who I am or I want to be!" '

Dylan: 'Oh totally, it was all about narcissism.'

George: 'Right, so you wanted validation within the scene?'

Dylan asked George if he had that too, convinced that he must have felt a similar urge of being validated by the scene. George agreed that growing up, he was involved in nightclubs and the music industry and whilst he may not have wanted to be a celebrity per se, he certainly wanted to be at the fore of the local scene. George continued that he went to Richmond College in Twickenham and during that period the dance scene was really 'kicking off.'

'Dance music had really kicked off and I was at college, I'd met a guy. His girlfriend, who was also at college, her brothers ran a successful club night called Milk and Two Sugars and it was up at the Cross and so we started to go to that and started to help them and dress the club and do flyering for them and just became their lackeys basically. Also you know, I was one of the kids in the record shop who knew everybody and at that point dance music was still quite a cottage industry so the guys who were delivering all the records from their vans would come in and they were the distributors and they also had an arm where they would press the records and the guys who delivered the flyers also knew the guys who designed them. So within a year of standing around you kind of knew the intricacies of how the little dance music industry worked and you knew the right promoters because they came in selling tickets and you kind of met everybody.'

Dylan: 'Which area of that did you want? Which part of that world did you grab and say I can do this?'

George: 'To be honest with you it was more, it was realising that I could see all of it and see how they all interacted, all these little key elements. I was at college and a mate of mine, Simon, said "listen, I want to make music, I want to make this music that we're going out and dancing to". Probably the same thing that I saw, we'd be standing in a club and going "I want them to be dancing to my tune" and I said, "all right, I'll be your manager then." '

On a more serious level, nearly all our contributors profess to having 'winged' it in some way at the start of their careers – passion and presence accounting for more in the early days than experience. George continued with his retelling:

'So we started to put records out, I used that whole infrastructure that I had...but we didn't have much success at the beginning. We kind of stood our ground and everybody, all our mates had gone off to uni and we said "we're staying and we're going to be in the music industry" and it was like year three, they are all at uni now going "Guys, this isn't really happening" and an old girlfriend of mine called me up and said "look, I'm working for the Ministry of Sound now and I need a driver to drive all the DJs in Ibiza."

So then I drive all these massive house DJs round and I'd make mixed CDs of all the big tunes of the day and just slip – track four would be one of ours and then track seven would be one of ours and we'd be driving around and I'd just tap the volume up on the thing. "Oh what's this one?" "This is one of ours actually, there you go, there you go."

By the end of the summer we had a couple of tunes that had blown up and my pal Simon and another friend of ours, Tom, they became this act called the Audio Bullies, we got them signed to Virgin and we went off on this mad trip for a couple of years going round the world DJing everywhere and having a wonderful time and I started my career into show biz really I suppose. So yes, that was how all of that started.'

Washed up at 22 – For the next chapter of the show, George asked Dylan how he initially got to write articles for magazines. Not only was Dylan's answer interesting but more so the fact that he was completely forthright in claiming he owed his success to one person – Terry Jones. Dylan was hugely magnanimous in suggesting that Terry was responsible for giving him his break, and he wanted to clarify that because he felt so many 'well known' personalities conveniently forget those who gave them a 'leg up' the ladder.

Dylan Jones (right) with Terry Jones (left)

Dylan: 'I owe my entire career to one man who…he invented my life. I left St Martin's in '81 and I was a layabout. I'd get up at midday, eat and then go to a nightclub and that's what my life was. It was awful. I mean it was amazing but it was…actually by the age of 22 I thought, "I'm washed up, I can't do anything at the age of 22."'

George: 'That's what I was feeling.'

Dylan: 'I just thought I was too old for everything.'

George: 'At 22?'

Dylan: 'Yes, when you're obsessed with youth and what happens at that age, when your 22 – 22's old! Then a friend of mine at the time called Mark Bailey said

"I'm photographing some people for *iD* magazine tomorrow and they need someone to interview these people". I had nothing to do that day other than get up, eat and go to a nightclub, so I said "sure". Literally, I did this thing and typed it up and thought nothing of it. Then I was in a flat in Oxford Gardens, I didn't have a telephone or money and then someone got a call on the house phone and said there was a call for me. I called this guy back, Terry Jones, who owned *iD*, still does. It's the only magazine from that era that's still going.'

George: 'Really, and still the same guy.'

Dylan: 'And he said, "would you like a job?" And my life just went like that and we're still friends. We live near each other in Wales and without Terry I wouldn't have anything. I owe it all to him and…I always find it interesting that many people who have a modicum of success in what they choose to do, they almost never talk about the thing that gave them the break.'

George: 'People forget.'

Dylan: 'Yes, but why would I forget because without Terry I wouldn't have a career. I started doing it, it was in his bedroom, the top floor of the house they still live in in Sheriff Road in West Hampstead and we made this magazine and in about six months I had become deputy editor and then editor and as soon as I started doing it, I realised I never wanted to do anything else and I actually feel privileged that at the age of 22 I'd found something and I still really don't want to do anything else other than work in that industry and I feel kind of blessed actually.'

Dylan then bounced the question back off George, summarising what we had all heard so far in that George was (managing and being entrepreneurial in that area) before asking when the emphasis changed. Dylan wondered if that was when he managed Lily Allen…asking was she his girlfriend…'See what I did there' he joked. George wasn't romantically linked with her, but picked up the story.

'No…that summer when I was working out there in Ibiza, she was staying out there with her family and then her family went back and she was having a little bit of a juvenile delinquent stage and she said I want to stay on. So she was staying in Ibiza.'

Dylan: 'So did you decide to take her under your wing?'

George: 'I called my mate actually and I said "you need to call your clients and tell them that their kid's not really having a good one and I think she's too young." I'd previously gone to Ibiza a few years before and I was like "I'm going to go to Ibiza and change the world" and all the rest of it and luckily some older people that I knew had seen me on a beach carrying my bag around and said, "do you know what, we're going to take you to the airport" and they took me to the airport. "Hi guys, where are you going?" "We're going to the beach; you're going to the airport." "Mum!" reversing the charges…"I need to come home."

So I just kind of repaid that favour for Lily and we stayed in touch and she at the time had a deal through London Records and I started to work in A&R when I got back and I was managing bands and doing A&R simultaneously and because I'd looked after her, I had that nice kind of brotherly relationship with her, a big brother relationship and she came out of her deal and London Records became a bit weird and I said "I'll help, I'd like to get involved". So we made a record and I got her writing songs and…'

The Audio Bullies

Dylan: 'So you were doing that and obviously being very successful at it because she became a star quite quickly.'

George: 'Well I helped her become a song writer and I helped her make that first record called *All Right Still* and I took it round all these record labels and Audio Bullies had just had a top five hit all round the world and we had sold half a million records and it was going very well so I could get in everywhere and I had a bit of clout.

For whatever reason I took this record to everybody and they wouldn't have it. We had eight of the eleven tracks, we had the big hit, we had *Smile* and we had all the other

George Lamb and Lily Allen

big hits on it and I'm sitting there playing this record going, "guys, this is a number one record, I don't understand this, look at her, she's a star." So we got to the point where we were like "look, it's not really happening, I don't know why." '

Dylan: 'So you dropped her like a hot potato.'

George: 'No, I didn't, no, not at all, not at all.'

Dylan: 'You cruel man.'

George: 'Not at all, not at all. What actually happened was they said "do you want Lily to come and have a go at TV presenting and maybe we can get her in that way?" We both went and I said "all right, but only if I can have an audition too" because I literally hadn't put in an invoice in for two years and at the time me and Audio Bullies, you can't manage your best mates and that all went west. So we both went down there, she did it and hated it, I did it and I liked it and we came out and we called my friend Adrian who was the only guy in the music industry with any clout who actually really liked her and we said "will you take her on?" and he said "Yes, absolutely" and he took her on.

They signed a very small deal, like a 25 grand deal just to develop it up and then MySpace happened and he called her in and said, "do you know there's this thing called MySpace?" We said, "I don't know what that is". But he was willing to get the tracks up there and then you know the rest of the story. It was an interesting period, this whole thing that you'd been trying to make happen and because it was such a quick transition, the success to happen, all my mates were like, well done mate, congratulations and I was, "yeah, well I'm not really involved in that any more, you know."

So that was a peculiar time but it's only having gone through that that I realised, now having this wonderful career and doing it for me and not living vicariously through other people, I realised that that was why but at the time I didn't get it at all. I was just like, "what have I done wrong? Why is the universe doing this to me? I don't get it." But it certainly taught me a lot about life and hopefully you learn some life lessons out of all that.'

Writing – George progressed to asking Dylan how he was able to make the transition from being someone with no formal journalistic background to being editor of one of the most prominent magazines in the world.

What he did he said was that he learnt to write very quickly, 'easy to do unless you're an idiot'...so for the series we have various authors and journalists chewing over the difficulties, laboriousness or downright ease of writing. Consequently the comments of our contributors throughout the series reflected many contrasting views, from which we can only surmise that writing itself creates either an expectation of ease or difficulty, depending on the contributors own personal expectations. Dylan explained in more detail.

Dylan: 'If you look at the four or five years previously, a lot of the people who were first writing about punk were writing about punk because they were going to the clubs and they knew the people rather than the fact that they could write because I couldn't write but you learn to write very quickly, unless you're an idiot. It's not the most difficult thing, you master it, it's a craft and so yes, it was fundamentally important that you knew that world, that you knew who everyone was, whether they were a singer, a club runner, someone who was about to become a successful chef, all of these different things, a video maker…'

George: 'So you just needed to know the scene inside out.'

Dylan: 'But it was very exciting because in a very small way you felt that you were the centre of attention for things and it did feel like our version of the Swinging Sixties. Youth culture was fracturing and expanding plus you were living in a…it is called pejoratively the *Designer Decade* but that's what happened very, very quickly. There was such an emphasis on visuals, on style, on design.'

George: 'So when did *The Face* happen? When was the transition from…?'

Dylan: 'Well then I had a career. I went from *iD*, went to *The Face*, went to Arena, edited that and then after, in '92 I'd worked in all the good magazines that I'd wanted to and was very lucky to have worked on them and then I went to work on newspapers. I went to work for *The Observer* and then *The Sunday Times* and then did that for much of the 90s...then I got the call to...or the opportunity came up I should say, at *GQ* and I went to do that and actually I thought...usually I'd done jobs for four years, if you've done a job for four years that's probably enough but I've been there for 12 years and it's an extraordinary experience and professionally it's been the best part of my life, although I couldn't have done what I did without any of the things I did before.'

George picked up on something Dylan had mentioned earlier when he described as a child on an Air Force base how he was motivated by the creativity of David Bowie and now all those years later he had probably not only met but had tea with Bowie.

Dylan Jones, editor of GQ, in his office

Dylan makes one of the most incisive points of the whole series with regards to celebrity/famous figures/well known 'stars' (whatever word we choose) that, for him, two things in relation to the 'Bowie factor' happen very quickly. Firstly that to go from being a 'nobody' to 'knowing people that are somebody's' happens very quickly. The second thing which Dylan stressed was fundamental was that some people think they are the same as the celebrities because they have met and they mingle together...but they are not. At the time of going to press, an article Dylan had commissioned should be published which states 'why you can never be friends with a celebrity.' Dylan felt they are a different type of person and become a different type of person.

Dylan moved the subject on with reference to George asking what his plans for the future are considering he is still at an age when he can largely determine what areas of work to pursue.

Sting Anecdotes and Being a Grown-Up –

'I'd like to have my own talk show and a show where you can just break bread with people and talk about what's going on in the world and actually...rather than just talking about someone's promo campaign and telling me a funny anecdote about when they met Sting, I'd like to…'

Dylan: 'Those are the best aren't they? The anecdotes about meeting Sting, you can't beat them.'

George: 'I'd like to talk about stuff I think is relevant and try and encourage a little bit of breadth of thought, so that's what I want to do from a broadcasting perspective, but at the same time I suppose because of watching how my dad's life has gone and watching how my mum has remained very constant and invariably the one we've all gone back to borrow money from when she has probably earned less than both of us…I'd like to have an array, a portfolio of interesting things going on in my life and one of those will always be broadcasting because I think I'm quite good at it and I really enjoy it and I do feel there is too much mundane information getting bandied around and actually if you a conscious human you have a responsibility to…'

Dylan: 'Elevate the medium.'

George: 'Totally, totally. I'm interested in how you've managed essentially to stay at the top all the way through what you're doing. You have worked as a guy who was basically, by your own admission, kind of bumming around and right in the middle of a scene that would have been full of excess and fairly wild one would imagine, to keeping your head and…at your core are you a 'Steady Eddy' kind of person?'

Dylan: 'I'm a grown up and also I'm not a celebrity, I'm not seduced into that world of huge highs and huge lows. I've had a career, I've had a very in some respects quite ordinary, prosaic job for the last thirty years. Neither of us are probably averse to a good time but we both know what we want and we both know what we have to do in order to achieve that.'

George: 'I'm a million percent the same. I had a couple of years having a bash at it when I was in my early 20s and then I just thought "it's not for me,"(excess) I'm too focused; I know what I want too much.'

Dylan: 'There's nothing wrong with being focused. We like focused.'

George: 'It kind of gets you where you are.'

George returns the conversational compliment and asks Dylan about the books he has written outside of GQ. Dylan attempts to skip over it saying he has written a few and is working on a couple of others although he won't 'tempt fate' and divulge anything about the new projects yet. George asks if Dylan fancies himself retiring to Wales to write. Dylan responds but very quickly the conversation turns to the stresses and strains of maintaining or managing a loving marriage/relationship when you are a 'well known' and busy personality.

The significant others –

'I often say that but like a lot of people, like a lot of men, the idea of actually retiring is not an option I think. Also if you are a journalist you can write until you die, if you're lucky/any good. I think to discuss a cliché, yes one has to have a well-rounded life in order to survive and you need the love of a good woman and a couple of beautiful daughters so yes, I'm very lucky in that respect. Presumably there's a significant other out there. You're out a lot, a man about town, putting your face about, on television, people know who you are, how does that affect your relationship, how does your girlfriend cope with it?'

Dylan Jones with his two daughters

George: 'She kind of works in entertainment and fashion and is around that world and gets it. Like anybody, she's not overwhelmed by the fact, I mean through social media now people can have access to you from all kinds of angles and she doesn't particularly like it but at the same time that's part and parcel of...she was conscious of my world when she decided to be a part of it and she also happens to be incredibly beautiful so even though she's not famous or whatever, she gets far more attention than I do, every guy chases after her and so you have to make a conscious decision in life – do you want to have a fight with everybody you meet or are you just going to let it roll and trust the person you're with?'

Dylan: 'Yes, of course but any partner would say that but my wife is as successful in her business as I am in mine, she runs her own business and she is as busy as I am so she probably...I know she does more home domestic stuff than I do, well she actually categorically does, for the record, let me repeat that. But yes, she has a very

George Lamb and his girlfriend Claire Burt

full professional life as well. Also bizarrely we have almost exactly the same background. Her father John was in the Air Force, the same rank as my father, had almost exactly the same background.'

George: 'So she gets you, you get each other.'

Dylan: 'Yes, it's odd, very strange.'

The two draw the conversation to its natural conclusion, as they thank each other for such an enjoyable conversation, before their busy schedules upped them away from the set in their separate directions as another episode is wrapped.

'Anyway, you haven't told me any Sting anecdotes but apart from that it's been a really enjoyable hour actually, it's been really good fun, really enjoyed it.'

George: 'Indeed. Well we'll save them for next time." '

Dylan: 'Absolutely.'

George: 'Wicked, nice one Dylan.'

Dylan Jones and George Lamb saying their goodbyes

BRIGITTE NIELSEN

Brigitte Nielsen is known as the Amazonian beauty who stole the heart of Sylvester Stallone, before appearing alongside him in 'Rocky IV.' Before Stallone, she was already forging a high profile career, starring opposite Arnold Schwarzenegger in 'Red Sonja.' Her height and looks set her apart from many of her contemporaries, where her film career also ran alongside modelling, including several appearances in 'Playboy' magazine.

Britt Ekland is the stunning actress who set hearts racing with her wide eyes, pouty lips and sultry good looks. Britt is a talented actress, epitomised by her turn as a Bond Girl and a memorable performance in 'The Wicker Man.' Overnight fame followed a whirlwind romance with Peter Sellers, whom she supported through their turbulent marriage.

BRITT EKLAND

6

BRIGITTE NIELSEN & BRITT EKLAND

A conversation of epic Scandinavian proportions was afoot with this episode of 'Living the Life'.

The Venue – For Britt and Brigitte we chose the luxury Pelham Hotel in Kensington, central for both contributors and with a set that was honourably feminine enough for 2 women renowned for their beauty as well as their acting and other creative skills. There were so many nuances that made this episode a real stand out for the series and especially for the crew.

The differences were more than being bi-lingual (or multi-lingual in Brigitte's case), there were definite Scandinavian qualities and quirks that brought a directness to the conversation, as well as an underlying feeling that the viewer can tell that Britt and Brigitte share a kinship of growing up in countries other than England that almost unites them in a joint joke we are only half grasping.

Despite the obvious Scandinavian connection, as a 'coupling' both Britt and Brigitte had similar childhoods and thrusts into film and modelling at an early age, as well as high profile marriages to movie stars that labelled them 'the wife of', even though they already had independent careers and have always been financially independent.

Tequila – The star of the show – or should I say 'other' star of the show was Tequila, the renowned chihuahua of Britt's who goes pretty much everywhere with her, including his own role in the annual pantomime Britt performs in. I say 'other' star of the show as Britt turned up to the shoot with three possible dresses to choose from, which is only to be expected from a former Bond Girl and feminine icon...But there were also 3 matching collars for tequila, depending obviously on which outfit Britt settled on.

Brigitte Nielsen with Britt Ekland and Tequila in 'collar' coordinated outfits

More of Tequila later...It is often said with 'well known' personalities such as Britt that they are the consummate professional, but with Britt (and Brigitte) this was definitely the case. Britt was on time, settled in very quickly, guided the make-up girl, chose her outfit, and was ready for her pre-shoot. Where her experience showed was just before filming her intro 'sound-bytes' she was looking in her little compact make-up mirror and directing the crew member in charge of lighting and our Director of Photography, knowing the perfect angles and perfect lighting to compliment her features – they

97

certainly learned a few things that shooting day...

Amazonian – Brigitte arrived, living up to the tag that was created in her honour – Amazonian – every bit the towering movie star. I won't be sharing anything that most people won't be aware of, but both ladies – who have obviously had to live with attention as a result of their physical beauty and presence – are very intelligent. Brigitte mingled on set flitting between speaking excellent English with Leslie Phillips, Rosemary Reed and the crew, to fluent Italian with her husband, to taking phone calls in her native Danish. Her comments and interactions with everyone were thoughtful, incisive and very much from someone who has an active and intelligent mind.

The ladies, once they had filmed their pre shoot intro's and were settled back upstairs on set, began filming, talking to one another in their native languages. If they hadn't covered so much material throughout the whole episode that made editing such a 'strict' job, we would have left in the fun exchange to see them both animated and yet with most viewers being unable to understand the language. However these two had much to discuss, and after Tequila decided to jump out of Britt's arms and bark at one of the cameramen, we cut and the main filming began.

Tequila on set

Brigitte kicked off the conversation in direct Danish manner, describing her early years.

'Brigitte, Copenhagen, Stockholm – I was a big city girl. I was born in the centre of Stockholm, it was me and three brothers and I was oldest. I was good in school, too tall, too skinny, you know, all that.

Britt: 'The interesting thing is that you said you grew up tall and skinny.'

Brigitte: 'Yes, I was six foot, I didn't have boobs and I had no hair.'

Britt: 'You see I was your complete opposite, I was short and fat.'

Brigitte Nielsen (left) with her borther (right) and friend

Brigitte: 'And I put three pairs of pants on so I looked like I had more curves and I started smoking at 14 1/2, they said if you smoke cigarettes you can be a part of the club and I was so sick, but unfortunately smoking has stuck with me. At 16 I was done with school...I actually liked school and I was good in school but when I was sixteen and a half I finished.

I was a grade A student but someone, this was a change in my life from being this tall giraffe, you know, whatever, this lady came up to me, I was together with my girlfriend and she came up to me and said "Come here." I thought, "Who is she?" She said "Do you want to be a model, become a model?" I said "Are you talking to my girlfriend or to me?" She said, "No, you." This is a long story however it was indeed Johnny Casablanca...'

Britt: 'Oh yes, yes.'

From the speedy introduction to each other Britt and Brigitte were instantly into full flow of conversation, and the initial turn it took was their physical shapes growing up and how that determined their entering of the modelling and acting worlds. Brigitte picked up again on her start at Jonny Casablanca's.

'...and I became a model and I remember after all those years of being laughed at, It made me stand up straight. All of a sudden all of the difficulties I'd had, they paid money for. I was thin, I was tall, I was this, I was that and it was a great thing. I was supposed to study but I didn't, I went to Hamburg, I went to Paris and Milan and this is how I went away from Denmark and became an international dame.

Britt: 'I was never a model, I was much too short but I did commercials, I did one for chewing gum, one for toothpaste and one for *Porla*, it was a mineral water.'

Brigitte: 'So you do a toothbrush commercial and then what?'

Britt: 'When I did these commercials, one of my school mates, and this was in the infancy of Swedish television, her sister was a presenter so they were doing a young people's

Brigitte Nielsen as a young model

programme and asked if I would come on the programme and do a sketch about Brigitte Bardot because I kind of looked a bit like her.'

Brigitte: 'But better looking.'

Britt: 'So that's what I did. I was still in school but I thought, hmm, I can do this, this is interesting. Because my dad said to me, "I give you one year of living at home then you go." '

Brigitte: 'But that's the Scandinavian way, you have to be responsible.'

Britt: 'And he was like, "After one year you're an actress, you go out and earn your money"." Okay dad".'

Fathers and Father Issues – One of the themes we talk about often in relation to the 'Living the Life' series is emotional intelligence. Without making judgements or fitting the jigsaw together for the viewer, we do strive to showcase the emotional relationships and events that shape – or at least in part – shape their lives. With Both Britt and Brigitte, they share the similarities of stern fathers. There are nuances of differences that come out of the show, namely Britt describing how strict and cold emotionally her father was and Brigitte's who although strict too, was the rock she relied on for validation of her choices.

Therapy – What is also interesting and worth highlighting here, at this point of the episode's transcription in this book is that Brigitte has undergone a lot of self-investigation and certain therapies so is, in a way, more honest with the struggles she had to contend with – with her male relationships and self-worth issues.

From a (slightly) older generation, Britt has never openly disclosed any therapy and even early on having described a stern, emotionally cold father (who any child would subconsciously try and elicit love and attention from) she went on to describe a stern, depressed and emotionally cold marriage to Peter Sellers, a much older man, yet categorically states she wasn't looking for a father figure – maybe not a father figure but a challenge to overcome the same emotional patterning? These are the pieces of the jigsaw that the show offers to the viewer for individual discernment.

On a final note, Britt describes below her father reading an Ian Fleming novel (something her father enjoys) and years later Britt is desperate to get an upcoming role in the Bond Film – is she subconsciously trying to please her father?

Brigitte: 'My dad was so strict and so mean...it was enough for him to look at us and we would be dead meat. We really grew up old school...respect, sitting with our elbows in, a book on the head, one glass of milk at six o'clock, one plate, finish it off, go clean it and goodnight. That's me.'

Britt: 'My dad went so far as to put a hanger between our shoulders...so that you sat really straight and you sat at the table like this and you asked if you could leave the table and...but when I started to grow up and was wanting to go out, I was probably 16 because that's when the...at 15 the switch came from being a little girl to looking pretty and he would put, he was the Swedish champion in curling and so he had these curling brushes, you know how they go, and so he had these brushes in the wardrobe, they are very important the brushes, so he would put the brush underneath the door handle and then he would sit like this, (Britt folds arms with stern look on her face) because his

Britt Ekland's father (second left) with his curling team

library was here and the front door was there and there were double doors here and he left them open like this, and he would sit in the chair exactly like this, in this position, with his whisky and his Ian Fleming in English and as I came home quietly opening the door, it fell bang. So if he had fallen asleep he would go..."Oh what time do you think this is?" Let's say I came home, I was allowed to be out until ten and I came home at 10.30 then he would take an hour off next week's going out. I bet you can't top that?'

Brigitte: 'Well I can. It got so bad with my dad, it was really strange growing up, not only because I was so ugly and such a misfit, at least that's how I felt, but my dad was still very protective but when they had said you should become a model, for some strange reason my dad said to me, "You've been through my school and I believe you are ready now, you may leave" and that's why when I was actually 21 and I would ring my dad and ask him for permission because I was so used to it.'

Britt: 'I hated my father because he was so Victorian and he wasn't nice to my mother, he felt she was too soft with me. He was so desperately afraid that I was going to become pregnant and have to marry like so many of his friend's daughters that he would do anything to avoid that and I just couldn't take the oppression so I moved in with my grandparents.'

Starring Movies and Shotgun Marriages –I described earlier Britt and Brigitte's shared Scandinavian commonalities, which surfaces in the next exchange where Britt talks of some early film stars she worked with (Alberto Sordi and Marco Toto) that Brigitte knows, and the genuine enthusiasm from Brigitte for them when hearing their names is a delight, as well as the insight Britt gives into their characters.

'...And then there was an Italian film company in town and they were making a movie with a very, very famous Italian actor called Alberto Sordi.

Brigitte: 'Grand Alberto Sordi!'

Britt: 'An enormously famous, famous actor.'

Brigitte: 'Of course, he's a legend, he is. He is.'

Britt: 'The film was about him travelling through Sweden to find someone to love and they interviewed me but I didn't get the main role but I did get the role at the train station, at the end when he has gone over all Sweden and he hasn't found it and I am at…and he goes "Echo, echo, echo." "Too late," so I left. But the director had my number and so a couple of months later he called me and I was on the road with the travelling theatre and he said, "I want to offer you a role with "– oh God, what was his name? – *Il Principe*, he was a comedian.'

Brigitte: 'Ah, Toto.'

Britt: 'Toto, Toto.'

Brigitte: 'Ah, Grande Marco de Toto! He was probably the best ever, ever.'

Britt: 'Well he, rather like Peter Sellers later in life, wanted to do a very serious movie and I played his secretary and I did the movie and my hair in a little pony tail and serving tea and…'

Brigitte: 'Sorry but how was he, how was Toto? Was he a nice man? Complicated or not really?'

Britt: 'He was nice, very tragic but you know, over the years I have learned one thing and that is that all comedians…'

Brigitte: 'Are tragic.'

Britt: '…are very sad people and most of them are bipolar or manic depressive if you want to use that word. I am in Italy, sitting like this with a girlfriend and we are sitting on the Via Veneto and just having a cappuccino and a man comes up to me and he says, "Would you be interested in a screen test for 20th Century Fox?"'

Brigitte: 'Wow!'

Britt: 'And I said, "Yes!" And he said "Okay, you have to go to the American Embassy and get the visa because the screen test would be in New York." I did the screen test, they filmed it in the studio in Manhattan, this is December '63 and my dad calls me and he says "There is a telegram here from 20th Century Fox and they have offered you a seven year contract and you have to be in London so you have to come back home." So I flew back home and literally the next day I flew to London and I stayed at the Dorchester in a room approximately this size…'(Britt mimes tiny)

Brigitte: 'A bathroom in the Dorchester!'

Britt: 'It is probably a cupboard now but then it was a room and the next morning, like at eight o'clock, I had a press conference and here I'm lying on the piano…'

Brigitte: 'To die for, beautiful.'

Britt: 'And that afternoon there's a knock on my door and there's a man outside who

Peter Sellers in his iconic role as The Pink Panther

said "I work for Mr Peter Sellers and he would like to offer you a drink." So now you know what happened.'

The dynamism of Britt and Brigitte sharing their stories of Peter Sellers and Sylvester Stallone were enthralling to watch not only because of their marriages to famous stars, but because both women were at the commencement of their own careers at a young age, amplified by 'fairytale' romances that was cinematic even in the retelling. Brigitte bounced off Britt's introduction to how she was wooed by 20th Century Fox with her own recounting of how she first made the leap into movies.

'I have to tell you because I have a couple of these stories too. So I'm a model, all of a sudden I'm 19 and I'm tired of being a model so I went into my modelling agency and I said, "Guys, it's over." They go, "What? Are you suffering from depression or something

Brigitte Nielsen and her first husband Kasper Winding

is wrong?" I said "No, I've had it, I've had three great years but I don't want to be a model anymore", and I went home and really what I was looking for was what my parents represented, so the white picket fence, getting married, have a kid, a dog, I really wanted that. I ended up marrying a Danish musician and I basically married him because I got pregnant, what was supposed to be a friend, a kind of an affair, whatever and to me that I was pregnant meant that I had to marry him.

So we got married and I gave birth to Julian but I felt I really had...I was back in Denmark,

Brigitte Nielsen with Arnold Schwarzenegger

I'm really Danish, got a nice man, I have a beautiful little baby boy, I'm breastfeeding like a rock star and everything was the way I wanted it to be until that bloody day the phone rings and it was my booker from Milan, David. He said, "Do you know, we have had one call into our agency from a film producer called Dino Di Laurentis, he's seen you in a picture and he wants to cast you in one of his upcoming movies," so I flew down and arrived in Rome.

Basically he says, "Richard Fleischer loves you, this is the lead role of *Red Sonia*, you will be starring – if you agree – opposite Arnold Schwarzenegger" and I thought, "Arnold who?" I had absolutely no idea, I said, "Who is Arnold?" "Oh you know, the guy with the big muscles." I said, "I have no idea who you are talking about," and I just realised today how ignorant I was. He had already done the first *Conan, Terminator*, they had the premiere about three months after but I was living in my world. Anyway, that day, so he goes "Here's the script, here's the contract, the role is yours," and that's basically when my life from that Danish bakery, go to school, bullied kind of person, nice family – my marriage broke up immediately, my first son I had to leave. My life took a turn forever.'

Britt: 'I never wanted to get married, oh God, I said, "Never, that is not for me." Then I arrive in London, I met Peter Sellers and I'm married ten days later.'

To pick up on what was written earlier, both Britt and Brigitte had manifested their own fledgling careers with opportunities on the rise, and it was at that point they got married, in many ways stalling the direction of their careers. Both explain below how for Britt, Sellers sabotaged her contract and hence film career, and Stallone controlled Brigitte to such an extent that she was only able to have roles in his films where, of course, he was the star.

Brigitte interjects after Britt had explained that she met and married Peter Sellers within ten days, wondering if that was 'good or bad?' Britt concedes it was 'very bad,' and genuinely amazes Brigitte when she confesses she loved him.

'...Oh yes, I fell madly in love with him.'

Brigitte: 'Really? The real thing?'

Britt: 'Oh absolutely, I was like a wet rag all over him and it was nothing to do with the father substitute because I had a perfectly good father at home.'

Brigitte: 'He was not that great looking and the body was a little bit like Woody Allen kind of thing.'

Britt: 'But you don't see the body with clothes on, you don't see that until that first night.'

Brigitte: 'No, because I love him. I love to see him in movies but from there to think you're going to go and marry the guy.'

Britt: 'I know, I know. He just sort of...he was so suave and elegant and knowledgeable and I come from a family where manners matter a lot so it is not like I was used to slobs but there was something about his whole behaviour and his whole treatment of me...I was like a little puppy and then he would give me all these gifts...but it was insanity, insanity. The man who came to my door was his valet, like his...he drove his car and looked after him so that first night I put as many clothes as I could because my dad had warned me about men and evil intentions so...I put a lot of clothes on, I went to his suite, the Oliver Messell Suite which is the finest suite in the hotel.'

Brigitte: 'He was divorced?'

Britt: 'His wife had run off with the architect to their new apartment in Hampstead so obviously he was very low and he said to me, would I like a drink? "Yes." "Would you like to see a movie?" I said "Yes." So we drove to Leicester Square, we walk in and the manager just seats us and gives us popcorn and soda and I'm thinking "God, we just walk in, we don't pay, this is incredible!" We sit down, it's dark and the film starts and it's him in the *Pink Panther* movie. And I'm just like blown away, I couldn't believe it.'

Brigitte: 'I can imagine.'

Britt: 'I am just peeing myself with laughter, particularly the scene with Capucine and all the sleeping pills going underneath the bed; I thought it was the funniest thing I'd ever seen. So we came out and now he's very pleased because at last...Now I know who he is, I know he is a big movie star.'

106

Britt: 'So he takes me back to the hotel and we are sitting like this and Bertie is there and he says, "Do you smoke?" I said "Yes, I smoke." He said "Have you smoked these kind of cigarettes before?" And he gave me marijuana and I said "No." He said "This is called marijuana" and I said, "Yes." I knew nothing about drugs, a completely drug free upbringing.'

Brigitte: 'Ah yes, but in Denmark.'

Britt: 'He said to me, "This is what you do, you take this cigarette and you go like this… Hold it, hold it, hold it…"and of course I did this and I remember the room is like this in a way and there is a huge terrace, here's Park Lane and here's Hyde Park, and I go out, he takes me out on this terrace and I remember him kissing me and that's all I remember. The next morning I woke up, in my little cupboard, completely dressed…'

Brigitte: 'How did I get here!'

Britt: 'Completely dressed and the whole little cupboard was filled with flowers, everywhere.'

Brigitte: 'Oh my God!'

Britt: 'So I'm thinking, hmm, I'm a star. All my fans who saw my picture in the paper, because that's how he knew I was at the Dorchester, he'd seen the picture in the evening papers. So I thought, I am now a star, this is fantastic. Of course I'm looking for a card and there's one card finally where it says, 'Hope you slept well. Inspector Clouseau.' So that was my introduction to Peter Sellers.'

It was a quick fire exchange between Britt and Brigitte, which not only covered the whirlwind romance of Britt and Peter Sellers, but also showed Brigitte's incredulity that Britt could have fancied someone physically shaped liked Sellers!

Brigitte then described how she basically pursued Stallone.

'Oh my God. You know things happen by chance and after I did my first movie, I'm in New York and I get together with a couple of girlfriends from my modelling days who were so nice but one of the girlfriends had a very annoying boyfriend, he kept saying "Hey, I know Sylvester Stallone, I know Sly Stallone."

At one point I thought, "Okay, if you know him so well, I'd like to meet him, do you have his number?"" Not necessarily his number but I know where he is staying"; he is in this hotel blah-blah-blah. I get back to my hotel, looking over what I have to do for promotion for the movie for the next day and I said, "If he is here I'd like to meet *Rocky*." Very few times in my childhood would my parents bring me to see something in the movies but I had seen *Rocky 1* and I thought, "Hey, if Rocky's in town, why not?"

So I got a typewriter from the hotel and I wrote, "Dear Mr Stallone, my name is Brigitte Nielsen. I have just finished my first movie, I don't want your autograph but I'd love to meet you." Then I left my composite, you know when you're a model you have…So it has the agency portfolio on and I said, "You know who is writing you." And I remember at the time I paid $20 to the gentleman in my hotel to have this hand delivered to Sly's hotel.

So I am in my hotel, I have red hair; I look nothing like I look on the picture that I sent him and the phone rings, "Hi, this is Sly Stallone." I dropped dead, I go "Oh my God, I've got Rocky on the line, what am I going to do?" because I never thought this was going to happen. He just said "Look, it is my last day in New York, I can be over in 40 minutes, we can have a chat" and that's that and I was like "fine." I hung up the phone and panic sets in, I have red hair, I don't know what to wear, I'm not really ready for it and one of the ladies that was helping me out with all the promotion was there and I said "Can you stay here, he's on his way, because I'm too tall so when he knocks on the door, you open the door and you leave and I'll be here on the couch!" I had it all figured out.

I ordered a bottle of red wine and a cheese tray because in Denmark if you have a bottle of red wine it is homely, cosy so it was like I was dining, I was meeting a Hollywood star and I had to look a little like I'm comfortable – not at all. He gets there, she's very good and he looked amazing, he was absolutely beautiful and he sat down and we started talking and strangely enough the first thing we talked about was divorce.

He was going through a divorce and I was divorcing my friend, the nice guy I'd got married to. It was nice and all of a sudden he said, "I've got to go, it was really nice to meet you, I've got a dinner tonight and I've got to be going and tomorrow morning I'm leaving for LA." What we do of course in Denmark, he stands up and I forget that I'm too tall and I stand up to show him the door and he goes, "Wow!" He said, "You are a big woman!" and he turns around he goes "*Red Sonia*, why don't you come for dinner tonight?" '

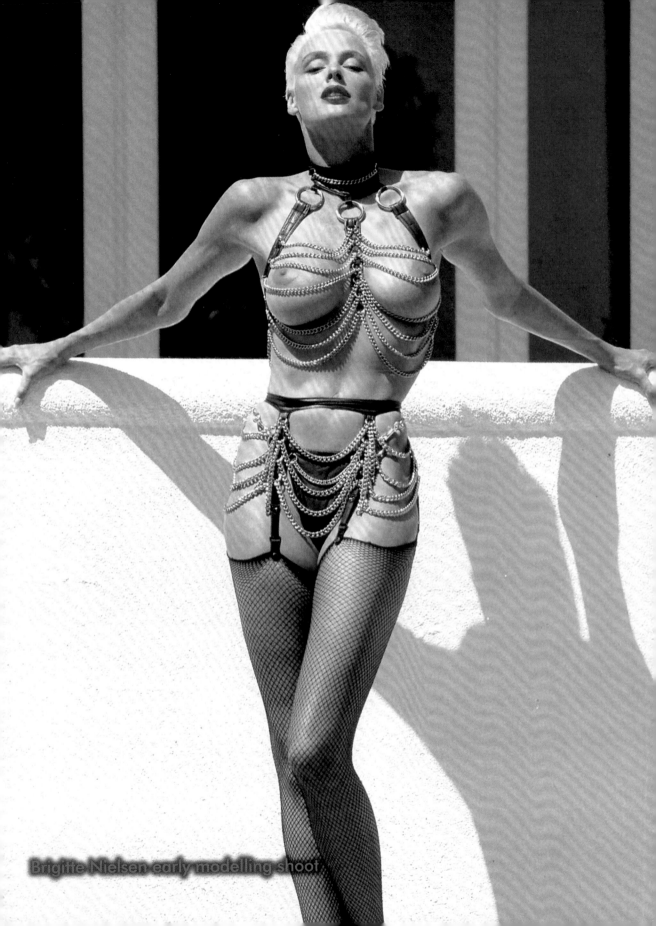

Brigitte Nielsen early modelling shoot

Britt: 'Oh really?'

Brigitte: 'Oh shit. But I said "Yes, I'd love to." He said, "My driver will pick you up in two hours." As I walk in, Sylvester's there and the girlfriend is there and the girlfriend is like, "mmm." Of course it was stupid of him to invite me, it was very embarrassing and I felt quite awkward and then I go, "Jake, oh my God, how are you, nice to see you" and I was so lucky he was there because that was also Arnold's lawyer so at least I had him to talk to.

All of a sudden, it is one and a half hour into the dinner, Sylvester stands up and goes "Okay, dinner's over." He leaves me, says "It was nice to meet you, see you around, if you ever come to LA give me a call." I mean it was just the weirdest thing. They leave in the limo, the father, the girlfriend and him and there I am, in New York with Jake and I go, "Jake, what did I do wrong? What have I done?" And he looks at me and says, "Don't you see it, he is already jealous." I said "Jealous of what?" He said, "You shouldn't be talking to me when you are in his company." I said "But he was there with a girl" and he said "Just forget about it, get over it, everything is okay" and that was the end of that.

Being the picky Danish weird person that I am, I thought "What an asshole, that was not very nice to leave me stranded like that." The day after he had given me his office number and his home number in LA and he had mentioned so many times, "If you ever come to LA give me a call." So here I am, midsummer, I don't have a lot of money, when the promotion time is over I'm back to Denmark and I have been through a divorce so it means going back to my mom and dad's house and okay, how can I get out to LA, what am I going to do? I call up *Playboy*.

Britt: 'You called them up?'

Brigitte: 'Yes, and I said "Listen, I've just finished my first movie, would you like to do something with me?" They said, "we'd love to do some pictures with you." I said "Great but it has to be in Los Angeles, at the Beverly Hills Hotel, I want a limo"– I had the whole thing – "And I want this kind of money." They said "Fine, we'll do that." Next thing I know I'm flying out to LA, I'm staying at the Beverly Hill Hotel, I've got my limo and the whole thing is such bullshit, I mean can you imagine? But I feel now I am at the right level now. So I think I'm not going to call him at home this time, I'll phone his office and notify them that I'm in Los Angeles and I can be reached at the Beverly Hill Hotel. And the phone rang again and it was him. I said "Wow!" He said, "You're here." I said "Yes, I'm here." We went out for a week. We never had anything sexual, like a little kiss or whatever. The truth of the matter is, *Playboy* is over, we have been going out for a week and that's that. I had no place, I don't want to live in LA, I'm not an American so I'm back to Denmark. The fairy tale is over.

I'm back home in my little room where I grew up with my mom and dad and with my son Julian, talking to my mom and dad about how nice he was and it was fun and Los Angeles is like this and that and the phone rings. It is 11pm and in Denmark, probably like with your dad, after 9pm you should not call the Nielsen house because my dad would be very offended. So my dad picks up, he speaks English and I think, "Oh my God it's got to be him, it's got to be him." The next thing I know my dad says, no one calls the Nielsen house at this hour, you may call back tomorrow. "Oh my God, please", I said, "That's Rocky, that's Stallone! What are you doing? Don't you realise there is a nine hour time difference?" Blah-blah-blah. He calls back the day after and he asked my dad permission, he said "may I see your daughter, I'd like to invite her to Malibu," and that's that.'

Britt: 'And how old were you?'

Brigitte: 'About 21 and he was 38.'

Sylvester Stallone with Brigitte Nielsen in Rocky IV

Britt: 'Okay, 21, 38, that's exactly the same difference. Sellers was 39 and...'

Brigitte: 'I was 21, so you see we have a very similar in the years...'

The Twerp – The ladies then spent the next part of the show in essence 'judging' the other woman's physical choice in men and such like. It was either a Scandinavian directness that our British sensibilities winced slightly at, or Brigitte's body fascism was so strong she was unable to contain herself regarding imaging a naked Peter Sellers. It was certainly an interesting exchange. Britt could understand why Brigitte had been attracted to Stallone, but Brigitte couldn't imagine a physical attraction for Britt towards Peter Sellers, 'a twerp.'

Britt never flinched, got defensive, or lashed out verbally, she just very calmly revealed that Sellers, was always dieting, which elicited more understanding from Brigitte who also revealed how rigid Stallone was about his diet, although Britt highlighted the obvious difference of someone like Stallone whose physique was his wealth and hence very rigid about maintaining it, compared to Sellers being upset about his shape and dieting to try and stay thin.

Body Fascism over, Brigitte moved the conversation along to the realities of her stifling marriage to Stallone.

'I don't know how it is about you, I was only with Sylvester for three years, he was very romantic to start with but it didn't last, it was a nightmare and it really became a nightmare. It is unfortunate to say but it was not an okay situation but I really till today, I still feel punished. If I could re-do my life I would rather not have married the guy because I had already done a movie and I felt always an ex-Stallone, you know. Thanks to him and this and that, being put on the black list now I was no longer with him and it was very, very difficult for me after the time with Sylvester.

My girlfriends said "Don't leave him, don't leave him" and I said (Because we're Danish and Swedish) "You can't buy me, because he will do the same thing with the press and stuff and that's all nice but I can't live with a fucking picture," you know, I need the real stuff and when I realised I don't have that, I've got to go" and I got punished. I felt like I was punished for so many years and most people don't ever look at Nielsen, they look at Brigitte Nielsen Stallone.'

Britt then went on to share a poignant retelling how Peter Sellers deliberately set about sabotaging the start of her film career and contract with 20th Century Fox, including how difficult it was to live with a manic depressive such as he was.

'I was this little fluffy blonde and I wanted to be that tall gorgeous thin person but I never had the model background so I basically just went in at the top, I married an actor who was at the top of his profession, I had my own contract and what he did, he pulled me out, he told me to leave the movie. I started my movie on the Monday, he started his movie on the Monday in Hollywood, I started my movie in London.

So we had been married for three days when he left, he is in Beverly Hills with all those Beverly Hills people and one day he just said, it's Easter, the beginning of April, I started the movie on 22nd February and it's Easter and he said, "Ask 20th Century Fox if you could come over for Easter, if they can give you a day extra." So I asked them and they said "No." So he said "When Friday comes, I'll have a car pick you up, fly you to LA, you can be back shooting by Monday." Well if the man of your dreams says you can do it...'

Brigitte: 'You can do it.'

Britt: 'I'll make sure you do it. So I took my handbag, a car picked me up, took me straight to the plane, I flew to LA, he picked me up at the airport, he had a doctor meet me immediately saying "You look very ill." '

Brigitte: 'Oh God!'

Britt Ekland with Peter Sellers

Britt: ' "You look very ill" and did I go back to the movie? Hell no. He made sure I didn't. My seven year contract cancelled, everything cancelled.'

Brigitte: 'Okay, but do you feel penalised? Do you know what I'm saying? Because with Sylvester, in the time we were together, *Rocky IV*, all the other scripts I got through, he made sure I was always in one of his movies. Did you feel that way?'

Britt: 'I did two movies with him. You see we had a child, I got pregnant immediately because I didn't know any better...'

Brigitte: 'With Victoria.'

Britt: 'I thought you're married and that's what you do. We did two movies together but he was a manic depressive and he did nothing but nothing but fight all through our marriage...and sit like this (mimes arms crossed, head down with a sullen expression) 24 hours a day.'

With Britt having been so candid about the harsh realities of her destructive marriage to Peter Sellers and having to live with his mood disorders, Brigitte senses a kindred spirit and asks Britt for some advice regarding her current marriage.

Insecurities and jealousies –

'But now I need some advice from you, please. I've been through some crazy relationships in my life, married and divorced, got four beautiful boys. One marriage really drove me mad, I became an alcoholic and I went through some really, really shitty times. I swore to myself, "Every time you have a problem you can't leave, you can't just pick up your bags and leave." Because of the kids I decided to stay and I should have left when I realised it was wrong, instead I stayed and started drinking.

However, finally when I was out of that relationship I said, "Never again am I going to marry, I don't want guys. I want my kids and my dogs and if I'm going to mess around I'll have a flirt, a little affair but out of my house and out of my life, not again." So I've come back from a reality show and I go to a restaurant where I often took the kids, a pizzeria and Mattia walked in anyway and he is my husband today and he lit up literally my dark grey whatever, so my question is: I ended up marrying, I am very happy, we have been together almost seven years, but he is 15 years younger than me and I have become what I never was before, a little bit insecure and jealous and I keep nagging at him. I say, "Do you love me?" I feel really that I am becoming someone that I'm not because I feel insecure and I am so worried that when I'm 60 – I'm 47 – when I'm 60 he is going to be 45.'

Britt: 'So?'

Brigitte: 'So what should I do?'

Britt: 'Peter Sellers was possibly the most jealous person on the planet.'

Brigitte: 'Really? Do you know, Sylvester was the same thing? He had statues of me, the table was covered in my profile, it was horrible. It was like, "at 8.37 Brigitte is leaving the house," a nightmare, an absolute nightmare. That's why you can't live with people like this, that's why it comes to an end. But now I've become that person. Well I'm not like that but I'm jealous.'

Britt: 'When we separated I swore never, ever to be jealous and I have never, ever been jealous. If your relationship and your life is based on what you look like and how old you are, then your relationships don't have foundations. He is madly in love with you but for you, gnawing away at this relationship with all this fear and security and you are so beautiful…'

Brigitte: 'I know, I've never been that way.'

Britt: 'So you just have to find either some way of talking yourself out of it, talking to your husband, talking to someone else.'

Brigitte: 'It is just that creeping insecurity that I don't want because…'

Britt: 'I would speak to my husband.'

Brigitte: 'I do speak to him and he says I'm crazy.'

Britt: 'Yes, of course, so you have to listen to him, you have to trust him and you have to believe him and you must not be jealous. Jealous is really annoying, jealous is the worst quality in a human being, the worst quality.'

By this time of the show, Brigitte had really opened up about her emotional challenges in life and love and having revealed previously how she felt insecure being the older woman in a relationship, she continued with the age theme sharing how in limbo she feels regarding suitable acting roles for her right now.

'So anyway, what I was saying, when I feel all this sorry and insecure with what I do, I am 47 and when you see in movies, the roles, it is either the action thing and I can't be bothered with it and I've never been considered either a comedian or a dramatic actress, I'm not good enough for that people think, I haven't had the chance and then the age, you're not old and you're not young, you're just in between.'

Britt cuts straight to the point – that at 47 you are considered old for the movies, Brigitte feigns feeling the sting of such a reality and Britt continues, telling Brigitte how she was the oldest woman to play a Bond Girl at the age of 35.

'Listen, at 35, I was old.

Brigitte: 'Yes, it's true though.'

Britt: 'I had just finished the Bond film. I have to tell you how I got the Bond film because that is one of only two times I've really gone for something. When I was a teenager and my dad had the broomstick underneath the door, his curling and he's sitting here reading Ian Fleming's *James Bond* books in English in paperback and falling asleep with them…Then I read in the paper, I was living in London and I had done *The Wicker Man* and had done movies and I was known and I read in the paper that they were doing another Bond film so I went out and bought the book, *The Man With the Golden Gun* and I dressed up like a secretary, called up and said, "Could I come and see him?" and "I was a well-known actress" so he said, "Sure."

I went up to see him and said "I would like to have the role of Mary Goodnight in *The Man With the Golden Gun*" looking just like a secretary. He said, "Well we basically sort of take the title of the book and then we write the story around it" and so he thanked me very much for coming and as I'm walking out – this is in South Audley street, his offices, Roger Moore was coming in and he said, "Meet Roger Moore." So "Oh hello, how are you?" and I left and went to LA to do a movie and I was away for six weeks and on the plane back, I'm reading the English paper that had come over with the flight and it says "Swedish girl cast in the new Bond movie." And I'm going "what!" I was absolutely, so upset…'

Brigitte: 'Why?'

Britt: 'It said "Swedish girl Maude Adams is cast in the new James Bond movie." So the plane lands, I get home, my agent calls me and says "You've got to go to Cubby Broccoli's office immediately." So I rushed up and I thought "Oh he is going to apologise to me for having giving it to someone else," that's how naïve I am. I go in and it's all wooden panels and I'm sitting there waiting, suddenly the door swings open like this, he comes out with the script and he says, "You're my Goodnight." I said, "What about Maude Adams?" "She's playing Scaramanga's girlfriend." '

Brigitte: 'Isn't that wonderful?'

Britt: 'And I'm probably the oldest Bond girl in the world and with two children.'

Britt and Brigitte finished on that note of other people's expectations and expressed a genuine pleasure for having shared their conversation. Brigitte invited Britt over to Denmark to cook Danish food for her and so she could meet Brigitte's dogs (Tootsie and Joker). Tequila, who had been fantastically quiet and good throughout the show, either knew intuitively that the show was over – or showed his disdain for the idea of Britt meeting other dogs, as he jumped off the chair and turned his behind to the camera.

Brigitte asked Britt to repeat her firm hand of words – 'Gitte, get on with it.' And it was a wrap.

Brigitte Nielsen and Britt Ekland saying their goodbyes

SIR IAN BOTHAM

Sir Ian Botham OBE, 'Beefy' is a renowned former England Test cricketer, Test team captain and commentator and he is considered to be England's greatest ever all-rounder in test cricket. To this day, Botham holds the record for the English bowler with the highest number of wickets taken, of 14 centuries and 383 wickets.

Sir Tim Rice is a genuine legend of musical theatre and alongside his long-time collaborator and friend Andrew Lloyd Webber, he is responsible for some of the most iconic musicals of all time, such as 'Joseph,' 'Evita' and 'Jesus Christ Superstar.' His lyrics have resonated in the hearts and minds of music lovers across the globe throughout several decades and he is truly part of the cultural fabric of the theatre world.

SIR TIM RICE

7

SIR IAN BOTHAM & SIR TIM RICE

Lords – For Ian and Tim's episode of the series, it wasn't a huge creative leap for us to determine Lords as a venue for the filming – the iconic ground of English Cricket, where the schoolboy Botham served his apprenticeship on the ground staff and later scored runs and bowled wickets with prolific regularity. For Tim we also debated filming in one of the West End theatres that had offered his musicals to a worldwide audience, but if there is a passion other than music for Tim – it is cricket. Tim was president of the MCC in 2002, and of the Lord Taverners from 1988-1990. He also runs his own amateur cricket team – The Heartaches Cricket Club. One of the defining reasons we brought together this meeting of minds, friendships and professional appreciation.

Intro's – For Ian's filmed piece to camera for our Introduction (exclusive to the DVD) we were lucky enough to have the run of Lords and hence we were able to film him from the lower stands as he sat on the boundary fence with the famous ground as his backdrop. Two things struck us from the outset with Ian; firstly how generous he was with his time. Between the main set and the outside pick up filming he said, 'Hello' to numerous members of staff, asking after families, sharing anecdotes and giving time to everyone. Secondly, having commentated for years with Sky Television he looked straight down the barrel of the camera, and delivered perfect 'one take wonders' for us. This was after he had managed to halt the grounds-men mowing the outfield and maintenance men drilling up in the higher stands so we could film.

For Tim's intro we were able to film him standing in the Lords Museum with famous memorabilia framing his backdrop. Also the consummate professional, it meant we were on set ready for the main shoot ahead of schedule.

Beginnings – Tim kicked off this episode of 'Living the Life' asking Ian if being a cricketer/ sportsman was always what he aimed for, even as a child.

'Yes, I made my mind up very young and I always remember at Butler's Mead Secondary Modern School in Yeovil, you had to queue up outside the library to see the careers officer and he said "Where are you thinking of going, what do you want to do?" I said, "Play sport." "Yes, of course, like everyone else but what are you really going to do?" And I said, "I'm really going to play sport." '

Sir Ian Botham and Sir Tim Rice in their pre-interviews

Tim: 'And were you good at that point, did you know you were good?'

Ian: 'Yes, yes. Somerset registered me at 14...and I signed here at Lords when Somerset sent me up here as a 15 year old.'

Tim: 'So you were signed to the MCC?'

Ian Botham (front row second right) as part of a school boy cricket team

Ian: 'No, Somerset owned my registration but in those days the way it worked was if you had three or four players or two players you thought could go all the way they used to send us up here to the ground staff, over the back there, the nippers.'

Tim: 'What sort of pay were you on then?'

Ian: 'I think it was £11 a week of which you had to pay £6 out of your £11 a week for your bed and breakfast, your boarding in the hostel so that left us, basically we got paid Thursday and by Saturday morning we were broke.'

The Articled Particle – Tim being (slightly) older shared the fact that his first job netted him 'a fiver' a week, and through explaining it exposed the zeitgeist of his generation being urged by parents to 'get a proper job' despite their creative talents or inclinations.

'I was an articled particle in a firm of law, a firm of solicitors, I got five quid a week plus luncheon vouchers. At the same time I was trying to sing with pop groups, I wanted to be – it's hard to believe I know but I wanted to be a pop star and it seemed to me that everybody else in my generation was in the charts except for me.

I sent this tape of me singing three songs to, well there were only about four record companies worth sending it to, and I heard nothing for quite a long time and then I got a call from a music publisher and these are the guys who look after the songs as opposed to the recording stars and he said, "Oh we've been sent this tape by one of the recording companies and we don't like the voice, terrible voice, but one of the songs is quite good. So we're going to record one of the songs with one of our groups."

I thought, brilliant, fantastic, is it going to be the Kinks or the Animals or Herman's Hermits or maybe even the Beatles, perhaps they've dried up, and he said it's a group called the Nightshift. I felt very sorry for the Nightshift because my song was their career and they recorded it and it came out...and it was a total flop and I was very depressed but I had my name on a record and gradually my career shifted, I got less and less interested in the law if that were possible and I eventually joined EMI records as a general dogsbody.'

The Nightshift record sleeve

Coincidence, serendipity, luck, fortuitousness... the list could go on but similarly to so many of our contributors, Tim, who was visiting a book publisher at the time, was asked what else he did. He replied he also wrote songs, to which the publisher off the cuff remarked, 'You should meet this bloke called Andrew Lloyd Webber!' Tim humorously related how he told the book publisher this bloke will have to change his name, 'He'll never make it with a name like that.'

Tim asked Ian how his early days on the ground staff had been – and talk about the polar opposites of today's pampered professional sportsman. For Ian it was about survival, playing cricket, moonlighting in pubs for a bit of extra cash and evading police as they were hopping over underground tube barriers to make some cricket match across London without money in their pockets. Two years of summers at Lords, and then returning to Somerset for the winters. Ian said one winter he moonlighted labouring for a couple of plasterers and made more in a day than his whole Lord's tenure. Although he spent his money on flared trousers and platform shoes, much to Tim's joking distaste telling Ian, 'You were very unlucky really to be a teenager in that era of fashion.'

In cricketing terms, Ian played for the second team in his teens (14 and 15) with a first class debut against Lancashire later on. What was interesting was how Lords kept Ian from bowling, again was it luck or circumstance – Ian bowled a lot for Somerset – that shaped the greatest all-rounder English cricket has had.

'I was a bowler primarily at the start…when I was at Lords, this is the turnaround, the ground staff here, they wouldn't let me bowl. They said, "You're not good enough." So I said, "But I like bowling." "No, you're not good enough, we've got other bowlers, they're better," they said, "You bat."

So I ended up batting three or four and never bowled. So I went back to Somerset where Tom Cartwright and the coach said, "Yes, you can do bowling" and I was opening the bowling for Somerset at second and in the various games and bowling for Somerset in the John Player League but I wasn't allowed to bowl here and if you look at the overs that I bowled here on the Lords ground staff, there probably wouldn't be twenty.'

Ian then raced through some stats and facts for Tim's mathematical and cricketing mind (Somerset debut '71, England test debut '77 and one day debut '76 against the West Indies – the hot summer that Ian wryly attests to being 'Before they invented global warming.' His test debut was against Australia at Trent Bridge which the queen also attended, 'So first test and meet the Queen, it doesn't get much better than that as a youngster, you can imagine, a Somerset bumpkin boy.'

Sir Ian Botham meeting the Queen

Thrown to the Wolves – Ian shared how 1981 was like flicking a switch – the legendary Ashes series where he broke the record for most sixes in an Ashes test match (6) hit huge scores 145 not out and took 6 wickets for 95 at the famous Headingly test. Tim did raise the point though that although other people share his great success in sport they weren't in the spotlight in the way Ian was. Ian agreed that to be catapulted into the world arena, in the days when professional sportsmen didn't get the guidance they receive now, was like being 'Thrown to the wolves.'

Ian flipped the conversation back to Tim, recapping that '81 had kicked him off, so when did it happen for Tim?

Sir Tim Rice (left) with Andrew Lloyd Webber

'It was in a way overnight because we'd been working for a long time, Andrew and I, since the mid-sixties, working on shows that hadn't made it. We did a musical about Dr Barnado, the Victorian philanthropist, we'd done *Joseph* which was good but it was only in schools and we didn't think it was ever going to make us any money. After *Joseph* the big break was *Jesus Christ Superstar.*

What we didn't realise was that one of the boys in the school (where we were performing Joseph) his father was the Sunday Times music correspondent, the serious one. He had been writing about Frank Sinatra or whatever and the next week in the Sunday Times, and we had no idea this was coming up, there was our little school concert being reviewed by Derek Jewell who was the Sunday Times music man. He said, "This is brilliant, these two guys are superb, great words, wonderful tunes, best school concert I've ever seen" and immediately – because nobody knows anything in show business, including me – having had nobody show any interest in us up to that point and we had been hawking our songs, Joseph songs, round to every music publisher and theatre man we could break into but once a newspaper said it was good we then had people ringing us and we made an album of *Joseph*. Even that didn't do particularly well but it was a good album and it was sent out to schools and sold a few copies.

A bloke who became our agent, our manager, David Land, heard that album and he said, "You two guys are good" and he signed us up and offered me and Andrew 1500 quid a year each for three years and Andrew of course didn't have a job at the time,

Pop goes Joseph

JAZZ/POP □ DEREK JEWELL

'*GIVE US food*' *the brothers said,*
'*Dieting is for the birds.*'
Joseph gave them all they wanted
Second helpings, even thirds ...
EVEN ON paper the happy bounce of lyrics like these comes through. They are exactly right for singing by several hundred boys' voices. With two organs, guitars, drums and a large orchestra the effect is irresistible.

The quicksilver vitality of *Joseph and His Amazing Technicolor Dreamcoat,* the new pop oratorio heard at Central Hall, Westminster, last Sunday, is attractive indeed. On this evidence the pop idiom—beat rhythms and Bacharachian melodies—is most enjoyably capable of being used in extended form.

Musically, "Joseph" is not all gold. It needs more light and shade. A very beautiful melody, "Close Every Door To Me," is one of the few points when the hectic pace slows down. The snap and crackle of the rest of the work tends to be too insistent, masking the impact of the words which, unlike many in pop, are important.

But such reservations seem pedantic when matched against "Joseph's" infectious overall character. Throughout its twenty-minute d u r a t i o n it bristles with wonderfully singable tunes. It entertains. It communicates instantly, as all good pop should. And it is a considerable piece of barrier-breaking by its creators, two men in their early twenties—Tim Rice, the lyricist, and Andrew Lloyd Webber, who wrote the music.

The performers last Sunday were the choir, school and orchestra of Colet Court, the St. Paul's junior school, with three solo singers and a pop group called The Mixed Bag. It was an adventurous experiment for a school, yet Alan Doggett, who conducted, produced a crisp, exciting and undraggy performance which emphasised the rich expansiveness of pop rather than the limitations of its frontiers.

A more predictable occasion was the opening, at the Talk of the Town, of Cliff Richard, who these days seems over-involved with what the disc jockey John Peel calls "wallpaper pop"—schmaltzy ballads intended to be heard but not listened to by the middle-aged young.

His show, however, was more interesting than this suggests. During one rocking number "Ain't Nothing But a House Party," the evening—enlivened by the backing of The Breakaways, a pretty female group—really ignited. But thereafter, excitement turned too often into mild diversion.

The Sunday Times newspaper review of Joseph

he was still a student and for him it was a no-brainer but I was thinking, "Mmm, well, we haven't actually written a hit yet, we may be promising but I've got a good job with *Norrie Paramour*." It was the first row we ever had because Andrew was saying, "No; we've got to do this." In the end I agreed with Andrew and said, "Okay, I'll take the plunge" but I thought, "I'm 24 maybe this is a big mistake," I really had this middle-class play safe attitude, very boring really but we want for it and the first thing we wrote was *Superstar*. Even then we couldn't get arrested with that. We had one record company say, "Well we quite like this Superstar idea, you could make a record of it," but to get the money to make the record we had to sign all the rights away for everything, which in a way was fair enough.'

Ian: 'They were taking the plunge I suppose.'

Tim: 'Yes, they were taking a bit of a plunge and even then they just said you can do a single and we did the one single Jesus Christ Superstar, with Murray Head who was an old friend of mine from the EMI days and he was cheap. He was also extremely talented but he wasn't a major record name at that point so we were really sort of flying by the seat of our pants even though we had our 1500 quid a year each guaranteed for three years. MCA put the single out and said, "If the single's a hit you can do an album, or you can do the album and if the album's a hit we'll do a show and if the show's a hit we'll do a Broadway stage show and if that's a hit we'll do a film." And we thought, "We'll sign this but none of it will ever happen" and of course it all happened, but not here, it happened in America, the record took off in America like a bullet.'

Ian: 'You talk about the musical side of it, but it almost seems as if the musical led to the pop songs rather than the other way round.'

Tim: 'It did really, yes. I mean I've never been very good at writing pop songs, there are those who might say I am not very good at writing musicals either, but nearly all the pop hits I've had have come out of shows and the first big song we had was *I Don't Know How To Love Him* from Superstar and the song Superstar itself. Well I would never have written that song, *I Don't Know How To Love Him,* if it hadn't been for a character within a situation in a show. If you have a good story which Superstar or the story of Jesus is undeniably a good story…'

Ian: 'Yes, it's quite a big selling book, yes.'

Tim: 'And also a song about Jesus, writing that was much more interesting, with a great tune from Andrew in each case, much more interesting than writing 'I love you baby, please be true', actually that's not bad, I must make a note of that! But again with *Don't Cry For Me Argentina,* nobody in their right mind would have sat down to have written a song, a big ballad, six minutes long, with a lyric all about Argentina. I mean this was pre-Falklands but it didn't really have much resonance with the Brittish record buying public. The only things that really are big are usually things that are totally unexpected, that come out of left field and obviously once you've established yourself, if you're lucky you can keep going.'

Tim, at this point of the show, asked Ian not only if he saw himself going into television (the best thing I did) but also why he never plays now. It is a great question for a sportsman, because so many come out of retirement to fight or play again, or join the senior's tour or turn out for charity matches and such like, and Ian explains it so well from his point of view.

Sir Ian Botham as a cricket commentator

'I've not played since the day I retired in '93 because where do you draw the line? I still get a sack full of requests to play in benefit games or charity events and there would be more if I were playing, there would be lorry loads coming and you have got to draw a line. The reason I retired is because the body was knackered, it was gone. This operation, that operation, when it got to the tenth operation to keep me on the field I thought "maybe there's a message there coming through." Also you set your standards and go out and hobble around as an old beaten up crony now, it wouldn't give me any satisfaction and I wouldn't enjoy it.'

Tim relates completely to Ian's explanation of not wanting to go on too long and said that after *Chess* didn't do as well, and Lloyd Webber had solo hits with *Cats* and *Phantom* he was sort of 'done' with the theatre and feeling a little bruised and then goes on to explain the new lease of life Disney gave him and also gives a fascinating insight into how that side of the industry works.

'I was saved by Disney because it was right up my alley, I loved – probably because I am still a mental age of eight or nine but I loved Disney cartoons as a kid and to be asked to come to Disney…to begin with they just said, "Would you like to be on Disney's payroll" – "Yes" – "For two or three years and we'll find projects?"

The first thing they asked me to do was suggest songs to be placed within a script for a Dolly Parton film and Dolly is fantastic and I thought maybe I could write a song for Dolly

Parton but that never happened, but I did get into the Disney set up and I was meeting the Disney execs. I kept saying, "I write words, I wouldn't mind having a go at one of your animated films" and they put me on to this project called *King of the Jungle*, they said, "It's about a lion and it is a bit like Hamlet with fur. It's about a lion cub and his evil wicked uncle and his uncle kills the father and all that, we haven't got much idea what we're going to do with it but would you be interested in writing the lyrics?" "Yes!" All they had at that time was a page of story, a couple of characters drawn on a board and a director. It ended up of course being *The Lion King* many, many years later, well two or three years later.

'I was in that process from literally starting with one picture and one story line and they said to me at one point, "Who would you like to do the music?" I said, "Well Elton John"...I think the best thing I did for Disney was to suggest Elton because it was a different sort of score. Ironically, when I was working with Elton on *The Lion King* and he of course was going round the world all the time, the words come first with Elton and that's quite unusual.

Sir Tim Rice (right) with Sir Elton John brandishing their Oscars

So I was working with the scriptwriters and getting the story together and it sounds an awfully long time to come up with just six songs but really we were all a team during this movie and whilst I was working on it, the brilliant lyricist Howard Ashman, who was working with Alan Menkin on Aladdin, died, he had been ill for a long time and they had hoped he would finish Aladdin but he didn't.

I'd done a bit of *Lion King* by then and they were obviously quite happy with it and they said, "Ere you, work on *Aladdin* for three months" because it was panic city, *Aladdin* was about to come out and they were three songs short. So I was pitched into this completely different animated film, with a composer I didn't know but he turned out to be, apart from brilliantly talented, one of the nicest guys I've ever worked with and we have done quite a lot together since. One of the songs which Howard hadn't done was the big ballad and I was pitched into this and had to sit through endless rough takes of the film and it was the song which turned out to be *A Whole New World* and that went to number one in America and we won an Oscar and a Golden Globe and I went back to *The Lion King* slightly sheepish and rather embarrassed that suddenly I was an Oscar winner, having been a bloke who didn't know the first thing about movies.'

An interesting fact was that Tim described how he was put on a Disney project to write songs for Dolly Parton and, completely unconnected, another 'Living the Life' contributor Robin Gibb, did write a song for Dolly – *Islands in the Stream.*

Swinging the conversation back to fame, Tim alluded to the huge amount of charity work Ian has done for Leukaemia research over the years,one obvious benefit for the charity was that so many people knew Ian. Ian agreed and described how his walks have changed – how they used to be huge treks the length of Britain but the literally massive increase in traffic makes walking down main roads of the U.K. impractical, so the structure has changed to long walks around cities culminating at a finale where in a 'well known' park or grounds where the public get to join him too. (The 10 Cities walk)

It was the 25th anniversary of Ian's walks in 2010 and he has raised a staggering 16 million pounds 'but that is the tip of the iceberg, that's just the walks because you get the big conglomerates now who say, "Right, we'll make you Charity of the Year" and

Sir Ian Botham on one of his 'Ten Cities' walks

that's where the real money comes in.

It's good and the real thing that drives you on, and this is the bit that I'm very proud of, 26 years ago now when we did the first ever walk, children with leukaemia had a 20% chance of survival. We announced last October that it is a 91-92% chance now of survival, in such a short time span...In 26 years that's an amazing effort and the research centre, just outside Glasgow, was funded from the first ever walk.'

Family and Friendships – Ian is a devoted family man and describing his own parents, he (like many of our contributors) recognises the sacrifices they made to enable him to pursue his dream. 'That's one of the things, people always say, "Who was your guiding light," at the end of the day when you look at the bare facts, you look back and think how did it all happen? "I'll tell you why it happened, because my mother and father made enormous sacrifices. They were working class, my father was in the Navy and then he went to Western Helicopters, my mother was a nurse, a dental nurse, but then she became a mother which was a full time job with us lot and they made many sacrifices. Weekends, driving me all round Somerset and the South of England to play cricket, and soccer at that stage, so that's where it all comes from. My old man was a gifted sportsman and he spent time with me.'

Sir Ian Botham with his father Herbert Leslie Botham

As Ian and Tim relaxed into the final chapter of the show Ian described how he relaxes through his love of fishing. 'And you get into that river wherever it is and you've got your 15 foot rod, you get your waders on and it's done. They don't flatter you very much but you've got your jacket on, your hat and you go down and get into that pool, you walk maybe 100 yards down the pool, the length of a good long pool, and you look at your watch and three hours have gone and you've just switched off. I've had deer swimming past me, crossing the river, otters, golden eagles, it is wonderful.'

A narrative on how arguably one of England's greatest sportsmen continues to live a full and centred life outside of the energy that fed him. Where so many have succumbed to drugs, depression and all manner of self-sabotage once their professional sporting career ends, Ian has maintained a loving marriage, given hugely of his time to altruism and philanthropy and balanced a high profile life with the quiet spiritual solitudes of time in nature. His persona with the crew, with others and what surfaced through his revealing conversations was a man who knew his own mind, and had found his own path for living this so called challenge of life.

A Cunning Ruse – There were many instances throughout the show where both contributors slipped an instantaneously witty comment into the conversation (Ian with invention of Global warming, Tim describing vinyl records, Ian's fashion etc) and when Tim and Ian rounded off their episode talking about the media change in their respective professions. Tim described the excitement of listening to a hit record on the radio compared to the repetitively and instantly downloadable access of today. He felt this probably made it harder to break through although conceded Adele managed it 'in a rather old fashioned way by the cunning ruse of having a very good song which people hadn't thought about.'

Sir Tim Rice and Sir Ian Botham saying their goodbyes

Television accessibility of sport led in Ian's view to overkill 'When you think when Don Bradman went to have a net at Lords there were probably 10,000 there to watch him have a net because they weren't getting it on the newsreel, *Pathe* news didn't have it out every day and people get into the habit of sitting at home and switching channels and they can watch two games of football and press the red button to be interactive, it makes it hard, hard work to compete but there is at the end of the day no substitute for actually going there and live sport does that as does the theatre and long may that last.'

The old antagonistic word of 'celebrity' reared its head again with both Ian and Tim detesting the moniker; as Ian so succinctly put it, 'I'm not a celebrity, I just happened to be quite good at cricket.'

The world put to rights, stories shared and emotions spilled, Ian wrapped up the show with the sensible suggestion that they do what they do best, and go and get a glass of red...and it's a wrap.

FAY WELDON

Fay Weldon CBE is the prolific author, essayist and playwright. Starting her career in advertising, Fay proceeded to write television plays for the BBC and subsequently made a career as a prolific writer of dramas and novels, for which she is best known. Her book, 'The Life and Loves of a She Devil' was a huge hit both as a work of fiction and later as a dramatisation for television.

Caitlin Moran began her prolific career as a journalist at the age of 16, writing for 'Melody Maker,' 'The Observer' and 'The Guardian,' as well as publishing a novel called 'The Chronicles of Narmo.' Caitlin launched her UK television career in 1992, hosting the Channel 4 music show 'Naked City.' and her best-selling book, 'How to be a Woman' was published in 2011. She is the tv critic and columnist at 'The Times.'

CAITLIN MORAN

conscious of 'the right fit.' Having enjoyed the writing of Caitlin Moran for a while, we mooted the idea of bringing them both together. Although we usually chose a pairing from different fields of excellence – with Fay and Caitlin we had two ladies renowned for their positive strides for feminism and both were writers. Luckily though, there was enough of a difference with an acclaimed novelist Fay and an insightful, polemical journalist and non-fiction writer, Caitlin. When we first approached Caitlin she had yet to release her book, so her time was a little less fraught than after publication and her consequent world domination of *How to Be a Woman*. It was certainly prescient of the team to push for Caitlin.

The Library of the Gore Hotel was for us the perfect fit for the shoot; a luxurious room, fit for two literary giants.

The Baby Machine – Once the 'girls' had settled into their chairs on set, the cameras were rolling and it was action, Fay kicking off proceedings asking Caitlin about her childhood. The hilarious exchange that followed set the scene for the whole show where there was a mixture of frankness, honesty, humour and strife.

Fay: 'So how many brothers and sisters do you have?'

Caitlin: 'Too many, not enough to be able to fit in an average sized car, we had to buy industrial vehicles. We had eight; I heard the conception of every single one I think. My mother would stop breastfeeding, then I would be given the child that would then come and sleep in my bed and then that night I would hear the next child being conceived and I would lie in bed with the sibling and just go, "Well you're going to have another brother or sister in nine months time my friend", and so it turned out to be.'

I think she liked being pregnant, she liked having babies and stuff and then it worked out that each child, once they had left the mother, would just come and join the gang of kids and we were very separate. There was my parents and whatever baby there was and then there were all the kids, because there were eight of us, and we were just a pack and we kind of brought ourselves up really.'

Fay: 'How many children do you have?'

Caitlin: 'Two. I thought that I would have eight, then I had one and I thought, "No, I might have six" and then I had two and it was like, "No two is enough." '

Fay: 'That's quite often the case, women think they are going to go one better than their mother and have one more, but you'd then have to have nine'

Caitlin: 'My uterus would look like a sock; it's not physically possible I don't think, I'd be like Octomom plus one that would just be horrible.'

Even from the start Caitlin had that ability to share what was obviously emotionally difficult times, with the same wry humour that has touched her writing, and Fay throughout the whole episode 'understands.' Usually, by the time I have chosen the final edit for an episode I have seen every clip numerous times – I won't say hundreds but it can feel like it. What was apparent was that Fay was measured in her responses but acutely worldly wise. She could say something that on closer examination offered a great insight into her empirical knowledge and wisdom.

Caitlin Moran tweeting before the show

Twitterati Anecdote No2 –

Caitlin is renowned for her avid attachment to *Twitter*, twittering and all things that tweet. For the opening intro of the episode (special feature for the 'Living the Life' DVD) I felt that during Caitlin's answering of the loosely standard questions about meeting Fay and what to expect, Caitlin could tweet Stephen Fry, one of our earlier contributors for a pre-filming heads-up and some advice.

Being so comfortable with the medium of social networking Caitlin was thoroughly relaxed, lounged on a chair of one of the hotel rooms, as she tweeted her participation for the forthcoming show. Stephen replied almost immediately.

It was a telling moment in terms of television interaction and also the interconnectedness not just of the series but also of the contributors.

@caitlinmoran
Caitlin Moran

@stephenfry Darling, just about to copy you and do "Living The Life" with Fay Weldon. Any tips?

5 Aug via Tweet Deck

@stephenfry
Stephen Fry

@caitlinmoran You're adorable. She's adorable. What could possibly go wrong? So long as Michael Winner isn't hiding under the table...xxx

5 Aug via Twitter for iPad

Home Schooling – The conversation moved on to Caitlin describing her unconventional schooling.

Caitlin Moran (centred in hat) with her six siblings and parents

'...so we didn't go to school. Well we did, we all went to school until 1986 and when people say "Why did you become home-schooled" I always jokingly say, "Because my mother couldn't get together eight pairs of socks and pants for the school run by 8.30 in the morning," but that actually was the truth of it. She was just furiously angry at the amount of laundry she was having to do and figured that if we all came out of school and were taught at home we could just walk around all day in our nighties, and so it proved to be.'

Caitlin Moran as a young schoolgirl

Fay: 'And was she a good teacher?'

Caitlin: 'Well she was, in that she realised that she would be a terrible teacher and never gave us any lessons at all. What you don't realise is that if you do home education you don't have to do anything at all and we didn't, we just sat around all day watching *Ghost Busters* and classic MGM musicals and drinking undiluted Ribena, because that gets you very high on the sugar, and occasionally we would have shots of vinegar in a shot glass and call it whisky and we would knock it back and go, '"That kicks ass!" and pretend that we were drunk. Sometimes we would spin round and round and round until we were very, very dizzy and then fall over. I enjoyed that.'

After such a sideways look at childhood from Caitlin, the conversation took a natural turn to Fay and her own childhood spent growing up in New Zealand. Caitlin had heard that Fay had grown up there and explained that when she was younger she used to read about New Zealand and see photographs, thinking it 'seemed to be one of those perfect places, so beautiful.' She asked Fay if people were ever unhappy there.

Native Buttocks – 'Oh terribly, yes, they are committing suicide all over the place. No, of course they were unhappy. If you were my mother you were very unhappy because you weren't in England and you had been kept in New Zealand because a war had broken out and she was a very sophisticated young English intellectual and

 was suddenly in New Zealand where there are a lot of farmers and she was really very worried that me and my sister would grow up to be farmer's wives which is a terrible, awful thing. So she was anxious, she was a really anxious person and we were very poor. Like you, this sense of not having what the other children had and poor really because she and my father got divorced and he never made any money, it was a depression.

Fay Weldon (right) and her younger sister Jane (left)

It was such a long time ago, it was such a different world, growing up was such a different business from the world you grew up in where nobody ever saw anybody naked, nobody had any idea of sex, you knew absolutely nothing about it. Boys and girls were not allowed in the same room together without a chaperone, it was a sort of rather extraordinary middle class respectability put upon a very energetic pioneering nation.'

Caitlin: 'Did you have a sense of that kind of repression and prudishness being wrong?'

Fay: 'All I can remember is going to a convent school and standing in a row waiting to go in to the class and the nuns saying, "Don't touch each other, stop touching each other, you must never touch another person." I just put out my hand and touched the person in front of me and got into terrible trouble because growing up is a very different matter and for me it took rather a long time, especially as I lived in an all-female household with my mother, my sister and my grandmother and went to an all-girls school.

I never saw a man and then coming to England at the age of fifteen after the war; it was again the all-girls school. You weren't meant to have a boyfriend until you were out of school uniform and since you stayed at school till about nineteen it could be rather sort of onerous. So this idea of the sexes joining was just not in the world. But got a lot of work done, got a lot of books read.'

Caitlin: 'I was going to say, nineteen is a long time.'

Fay: 'Well actually I left school when I was seventeen and I got to university then.'

Without labouring the point regarding the mission statement for the series, it was important that although we adhered to the certain programme goals, we worked hard not to become rigid or negatively formulaic. A good example of this was that although Fay and Caitlin still shared emotional journeys from childhood to the present day, the nature of the conversation became related to and observational about feminism. This may seem obvious and to be expected, but it wasn't directed that way, the themes just naturally ran to the sensitivities of the contributors.

Similarly Lord Sebastian Coe and Gary Newbon shared their emotional time-line journeys and it became naturally 'Olympic' centric. Seb's early childhood motivation for taking up running was the 1968 Olympics, he starred in two legendary Olympics (1980 and 1984), and he was also an integral cog in winning the 2012 Olympics for London. Also some of Gary's career highlights involved anecdotes from the Olympics. Hence their experiences came out through their respective interests.

A Man To Share My Bed With – Caitlin pushed the next line of questioning in the direction of 'The Patriarchy', asking Fay what her idea of men was and how she thought of them coming from an all-female household.

'I thought men were amazing and wonderful people, you see. My mother kept us and worked terribly hard and made such money as we had and my father lived in New Zealand, very rarely sent the money back that he was meant to, he somehow never quite managed.'

Caitlin: 'Were you aware of men generally or was the only man in the world your dad? Were you seeing men by that time?'

Fay: 'Well no, I saw him once a year and could never think of anything to say to him when one did because they seemed so strange and foreign and they were but they bought life and energy into the house, they bought something else other than housework, cooking, worry, anxiety. What they bought with them was a sort of cheerfulness and energy and a lack of anxiety and it was, I think, a sort of sense of anxiety that we were brought up with...from the age of about 13 seeing my mother's lonely bed and my own lonely bed and thinking all I really want in life is to have a man in the bed beside me, what a very odd thing to think, not knowing anything about sex which one didn't really at that age, nor did one again because of the complete lack of information which was both one's own, a sort of sense of what was taboo that one was brought up very much so you didn't really work it out.

Reading your book, you're longing for information – the only naked person you ever saw was in the National Geographic which it's true, me and my friend Nancy Bell would go on such days as the National Geographic was delivered, we would go to the bookshop and open the pages in order to see a naked woman. A naked woman, not even a naked man but if you are a native woman you're allowed to be photographed going round without your top on.'

Caitlin: 'Yes, foreign buttocks are fine but British buttocks are absolutely wrong and must be covered at all times or the Empire will crumble.'

The whole section of this chapter began with Fay describing her absent father. Not only had her parents divorced in a difficult social time but her father had rarely managed to send the money home to support the family like he was meant to. Fay handles this retelling in a way of acceptance of the nature of life. It doesn't discolour her idea of men or her attraction to men; she goes on to say that in fact her mother and her own bed had an aura of loneliness without a man in it. The taboo of the naked body closed out her theme of the subject.

Both contributor's emotional challenges with being overweight revealed some interesting insights (below) before they went on to explain in their own humorous and inimitable styles the start of their menstruation and of both never really feeling as though they fitted in.

A Head in a Jar –

Fay: 'In your book you refer to being…and again I was fat as you were so you had this extraordinary sense of turning yourself into a head in a jar, so I tried to remain a head in a jar forever no matter what was happening and I think once you're that, you stay that really.'

Caitlin: 'There was a kind of comfort to it, because when awful physical things are happening to you – and it's something that I say in the book – that oestrogen is a bitch but the idea that you are a girl, you're like a little kid and you are just playing your games and then one day oestrogen happens and suddenly you're turning into a woman. You're given these breasts and you're bleeding and you have pain but you are still a little girl, mentally you are still a little girl when these things happen to you. I think most girls that I know kind of … and if you don't have any information and you're not expecting it to happen, I didn't expect it to happen.'

Fay: 'No, you just think you've got terrible wounds and you are bleeding to death. I asked my grandmother and she looked very alarmed and said, "Oh you'd better ask your mother" and she was out. And then your mother says, "Yes, this is called a period and you're much too young to have one but I'm afraid this country, it's just like the cabbages, they grow much too fast." '

Caitlin: 'So how old were you when you started?'

Fay: 'Eleven.'

Caitlin: 'That's terrible but she blamed the whole country for your starting menstruation. I found out about a month before it happened, someone had stuffed a Lillet's leaflet in the hedge down the road from the school, they would leave porn mags in occasionally or Coke cans and on one day this fabulous bounty of a Lillets leaflet and it showed a kind of cross section of the internal organs or the burrows as I referred to them.

When I read it I genuinely thought it was optional, I was just like, "I don't think I'll do

144

that, that seems like a really bad idea, what fool would do that?" Then when I realised it was coming to me I was exquisitely outraged and furious...and at the time the idea of being a woman just seemed to suddenly make you very vulnerable, it seemed to be a massive pain in the arse, I had no idea how you'd do it.

Being a woman seemed to be about being smooth and serene and being beautifully dressed and glossy and just being and floating around and stuff and I just couldn't see any way that I could do that. I was enormously fat and loud. I liked the fact that our family was weird, we were very ostracised. There was never a sense of ever...basically society and people and life was happening over there and we were always watching it and that is the classic set up for being a writer, isn't it, watching?'

Fay: 'Yes, being the outsider all the time which certainly happened to me because again my parents were divorced and nobody else's parents were divorced and I was an English child in a New Zealand culture and my mother was determined that we would be English and I was determined that I would be a New Zealander. Then when you finally arrive in England you are an outsider again because you are a New Zealand child so nothing that you saw ever seemed quite normal, everything is a kind of marvellous and extraordinary and bizarre thing that is going on in society outside you so you can actually look at it.'

Body image and the feminine representations of beauty and expectation in the world kept the conversation moving on at a scintillating pace, both contributors precise in their arguments and observations.

Fay: 'I think now and I see this in the students, is if they come from two cultures you are much better at everything than if you come from one because they take nothing for granted and everything that is proposed to them they look at very carefully and scrutinise it in order to come to...they are in the habit of only coming to conclusions when they have looked at all sides and it is really good for them. If you look at school photographs of fourteen year olds as it was, there are about three of them that'll look good out of a class of 30, that's 1 in 10 is a natural born looker and all the others are good women.'

Caitlin: 'When I was a teenager it was around the time of Britpop and grunge and it was quite a dressed down era and you'd look at pictures of teenage girls then and they are not really wearing any make up and their hair is just washed and clean and they are wearing Doc Martin boots and jeans and it is a very low effort look compared to now.'

Fay: 'Well I think it's because there are so many cameras out there, you're looked at all the time if only it's a street camera, so you become very conscious of what you look like and in my childhood you looked at the world from the inside out, you weren't conscious of being looked at.'

Sexism; but a Man Buffet – Fay went on to share an incredible story of being in university in 1952 and although it had to have a quota of 20% women, the Professor of Moral Philosophy didn't want to teach girls. After a bit of banter between Fay and Caitlin where Caitlin saw 20% as a token gesture and easily crushable from having a majority voice, Fay lightened the tone saying she felt rather lucky as a female with so many men. 'It's sexist but a man buffet,' as Caitlin put it. Fay expanded on the experience.

'The Professor of Moral Philosophy as I say didn't want to teach and objected very strongly to having to teach women and there were four of us in our class that he ignored totally and wouldn't mark our essays and he kept saying to the boys that women had no capacity for moral judgement or independent thought because they were too emotional. We didn't sort of object, he was a terribly good teacher, very interesting but he just had this odd eccentricity in saying this and all you could really…all I thought was, well I'm not a woman. You just sort of involved yourself amongst the men and went on being, for the purposes of your instruction, this head in the jar.'

Caitlin: 'What was happening in your life when feminism came along, because that is the great revolution?'

Fay: 'I was working in an advertising agency and I was doing all the women's products and I was being paid rather less than anybody else and you just sort of began to see that men behaved … I mean the change in society changed so rapidly that again, with the contraceptive pill I think that made a great difference so as soon as you could have sex without babies everybody just had sex all the time. The more a girl had sex all the time, the more the men despised them so by the end of the sixties men were behaving so badly towards women and talking of them so rudely…'

146

Caitlin: 'In what kind of way?'

Fay: 'In the 50s they didn't, while men were in charge of contraception, while the responsibility was the men's and you made a girl pregnant, on the whole you married her because there was no other way she could survive because the whole country was set up in that you were a bad girl. I had a baby when I was 22 without a husband so one was trying to live with all this and support yourself.'

Leslie Phillips and the Hitchcock Cameos –

Fay and Caitlin had been pouring out their souls and speeding through their own lives and parallels with feminist arguments. They were both in need of a rest and both suggested a glass of bubbly. The quickest way not to interrupt filming and explain continuity was to have Caitlin share an anecdote about dreaming about Leslie Phillips and then have him deliver them a glass of champagne on set.

It was a light moment and welcome pause for the cast and crew. We considered a 'Hitchcock' cameo for Leslie Phillips throughout the whole series as we had also, for the filming of the final exit scenes with Bill Wyman and Stephen Fry, had them both walking through the bar of the Gore Hotel where there are large framed photographs of the Rolling Stones at a party in the seventies. The Hitchcock moment involved Stephen and Bill walking past Leslie and in an instant of recognition, miss-step and then point to the framed photographs of Bill In.

They were fun anecdotes but to sustain a fresh inclusion of Leslie in all manner of different scenarios throughout the whole series would have become, we felt, a distraction from the gravitas of interviews, but the unseen photographs are below.

Leslie Phillips (left) with Stephen Fry (right)

Leslie Phillips, Hitchcockian cameos

Caitlin, after the refreshing break, picked up on something Fay had said earlier about only being 22 and a single mother, wondering if she was ostracised from society for being so and 'painted with a scarlet letter and beaten with sticks,' to which Fay replied that oddly enough she wasn't. Again she explained further.

'No, no they didn't but then I didn't set myself up. I'm sure it did happen to a lot of people but I don't know, I was always perfectly amiable and didn't pity myself.'

Caitlin: 'Do you think it was that you were radiating an air of I find this acceptable so you have to deal with it?'

Fay: 'Yes, I think so. Then I went and lived in sin, as it was known then, and I didn't even notice that!'

Caitlin: 'What was it that gave you the courage to break all of these rules? It was a very stratified and codified society, this is how you are supposed to live and you weren't doing any of the right things. You were foreign, you came from a broken family, you'd had a child on your own, you were living in sin, you were earning your wages.'

Fay: 'Well I just liked sex I think! All these sort of odd things didn't really seem to apply to me very much and so this sense of respectability never sort of afflicted me at all or the need to be accepted particularly so if you were pregnant, then you were pregnant,

148

you know.'

Caitlin: 'It's one of the things that I put in the book, discovering my sexuality suddenly felt like having an energy and if I followed what it wanted me to do then I'd go and have amazing adventures and find the right people and find the right career and also I find writing is kind of sexual, not that I'm rubbing my laptop on my crotch but that kind of showing off and peacocking. I suspect if I had no libido at all I wouldn't write because I just kind of want to make people fancy me from my writing.'

Fay: 'Yes, it is a sort of excess of creativity I think that makes you want as well as to have sex, to have babies and when one's had babies, to write a book or more books and then another book and another book and another book and so it goes on.'

Caitlin: 'Insatiable writer, yes.'

Having introduced the subject of writing through the medium of sex and libido, Caitlin asked Fay how she started writing. However Caitlin wasn't finished with the theme of all things masturbatory and it swung back in that direction.

Sexual Adventures –

Fay: 'Well I never wanted to. I came from a family of writers and it had never done them much good so I didn't want to be a writer, I didn't set out to be a writer, I just could write as I discovered in the advertising agency. I thought everybody could make up little stories all the time and then one day you realise that they find this terribly difficult and then I got into advertising because I was having an affair with somebody in advertising, which was really…'

Caitlin: 'It's your sexual adventures just taking you off, it is, your libido just takes you to exciting places. I love that. Women never talk about these things, it makes me sad. One of the things I really wanted to do in the book was just be very, very frank about everything.'

Fay: 'Well you were which is why I'm here talking to you about these rather frank and alarming things.'

Caitlin: 'But we shouldn't be embarrassed about things that make us vulnerable. If there are huge areas of your life that as women, that's 52% of the population, can't talk about these things and feel embarrassed about them...secretly these are the concerns that we have, we are going off and having abortions but we do not talk about them. We are in pain when we menstruate but we don't talk about this. We masturbate but we don't talk about this, we have these sexual desires and some of us passionately don't want children but it would be very difficult to talk about that in mixed society. All these things that are our normal lives, if we can't talk about that...it's oppressed behaviour and it makes me cringe when I see it so I thought I want to write the frankest book that I can.'

Prostitution –

So I ask you how you started writing and then talk all over you first by telling you how I started writing first which was because I was poor and I wanted money and I realised that the only way that I could earn money, because I wasn't going to school and had no qualifications was either to be a writer or to be a prostitute. I genuinely thought about prostitution for a while because a) it would get me laid and b) it appeared to need no qualifications at all, but my mother said I wasn't allowed to be a prostitute until I was 16 so I started to write a book.

At the time, the only way that I could write is that we had a family computer and all the eight children were allowed to use it for one hour a day each, so I was allowed one hour on the computer where I could start writing my book and I would be wildly resentful of them. After the hour they'd just stand there going, "We want to play *Sabre Wolf* and *Castle Speller*" and I'd be like, "I'm writing a novel!" and screaming at them that Mary Shelley didn't have to put up with this kind of BS but they would kick me off and I would have to wait until the next day to write the next bit of my book and I sent it off to the publishers and they accepted it. It was just literally sent off in a parcel and accepted and I said "How much will I get for this book?" And they said, "It will be a thousand pounds..."

The Chronicles of Narmo

'Oh God, this good already, and she's only *sixteen*.'
TERRY PRATCHETT

Caitlin Moran

Caitlin Moran's first novel

...and I realised at that point I was completely screwed because I would need more than a thousand pounds for two years work and to sustain me for the next five years so I said to them, "How else can I earn money from being a writer?" And they said, "You should be a journalist" and he did a face which suggested that they did not think I would be able to be a journalist and so I went, "Okay I'll be a journalist." I went away and wrote some things and faxed them to *The Times* and they published them too. So I got money finally.'

The initial question returned full circle and Caitlin asked Fay again how she started writing.

'Well I was writing television commercials and in those days I was the television commercial department. I just thought one day, "There wasn't much street cred in this", a commercial is just a little story selling a product so you might as well use an idea by using a longer story and it is probably exactly the same thing except you would have done something more sensible than selling a fish finger or an egg. You could sail whither the future, you could do anything.

So when I was waiting for the second baby to be born, I was three weeks late and I couldn't stand up because I was so heavy, so I had to do something and so I started writing a television play. I wrote it, then the labour pains came and I took myself off to – with none of my babies was the father ever present – so I took a taxi to the hospital and stopped off and posted it off to Granada Television on the way and went and had the baby. Now when I came back there was a letter saying, "Thank you very much for this, we'll do it." '

Caitlin: 'That's an enormous amount of multi-tasking, basically setting up your second career while you're in labour.'

For a concise retelling by Fay of how she wrote her first book she related how she handled the full scope of television advertising from writing, through editing and polishing to delivery, to how she wanted to 'up the value' of her writing to plays and novels and also how – as an almost incidental observation – the men were never around or present at the birth of her children.

Fay continued the story exhibiting the same forthright manner that has earned her success. Granada got back to her after the birth of her child saying they wanted to make the play and sent her an advance for it – which Fay gleefully shares that she promptly spent – only for Granada to change their minds. So Fay did nothing with the play for a further two years as she continued working in the advertising agency.

Some Fruity Stuff – Two years later a different executive had taken over and re-contacted Fay, interested in her script, 'He had just found lying around in a desk.' Fay picks up the story again.

'He said, "Would you write me another one" and of course those were the days of full employment and one was young and had a lot of choice so I said, "No, you've got one, if you want to do it, do that one." And they did it.'

Caitlin: 'Oh brilliant.'

Fay: 'Then it worked very well and they asked me to write another one, then another one and another one and then one day I thought, it's all very well, there are these actors and there are these directors and there are these designers and they all have their views and what comes on the screen isn't exactly what I meant and the only way to get them to do exactly what I meant was to write the whole thing down as a novel. So I took the play and wrote it as a novel, which is why all my writing is in the present, or used to be, is in the present tense because I was just transcribing from a play, which you do automatically, as a television commercial, in the present tense. So much for literature! What you end up with, you then sort of improve on that and then you realise that actually a novel is much more complicated than a television script turned into a novel and there is something else going on here.'

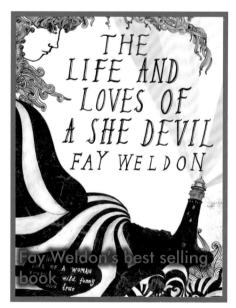

Caitlin: 'I got one of your books out, one of the first ones that I did because I was just looking for books with sex in and *The Life and Loves of a She-Devil* was on the telly at that point and it was like, "There's going to be some fruity stuff in this book, I'll get this book out," because all I wanted to do was read rude stuff and there was plenty in it, so thank you.'

Caitlin had loved the fact Fay had held her ground with Granada, but also went in for the next 'patriarchy' comment after Fay describes below how she used to write on the stairs and why. It is interesting to note that a discernible difference between the contributors became apparent as the episode progressed. Whether it was age, era, experience or innate nature – up to the viewer to discern – Fay was certainly more matter of fact about her experiences and more relaxed at what Caitlin would pick up on as perceived slants at women by the Patriarchy…

Fay: 'I was married to a husband who didn't like the sound of the typewriter so I started writing by hand which was a very good idea because I wrote much better. So I just simply sat on the stairs and wrote…he was an antique dealer and if you wrote on the table it would be sold from under you anyway!

Caitlin: 'Do you think he really didn't like the sound of the typewriter or was he just trying to stop you from writing?'

Fay: 'He didn't like the sound of domestic machinery which was rather embarrassing if you had rather a lot of small children, you know.'

Caitlin: 'Most women writers are having to write around children, J.K. Rowling sitting there with her baby in a buggy and stuff, and you are writing in chaos and you are… you can be in the middle of an amazing profound thought and suddenly someone falls off a rocking chair and boom, it's gone.'

Fay: 'Well the whole thing as you're doing it is to make order out of chaos. You are taking all these random bits and tying them together and getting them together somehow in order to make them into a shape, some sort of purpose.'

Caitlin directed the conversation back to relationships.

Fay: 'I mean certainly my ambition was to lose my virginity as early as I could but it was very difficult in those days because men were so honourable and nervous that you might have a baby, there being no contraception, so it was rather a difficult task.'

Caitlin: 'So how did you manage to trick one into doing it then? How did you manage to disable their honourableness and do it?'

Fay: 'Well it wasn't quite like that. There were enough dishonourable people going around!'

Naked City – Caitlin likened her first kiss to another 'full body flush' powerful feeling – that of when she first got recognised from being on television. At just 18 years of age, Caitlin presented channel 4's pop show *Naked City*. The first day it went out Caitlin was aware that it had just been watched by 2.9 million people and because she hadn't experienced the consequence or experience of fame, she thought 'I am now famous.' In her usual self-depreciating humorous style, Caitlin then went on to regale Fay with the how people were coming up to her in nightclubs saying 'ah, you're rubbish.' Dampening any reflected glories.

By instantly flicking that switch and not wanting to be famous Caitlin could see how being famous not only meant you were watched, but judged to.

Fay: 'I managed to keep the family and the career completely apart so that if I was on television or had a television show on, I would remove the fuse from the plug so the television would appear to have broken down so if anybody wanted to see it they never could. If I had an article about me, I would tear it out of the newspaper so nobody could see it.'

Caitlin: 'Why's that? Is that so your children didn't have a sense of you being famous?'

Fay: 'No, I didn't want to disturb my family relationships by being anything other than a mother because who wants their mother to have any interests except them?'

Never Complain, Never Explain, Never Eat Food on a Plane or a Train – The final chapter of the show covered regrets and offered another insight into their views on writing. Both Caitlin and Fay were from the school of thought of seeing regrets and guilt as a useless emotion, choices were made and life was lived. Caitlin agreed that she'd done stuff but in terms of apologising she thinks 'fuck them all' and raised a laugh from Fay when she said she 'never complains, never explains and never eats food on a plane or a train.' A sound 'byte' that rolled off the tongue but set her stall out on the subject of regrets.

Fay explained her side.

'You did because you thought you had to at the time therefore what is the point of regretting it anyway and if you do what's in front of your nose it will kind of push you somewhere where it's going to push you anyway so what's the point of trying to organise things or look after your own interests when looking after your own interests very often fails. You would have done much better, you see in retrospect, not to have tried to look after your own interests so I don't know...I was just sort of born smiling and that was what got you through, that is your basic nature.'

Caitlin: 'So you are an optimist then, you're cheerful?'

Fay: 'Well yes, you just welcomed what happened next, no matter how alarming it seemed at times.'

Caitlin asked Fay at this point if she had had any books that had just died on her which elicited a telling response from Fay concerning the art of writing.

'I think I probably did at the beginning but after you've written a few books you know not to waste time doing the impossible so you sort of screen it out really before you begin. Some people will come up to you and say, "I've written three chapters and I'm stuck" and then you reply to them, "You aren't stuck, you've just finished." '

The show began to draw to its natural conclusion, and Caitlin spoke of her now having to adapt the book of *How to be a Woman* into a screenplay with her sister Caz – by Christmas 2011. Fay explained that it was easier because by having the help of directors and producers, certain descriptions could be kept to a minimum as that was the domain of their creative skills.

Caitlin relished the word easier saying that as soon as she heard that she was off shopping after the show (instead of going back to work)- to buy knickers.

Fay laughed, agreeing she should spend the money in advance like she did with her first commissioned play.

Fay Weldon and Caitlin Moran saying their goodbyes

LORD SEBASTIAN COE

Lord Sebastian Coe, Baron Coe KBE, is the legendary English middle distance runner, winner of four Olympic medals, holder of eight outdoor and three indoor world records. Alongside his athletic feats, Coe has served as a 'Member of Parliament' for the 'Conservative Party' and was instrumental in securing the 2012 Olympic Games in London.

360°LONDON

Gary Newbon is the sports commentator who covered seven World Cup football finals, three Olympic Games, European Champions League matches, many world boxing championships and a myriad of other sporting events. Gary Newbon is one of the most respected sports reporters the country has ever known.

GARY NEWBON

9

LORD SEBASTIAN COE & GARY NEWBON

Olympic Sensibilities – The pairing of Lord Coe with Gary Newbon created a theme within the theme of the show, very similar to Fay Weldon and Caitlin Moran. With Fay and Caitlin, although they shared their journeys through life, it was very much underpinned and referenced to a feminist sensibility. Although it wasn't our intention, Seb and Gary underpinned the trajectory of their life journey's by the Olympics and all things Olympian, which made for a fantastic show – particularly considering their episode was broadcast on Sky Arts in the first month of 2012 amid the immense build up to the London Olympics.

We chose Lord Coe for obvious reasons as one of our favourite sportsmen – OK my favourite sportsman of all time, but I'm sure he is up there with the nation too. Gary Newbon also became the perfect partner for Seb. He has had a huge career in Sports reporting and was also present at the start of Seb's career, so their professionally entwined lives helped share the stories from both sides very smoothly.

The Four Seasons – The Hotel that is, not some training programme for Lord Coe – was chosen as a venue in Canary Wharf solely for practical reasons. As you may imagine Seb's schedule is a highly efficient and jam-packed affair leaving very few windows of opportunity. We finally settled on a day that suited both contributors and it meant we were lucky to have Gary on set a couple of hours earlier to help film his intro's and complete preparations before Seb arrived. Seb raced, literally from his office to our deliberately chosen hotel in close proximity and what followed was the quickest turn around for any of the episodes of the 'Living the Life' series.

From the moment Seb entered the suite he had quick introductions, and went straight into the make-up chair as I briefed him on the format and themes of the show. We filmed his special 'piece to camera' intro (exclusive on the DVD) in a corner of the make-up room, before he sat down with Gary. 1.41 hours later with filming finished he rushed downstairs for a meeting in the lobby as his busy schedule continued. I've referenced the time the whole shoot took because by wondrous serendipity it was the same figures for his 800m World record of 1.41.73(a record he held for 16 years – but in minutes rather than hours).

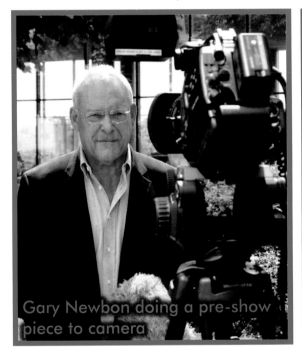
Gary Newbon doing a pre-show piece to camera

Lord Sebastian Coe pre-show interview

Flying Coffins – After a brief conversation about how Seb, having been born in West London, migrated north to Sheffield where he spent his early years (11-18) and where he still considers home, Gary revealed how lucky he was to even be here.

'My home town is Cambridge, actually I still miss it. The reason I was brought up there is my father comes from that area, but he flew forty times in the war...forty times in Hampdens, they were the slowest planes in the war and they were known as the flying coffins so as he flew in '40, '41 and I was born in '45, I was pretty lucky, I was lucky to be around. But then I went to school in Suffolk at the age of nine and at that school,

Culford School, two years later one John Motson arrived and is that a coincidence?'

Seb: 'There's only one John Motson.'

Just as a certain secondary School in Wales (Gwendreath Grammer) spilled international Welsh Rugby playing number 10's off their conveyor belt, it certainly is pretty coincidental to have two such well known sports commentators and journalists go to the same small Suffolk school. Gary also described how to his dismay, he had to take elocution lessons to lose his Cambridgeshire accent at school, forfeiting football lessons. Seb, in a similar quandary, offered that with a name like Sebastian, and arriving in Sheffield aged 11 – 'you either learned to run or to fight' – he famously chose the former.

Sebastian Coe and his younger sister

Hallamshire Harriers – The Olympic theme surfaced very early on in the chat as Seb described his exposure to the 1968 Games and consequent enthusiasm for athletics.

'I didn't really think about being an athlete. I always enjoyed running and people say you pick a sport but actually, funnily enough I think on balance the sport picks you and it was very much my temperament, I enjoyed running, I still do.

If you talked to my lovely mother who sadly is no longer with us, she would tell me that from the age of two and a half I ran everywhere, I never rode a bike, I used to think nothing about running two or three miles into the local town. I found it, I have to say, I found running easy. I then saw something that changed the whole direction of my life because one September, literally as I had pretty much arrived in Sheffield, I had only been there a few weeks, I had gone to the local secondary mod and we had a headmaster who was into sport and I remember coming into the school one September just as term started, 1968, the Mexico Olympics.

Instead of having the serried ranks of teachers on the platform looking down at you, I remember coming in and there was just the table and a television and what he was showing us was some of the BBC early highlights in the morning from the night before and the reason we were in there was John and Sheila Sherwood, recently married Sheffield athletes. John got the bronze in the men's four hurdles which was famously won by David Hemery in the world record and Sheila, his wife, narrowly missed out on gold in the women's long jump. I remember looking at this and I was too young to be able to articulate it but I just thought, "this looked really sensational." It was an Olympic Games, it was huge, the commentary, I just thought there was something here.

Then I joined what I thought was their Athletics club but it wasn't. There were two clubs in Sheffield – Sheffield United Harriers and I joined Hallamshire Harriers and to this day I'm still a member of Hallamshire Harriers. Then two years later Sheila gave me the first pair

Sebastian Coe as young athlete

of track spikes which I really ever owned and the reason she gave them to me was because I qualified for the English Schools Track and Field Championships and I was about to go down in something like probably Dunlop Green Flash or something and she said "No, no, no, these are rubber surfaces and you need spikes." I'd never heard of spikes, I'd run on…the workings of a mine (cinder) actually is probably what most of the tracks in South Yorkshire were. So I owe a massive debt of gratitude to that headmaster that day that introduced me to something that changed the direction of my life.'

Gary revealed that rugby had been his main passion in school but Gary's father offered the harsh realities of trying to play sport for a living.

'Then my father said to me, "Right, whatever sport you are going to play, when you get to thirty you're not going to be able to make a living" because there was no money in sport…"Then when you get to thirty you've got to do a job for the rest of your life that you don't want to do?" I said, "No, if I can't play it I want to write about it." My father knows all these journalists and he said they were all alcoholics, and they did drink a hell of a lot in those days. I said, "I won't be like that." '

Seb: 'Your dad wasn't a bad judge was he'

Gary: 'No, he wasn't actually! You knew a lot of them. So I then went into…all I wanted to be was a sports writer and I sort of fell into television.'

Gary then shared a story which the extended version didn't make into the final edit, but the upshot of it was that both Sam Leach and Cliff Morgan suggested he would be a great fit for television. Gary's first television job at the Olympics was 1972, and he shared with Seb the distress of covering the infamous terrorist act in Munich.

'I'll tell you what, 26, thrilled to be there, Germany trying to rebuild their image, West Germany, after the war. September 4th, I know that September 5th is a rest day, I go out with my mates, have a few beers and I had been given by the Germans two air tickets to go and see the Berlin Wall. Gerald Seymour who went on to be, and is a great ITN journalist…shakes me at some unearthly hour, I've got a hangover, and says "Get out of bed, put your shoes and trousers on and a shirt and just come on." I was trying to put my underpants on; he said, "You haven't got time for that." I didn't know what was going on, we get in the car and he is telling me about how the terrorists…we were only ITN, ABC, Howard Cosell and Israeli television knew about it. We got in and I got trapped with the film crew between the terrorists and the police, I think the police were even more scary and I have to say I was sickened that day.'

Seb: 'Well it changed the face of the Games.'

Terrorist at 1972 Munich Olympics

The Genetic Lottery – Keen to cut to the chase of Seb's development into a top class runner, Gary continued.

'Let's talk about you being a very good runner because you were smashing world records for fun weren't you? You did three different distances in 41 days at one point, how did you get so fast?'

Seb: 'I was very lucky. Yes, all right, I had some natural ability and I think I had the focus to be able to convert the natural ability into something more sustainable by just hard work and I also enjoyed doing it which is the big thing. You can't ask someone to run 100 miles a week unless they get at least some pleasure from it. I am not going to sit here and tell you every training session was a joy, it wasn't, some of them were bloody horrible but I basically enjoyed what I did but I did have the great good sense to pick my parents. Now clearly through them I won the genetic lottery but I also had in my coach and my father, one of the smartest people I have ever met. You knew him, I mean he was clever...He was a clever guy. He was a maths graduate...'

Gary: 'Hard.'

Seb: 'Hard, oh yes, yes. But he was a maths graduate, he then got a degree in engineering, he was a smart guy. He wasn't afraid to challenge orthodoxies and if you remember, Gary, I came into the sport at a time when everybody was just running mileage. The whole thought was that if you want to run quickly, you've got to run long mileage and he always came out with a great quote, he said, "If you want to run slow long mileage,

Sebastian Coe with his father Peter Coe

you will become a slow long runner." So he always focused on the quality of the stuff rather than the quantity and of course what he was proposing at that stage and challenging the norms, it's bread and butter stuff now but a lot of it then was very new.

I just trusted him and of course the programmes he was putting together were consistently making me faster. He set out a schedule for me at the age of 14 which is slightly unnerving really and he said, "Look, this is the progress you are going to make and at 22, 23, 1980 Olympic Games, you're going to get there." I can remember walking off a training track in Sheffield at 14, it was a windswept horrible, horrible Yorkshire night and he was standing there with a tracksuit and a stop watch and he slung the tracksuit out and I put it on and he said, "Oh by the way, there's a concept that I want you to start getting used to." I said, "Oh yes, what's that?" Barely understanding what the word concept meant.

He said, "you'll be going to the Olympic Games in about seven or eight years' time and I want you to start thinking about it now, I've seen people get there and it's all become a bit too big for them." He's saying this to me eight years before so he is thinking eight years down the track and I hit every one of those targets, apart from one year when I think I was out injured. I instinctively trusted the guy to get it right when it mattered and he had that crucial quality, all good coaches have it, Ferguson has it with Manchester United, Clough had it, the good coaches get the teams ready not the week before, the month before, not the hour before – they get them ready to the minute. I didn't always get it right and if I didn't get it right it was normally my fault and not his but he did produce me for major championships in the best form and with no stone unturned. I don't think any athlete ever went into a major championship better prepared mentally and physically and I owe him, I wouldn't be sitting here doing this interview had he not been my coach, it's as simple as that.'

It was a reverential part of the conversation, with Seb revealing his love and respect for his father as well as certain influences from him that Seb had picked up on. In the whole series of 'Living the Life', most contributors have shared strong experiences linked with their parents. On a psychological level, much of our patterning can be determined as having been shaped by our experiences with our parents in our formative childhood years. Stephen Fry confesses his difficult relationship with his father, Bill, Britt and Brigitte had very controlling stern fathers, Leslie Phillips lost his at an early age, and Peter, Joanna and Ken suffered bouts of enforced abandonment due to the world war. On an emotional level the patterning runs deeper, any trauma that triggers feelings of abandonment of father/mother love in a child can shape self–worth and drive to succeed, or punish very easily.

When Seb is explaining all the merits of his father, Gary, who met him, suggests how 'hard' he was which Seb agrees on but has shaped that into a positive for how he handled it then and continues to handle it now. Gary introduced the 1980 Olympics into the conversation revealing a 'dirty trick' played by ITV.

The Confession – Gary at this point, dropped in an exclusive for the show, about how he found out ITV were actually paying for Ovett's interviews but relying on Seb's goodwill in order to not offer him the same deal. The discipline we talked of earlier with Seb shone through in this exchange because even though he hadn't heard Gary's retelling before, Seb genuinely took it in his stride, unflustered and unmoved. Here was someone very comfortable in his own skin. Seb also then explained in thorough detail his emotions and reflections from the famed silver (not gold) medal in the Moscow 800m. It was a retelling of something that has etched itself onto a nation's consciousness, and here we had Seb explaining it in fine detail himself.

Gary: 'It was fantastic interviewing and we'll come on to the races in just a moment but ITV did a dirty trick on you and me, I might as well say that now, I've never talked about it before. You were fantastic with me, Steve Ovett wouldn't talk to anybody and suddenly I walked into a room one day and...'

Seb: 'Don't feel too alienated by that, it wasn't the most exclusive club at the end of the evening,

Gary: 'Remember, he wasn't talking to any journalist.'

Gary Newbon interviewing Sebastian Coe

'Yes, but we did something that I thought was dishonest because they didn't tell me. They decided to pay Steve Ovett quite a bit of money to talk and there's you co-operating with me and they decided, "don't tell Newbon". So I didn't know and I walked in to a left hook from you. I don't know if you remember this but you were quite understandably a little upset because you had been terrific with me and David Coleman has quite rightly wound you up by hearing this and telling you about it and I didn't know anything about it. And I thought, "I've lost it and

165

I'm not going to get any more", but you were absolutely brilliant. You were annoyed, you said you didn't think much of it but "Hey, let's carry on" and I'll always be grateful to you for that because if I'd have been in your shoes I'd have been well hacked off.'

Seb: 'I think I probably was at that stage, I was not as long in the tooth as I am now...'

Gary: 'You'd have been hacked off now would you?'

Seb: 'Probably not but I certainly know enough about the machinations of television to know how it works now.'

Gary: 'So I'm rooting for you now because I'm so involved with you and the 800 metres, well Coe is stitched on to win this one, this is his event and we all know what happened, that tactically you got it wrong and it was a shocker...You got a silver but you might just as well have come last, Ovett wins it.'

Seb: 'No, it was nothing to do with Steve actually, I could have been beaten by anybody that day and I would have been gutted because the litmus test is are you running at the top of your form, have you given everything you possibly could have done and on every count I knew I hadn't. I had underperformed that day. Inexperience, I'd not raced at championship level more than...that was only my second championship race.

I went off for a couple of reasons: I wanted to escape the classic Yorkshire winter and also it was getting a bit frothy politically. We'd already had the overtures about not going and all that stuff and I thought, well when the going gets tough, the tough go to Rome. I had a former teacher at my school in Sheffield who had taken a PE post and taught at the English school in Rome, at Algiatta, and he rang me up and said, "Why are you pounding the streets in Sheffield when you could be down here? My house is next to a golf course, I've got a gym at the school, come down." '

So I did and although I got myself into supreme physical condition, I was probably never in better shape in my career, looking back I think I just distanced myself from friends and family and the training routine, the ribbing from your training partners so I think a combination of inexperience, mentally having slightly switched off because I was in very comfortable surroundings and not in the ten previous years I'd had in Sheffield.

In an 800 metre race, which is the most difficult race to get right because everything happens so quickly, by and large you make a mistake, its pretty terminal. I made four mistakes and I still...I came into the finishing straight in joint 7th so actually I did pretty well in the finishing straight to get a medal but it wasn't that, it was just that I knew that I so under-performed. Really I had four days to try and pull it round and some fairly earthy conversations with my old man who did not pull his punches as you well remember.'

Gary: 'I certainly do. You see if I had a problem I'd always turn to my father. My father died young in 1982 at 62 but up to then I'd always talked to him about it and I suddenly thought, "Who have you got to talk to because your dad was not happy with that," so we now get the situation where Steve Ovett, painted as your great rival but you just didn't know each other really, I know that, you lived in different sort of worlds but still painted as your great rival. You are now going to his event that he hasn't lost at for three years and I'm thinking, "Well I'd better get to know this Ovett" and they said "No, stay with Coe." So I sat up in the stand and I thought, it was like a racehorse, the favourite is going to win this one, Ovett is going to win. "What happens? "You win it and a fantastic last part of the race and still one of the fastest I think sections and you win it and you go over looking like a startled gazelle really, the relief of it must have been fantastic.

Seb agreed that it was always a sense of relief, and that when he started his lap of honour, he was thinking he didn't want to through it again, yet by the time he'd finished the lap he was already planning in his mind what he needed to do to defend the title in Los Angeles four years later.

Seb also expanded on his relationship with his father through the medium of that historic win.

The Coaching Dilemma – 'He took it (the loss and the win)...he was great, he was great and everybody thought that...yes, he was tough on me, he was tough on me but the thing was that what he actually tried to say and I do recognise the words he chose were the £50 notes of journalistic currency, using the words ashamed and all that sort of stuff but actually what he was trying to say in his slightly logical way was, "Look, I can't disassociate myself from this. This was never about we win, he loses" and to his dying day he tortured himself about one thing and he said on the night before the 800 metres he could see that I wasn't quit...it wasn't me. I remember during the course of the day I was feeling unusually clumsy, I remember dropping the milk in the canteen and I always sleep well but I didn't sleep well that night. He was then left in that classic coaching dilemma – do I say something and risk introducing some negativity when he may just be withdrawing a bit and focusing or do I say nothing at all and then look back and think oh if only I'd said it? Literally to his dying day he often used to say to me, "I still don't know whether I should or shouldn't have said anything." '

Gary: 'It was a pity.'

Seb: 'Well he shouldn't have done because actually it was nothing to do with him. He got me into great physical condition and I blew it. The thing about track and field is that you have got nobody else to blame. You haven't got a referee arguing whether the ball went across. You've got a photo finish, it's time, it's distance, it's height, it's measurable, full stop. No argument, the fast win and the not quite so fast get second.'

Gary: 'For me, and I use you as an example for everybody, it's what champions are all about. You've got to be fit, you've got to have the ability or you wouldn't be there in the first place but it's the temperament. You were classic where your best event at the time was the 800 metres and Steve won it, Steve's best event was the 1500 metres and within three or four days you've come back and won it. That's what makes champions and that changed your life really didn't it because you then went on to win in LA and everything else changed with that gold medal…'

Seb: 'I thought, well I've just got to get on with it now. I then got into that really important space for anybody that's an athlete, that actually it then ceased to be important who it was that was in the race, whether it was Steve Ovett or a Kenyan, it didn't really matter. I got into the mind-set that if anybody was going to beat me, they would die that day with blood in their shoes because I just never wanted to walk off a track feeling that bad again. Actually, as it happened, the race was an 800 metre men's race because if you remember the first two laps, we dawdled and then it all kicked off because Jurgen Straub picked up his marker on the track from about 700 metres out and went off like free beer so really what I had was two warm up laps and then an 800. So actually the 800 metre runner did in the end get the last laugh because my last 800 was something like 1.46.'

Gary was smiling throughout Seb's retelling of his Moscow exploits and remembered only too clearly how ITV needed him to bring Seb across town to the other side of

Moscow and do a studio interview and also a live link to Seb's worried mother back home. For Gary it was the professional quandary of having to chivvy Seb along (they ran to the waiting car) knowing that the guy had just won a gold medal for three and three quarter fatiguing laps around the track.

As a humorous anecdote, Gary explained he was 'pissed off' because as they got into the car – Chris Brasher jumped in between them and was talking to Seb all the way, with Gary thinking it was a bit rude, only to find out later that, Seb had thought Chris was with Gary and Gary had thought Chris was with Seb – and Chris was just a wily opportunist journalist (and of course a famous runner from the Roger Bannister era).

The Cutting Room Floor –

In 1987 Gary made a programme called *The Royal Champion* which was the story of The Queen Mother and her support of National Hunt racing. It was Gary's concept and Central TV made it for ITV Network and it was shown the night before the 1987 Grand National. Sir Martin Gilliot, who was the Queen Mother's private secretary, was instrumental in getting the programme off the ground, as was Terry Biddlecombe who rode for the Queen Mother.

There were so many jockeys and trainers to interview for the programme that it was going to be difficult to get them all done in time, as it would mean going round the country interviewing them all so Fulke Walwyn, who was a main trainer for the Queen Mother, and his wife Cath threw a cocktail party and invited all the jockeys and trainers as well as the Queen Mother. Everyone turned up and was interviewed during the evening for the programme.

Gary Newbon (far right) and the team pose with the Queen Mother

Gary was under pressure to get an interview with the Queen Mother for the programme, but she didn't do interviews, so Terry Biddlecombe spoke to her and said he needed to have a 'jolly' with her, as he called it, and she agreed to have a chat with him which was filmed at a later date and included in the show.

On the night, Gary persuaded the Queen Mother to pose for a photograph (against protocol) with all the crew including himself who was the producer, the editor Jeff Farmer, the director Gerry Harrison and the consultant Terry Biddlecombe.

Having shared some fantastic anecdotes and emotional memories of some of the highlights of their careers Gary asked Seb to explain the how's? and why's? of his foray into politics.

Sebastian Coe
Conservative MP

'It was what I'd always wanted to do and I'd not wanted the politics to seep into my career but I decided to throw my hat into the ring towards the end of my career and the reason I did that was during my years as Vice Chairman of the Sports Council, I started working quite closely with government, understanding the buttons you press to get changes and the buttons you leave well alone so a more general interest became hardened into something much more profound during my time at the Sports Council and I thought, actually I looked forward and wanted to enjoy a stint of doing that on behalf of constituency.

Then I ended up in Cornwall which was about as far away...but I like Cornwall, I got to know it when I was Vice Chairman of the Sports Council, got to know it when I was Chairman of all the regional councils and I guess, I sensed in Cornwall an element of what I really liked up in Yorkshire which was a slight bloody mindedness, a good streak of individuality and I thought I don't really want to represent a Home Counties suburb, I actually want a constituency with real people and fishing boats and coastlines and tin mines. I had a great time, had a great time.'

Talking of politics and the Conservative era Seb was discussing, Gary shared an hilarious account of his mother coercing the then Prime Minister John Major into helping Gary out with a televised sound 'byte'.

170

'I mentioned my father died in 1982, just before he died John Major became the local MP, they were living just outside Huntingdon and my father said to me at the time, "This guy is going to be a future Prime Minister" and he used to talk to my father about business, they used to go on the lawn there and when my father died, my mother threw herself into the local politics and my mother, who sadly…I've lost my parents as you know but my mother was a very, very strong person. I always thought John was on the back foot with her a bit.'

Seb: 'Strong Tory women are certainly a breed apart.'

Gary: 'She was certainly very strong.'

Seb: 'What the Empire was made of.'

Gary: 'Absolutely. I said to Major one day, "my mother is slightly right of Genghis Khan" and John said to me, "Next to your mother Genghis Khan was quite a trendy guy." Anyway, there is one great story, your team Chelsea again. I told my mother I was doing the Chelsea match against Manchester United and ITV want me to talk to John Major so she got hold of John Major and said, "You've got to give Gary and interview." So he said, "Fine." So I turn up at Number Ten, there's a slight delay and I'm standing outside Number Ten with a camera crew, there's nobody about and a message comes out, John is in a very important meeting but he will come out.

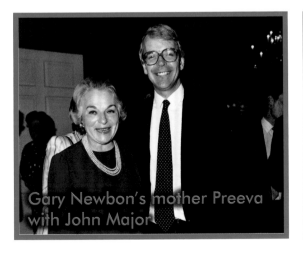
Gary Newbon's mother Preeva with John Major

Gary Newbon (right) meeting John Major

He came out and gave a brilliant interview all about his love of Chelsea and everything, then went back in again and it wasn't till two days later that I found out he had broken up the Cabinet meeting about the decision to go to war, The Gulf War, to come and do this interview, which was very kind of him but I think he was probably more worried about my mother than he was about…'

Seb: 'No, no, I can imagine, I can imagine.'

Gary did ask Seb how it felt becoming a Lord and he very humbly describes how William Hague nominated him and he was 'very flattered and will always have a huge debt of gratitude to him.'

Gary: '…but what you have done by bringing the Olympic Games here does cap off a remarkable life. Two Olympic gold medals, all those world records, an MP, a Baron and now bringing the Olympics to London, I mean it was fantastic the way that you led that bid to win it.'

Seb: 'I was very lucky because I had a remarkable team of people around me and the great thing about the Olympic project is that it has been politically seamless.'

Muhammad Ali (left) with Gary Newbon

Muhammad Ali and Brian Clough – Seb wasn't going to let Gary off lightly and asked him to share some of the highlights of his career, which were astounding really in revealing how much of a long and varied career with televised sport Gary has had.

'There have been so many but let me get one out the way because it sounds patronising and it's not. Seeing you win the 1500 metres after the 800 metres meant so much to me.

Gary Newbon meeting Sir Alex Ferguson with the Champions League trophy

Our relationship, I've always valued it and I didn't think you'd win that day so that was fantastic. Funnily enough, of seven World Cups and three Olympic Games, probably the highlight of the lot was when Manchester United did the treble. Ferguson has always been fantastic to me, like Brian Clough, and I thought they'd lost it. He did, hence his mind went blank in the after match interview when he said to me a famous quote – he thought it was a disaster but everyone else thought it was brilliant – "Football, bloody hell!" His mind went blank, I looked at him and his mind went blank. He just didn't think they were going to win and they won it and that was fantastic. I was up all night with the players, I got invited to their banquet at the Hotel Arts in Barcelona and that was fantastic. There are so many. I did enjoy the boxing, Interviewing Mohammed Ali was fantastic, I'm sad to see the state he is in now but he's the greatest athlete during my career, a great sportsman.'

Seb: 'Unquestionably.'

Sporting childhoods through to professional sporting careers, one on the track, one ringside and trackside, and Seb developing into a political heavyweight and figurehead for the next greatest sporting event this country will witness in 2012 – this episode of 'Living the Life', was certainly a ride. With our 1 hour and 41 minutes just about elapsed,

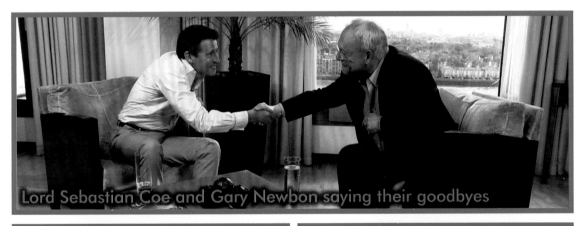

Lord Sebastian Coe and Gary Newbon saying their goodbyes

the guys thanked each other and Seb promised to surface sometime in 2013, for a breather, before they went their separate ways.

Gary: 'I'm grateful to you for sharing those memories but all I can say is, Seb, I have always admired you and I have always valued our friendship and long may it continue.'

Seb: 'I'm sure it will.'

SIR PETER BLAKE

Sir Peter Blake is, above all, recognised as a pioneer of the British 'Pop Art' movement. He studied at Gravesend Art School and later continued his studies at The Royal College of Art after a break serving in the R.A.F. Peter has produced collage, sculpture, engraving and printmaking, and has created many iconic pieces of British Pop Art such as 'On the Balcony' (1955-57) and 'Self Portrait with Badges' (1961) and the album cover of the Beatles 'Sgt Pepper's Lonely Hearts Club Band.'

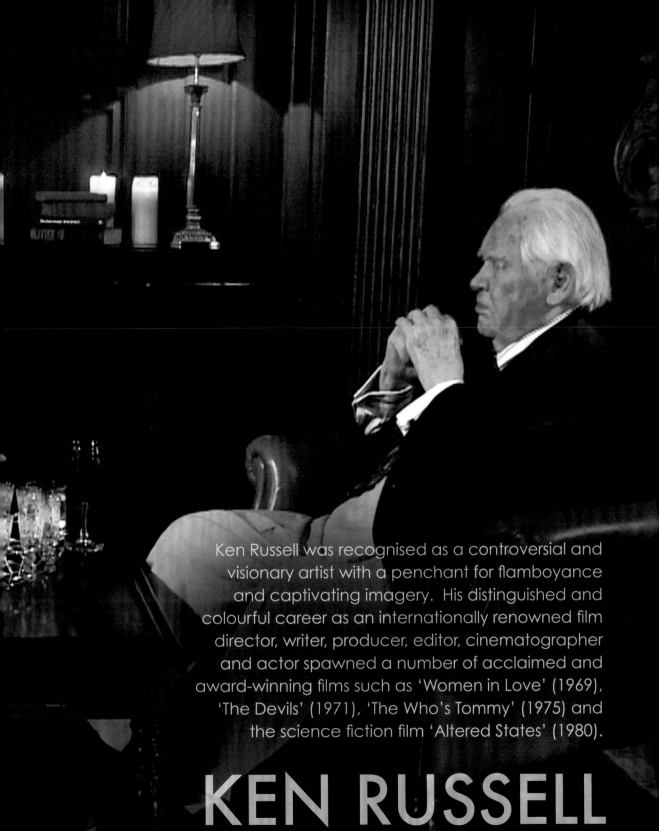

Ken Russell was recognised as a controversial and visionary artist with a penchant for flamboyance and captivating imagery. His distinguished and colourful career as an internationally renowned film director, writer, producer, editor, cinematographer and actor spawned a number of acclaimed and award-winning films such as 'Women in Love' (1969), 'The Devils' (1971), 'The Who's Tommy' (1975) and the science fiction film 'Altered States' (1980).

KEN RUSSELL

10

SIR PETER BLAKE & KEN RUSSELL

Rest In Peace Ken –

Ken Russell was an icon of British cinema and somebody who we always felt was perfect for 'Living the Life', and who better to join him in conversation than Sir Peter Blake the iconic pop artist, long- time friend, early collaborator and muse to Ken. This episode of the series holds bittersweet memories for us though as it turned out to be Ken's very last interview before his sad and untimely death in November 2011.

We were aware before filming began in August that Ken had suffered a stroke and was physically limited, spending much of his time in a wheelchair. However he expressed an enthusiasm for taking part and his loving and supportive wife Elise reassured us of his interest and commitment to filming.

It was a challenging shoot on the day, because Ken's conversational ability had been impaired by the stroke making a fluid exchange difficult. As a result though, with patience and sensitivity towards Ken's condition we truly feel the episode brought to light previously unknown incidents from Ken's early life that built an emotional picture of his early traumas that certainly shaped his life's experience.

Also it was the perfect example of what makes 'Living the Life' unique within its genre – i.e. two legendary contributors, no interviewer. It would have been impossible for an interviewer to have created an enthralling show with Ken in his condition, but by having Peter share his own story and segue his own life with crossovers with Ken it firstly took the conversational pressure off Ken and secondly allowed more of Ken's story to be fleshed out retrospectively with Peter too.

Ken had also at previous times of his life given very direct, forthright and animated interviews that regularly covered certain well-known anecdotes of his career. This episode though we had Ken – having experienced a severe health scare – undoubtedly triggering emotions of mortality and resurfacing traumas from the past we see a different side of Ken and share some heartfelt revelations with him.

The 'Monitor' Clan – It was interesting that both Ken and Peter worked on the early *Monitor* series for the BBC, and that also another of our contributors – Lord Melvyn Bragg – did too, with Joanna Lumley making a cameo as well. I mention that as Lord Bragg, wrote a heartfelt commentary on Ken's career in *The Guardian* in tribute to his life. There is a printed excerpt below.

Melvyn Bragg Tribute to Ken Russell in the Guardian

I met Ken on [BBC arts programme] Monitor, where he was the star turn. He had just done Elgar, which had expanded people's appreciation of what an arts programme could do. It was bookended by two glorious shots: one of a boy riding a white horse across the Malvern Hills; another of men with bandages over their eyes, stumbling across the detritus of war, with *Land of Hope and Glory* playing in the background. It was shattering.

It was also an area of arts programming that hadn't been explored before; using fiction to make a documentary, and it caused a hell of a row. I was 24 when we worked together on Debussy, and it wasn't done to say: "This actor, Oliver Reed, will play Debussy." People said we were degrading expectations of what BBC documentaries should be.

Ken didn't go to university, but he knew more about film than anyone else. At Oxford, I'd been the film critic on the university newspaper; when I met him, Ken was this innocent Friar Tuck character who had seen every film ever made. Thank goodness Huw Wheldon gave him a job at *Monitor*. Ken scarcely spoke in those days; he was just waiting to get hold of a camera.

I wrote the screenplay for *The Music Lovers*, and we made a dozen or so documentaries for the *South Bank Show*. For the last 15 years of his life, I was his major commissioning editor. The critics had rather lost interest in him by then. He didn't get the backing of a Hollywood studio, or a British funding body, and so was slightly abandoned– a difficult place to be.

But he was fearless, eccentric and silly; I liked the first two and excused the last. Nobody else played with music and imagery the way he did; in *Tommy*, he cracked the rock world, and it's a very powerful piece of film-making. Ken didn't lack for boldness. I liked him a lot.

Movie Going Mothers – Peter began the conversation reminiscing about his own childhood when he used to go with his mother to the cinema most days to watch a film with her – especially his favourite Shirley Temple ones. It was quite a coincidence because Ken used to also go regularly with his mother as a child too. They shared stories of the movies they used to watch and also Ken explained how after his childhood, cinema just remained a potent part of his life. Peter talked about their first early meeting.

Pop Goes the Easel –

Sir Peter Blake in Pop Goes the Easel

'We first met in '61, so 50 years ago, and we had mutual friends and you had made...with Angel in the title, a short film, something and the Angel?'

Ken: '*Amelia and the Angel*...It was one of my favourite films, it was about children dressing up and going to films and they all had stories of their own.'

Peter: 'Do you think that was an influence?'

Ken: 'Definite influence, yes.'

Peter: 'The first time we worked together, the first time we met was *Monitor* wanted to make a film about pop art and they suggested that John Schlesinger make it and we met and just didn't get on, I don't think he liked me and there was nothing in common. Then you took it over for *Monitor* and if you remember, we met in the Downbeat Club in Old Compton Street and talked about the film and about pop art and I proposed as a joke the title *Pop Goes the Easel* as opposed to Pop Goes the Weasel, which you adopted and the film became Pop Goes the Easel.

And for its time, as I say it was 1961 when pop art really hadn't taken off, as you remember it was about four young British pop artists – myself, Peter Phillips, Derek Bosher and Pauline Boty.'

Evacuation and Tragedy – Both Peter and Ken had been evacuated during the war and both had suffered tragic experiences that shaped their lives afterwards. Peter began the topic of conversation.

'Anyone of our age who went through the war, the beginning of the war was an extraordinary change of childhood wasn't it? Whenever I'm doing interviews, it comes up again and again, that one's life kind of stopped. I was seven when the war started and I was evacuated and came back to Dartford at the end of the war when I was 14 and went straight to arts school so there was a whole chunk of childhood which was taken away, wasn't it? You were evacuated, Ken, weren't you?'

Ken: 'Yes, I went to Bournemouth...We were bombed so we didn't escape the bombs and we went back to Southampton and lived there throughout more bombing.'

Peter: 'I was evacuated to an extraordinary household. It was a little village that was right on the intersection of Essex, Suffolk and Cambridgeshire, a little village called Helions Bumpstead.

The household consisted of the man and woman, the man was in the Navy but quite elderly by then so he was stationed at Greenwich and was a batman and would come back every six months. The woman, called Mrs Lofts, I suppose she would have only been in her forties but she seemed incredibly old and she had a son, Peter, who was 12 to my seven and a daughter who was disabled and a farm labourer lived there. It was a tiny house, I don't know how all those people got into it.

Every lunch time we were given a penny to get our sweet ration but also as a task, we had to go to the nearest field and collect the mole hills because they were very good soil so we'd go with two pails, fill these pails with mole hill soil and come back.

One day I thought, "I can't go on with this" and I tried to strangle myself in the middle of the field but of course it is very difficult for a child and you stop very quickly, but it was a strange, completely time out of one's life. So from seven to fourteen, apart from these strange things, didn't exist, you know. It was an odd time wasn't it? You were 12 when it started so were even more aware of it.'

Ken Russell and his cousin Marion.

Ken: 'During the war I did, I had a bit of a tragedy. I had a cousin called Marion who became a casualty; she trod on a land mine… she just trod on this high explosive that just blew her apart and it was tragic.'

Peter: 'And you saw that?'

Ken: 'Yes, there was nothing I could do, that was the end of her. She was blown to pieces.'

Peter: 'Have you talked about that over the years?'

Ken: 'No, I more or less kept it quiet.'

Peter: 'But it would stay with you constantly I suppose as a memory.'

Ken: 'Yes, I never really forgot it and I never really…I never could get the image out of my mind.'

Peter: 'Did it affect your film making do you think?'

Ken: 'Well I think it did. It was something I couldn't get out of my mind and it remained with me forever.'

The war seems to shape many of our contributors by having such a huge effect on them during their formative years. Peter shared quite matter-of-factly how he felt, but if you stand back from the narrative for a minute, he is actually saying how traumatic it was for him, so much so, that he physically tried to strangle himself. Ken had carried the burden of Marion's death his whole life, and in essence had only publicly shared the story towards the end of his own life where commonly the traumas that haunt us resurface near death searching out for reconciliation.

Without being an academic student of Ken's work, I can't comment on what has been surmised about any imagery or literary allusion to his films, but I would offer an opinion that having suffered the trauma of seeing his little cousin being killed in such a way, he subconsciously tried to bring Marion back to life through films like *Amelie and the Angel*, perhaps to assuage the huge amount of guilt and abandonment he would have felt at being unable to save her (obviously it was impossible for Ken to have done anything, but that doesn't stop the subconscious looking to alleviate the trauma and prevent feeling such pain again.)

Des O'Connor experienced the German bombs first hand, having to be dug out of the Anderson shelter, and Bill Wyman raced for cover as an enemy plane strafed his street with bullets. Leslie Phillips was invalided out of the Army during the war and other contributors were affected indirectly such as Joanna and Howard owardHowanot seeing their fathers for a period of their childhood.

Sir Peter Blake ABC Club painting

Although no association was made with Marion's tragedy and Ken's early films, Peter clarified that *Amelie and the Angel* was Ken's third film and his first also included a child and her angel wings. They both then went on to discuss the influence of children and childhood on their work and also how Peter began his art career.

Ken: 'The first one was a very simple film, it was about a child who lost her angel wings and was going to make another pair and finally does so, before they fall apart.'

Peter: 'I think that's another strong link isn't it because a lot of my work, certainly the very early work, was about children and it was autobiographical and it was about cinema clubs. I did a painting called *ABC Minors*, there were two little boys with their badges on including belonging to the ABC

Minors Saturday Morning Club and maybe this whole thing about being that age and having this chunk of life taken away by the war isn't a coincidence, that we both have worked a lot and I still, childhood is still a theme as it were, an important theme. In a curious way I still feel very child-like, my work is often – I mean it is more sophisticated because I'm older and I can do it, but it is almost as if it is done by a child often and it's no coincidence is it?'

Ken: 'No, I don't think so. So can you tell me how you actually started art?'

Peter: 'It was a coincidence really. I'd come back from the war, I went to a really terrible secondary school in Dartford and then I got an interview and at the interview at Gravesend Technical School, they said if you wanted to go to the art school, it's part of the Technical School, you can just walk round the corner and do a drawing examination and go to the Art School.

I thought, well I might as well, so I went and did a little drawing, got into the art school so started at the age of 14 into the junior art department for three years and then the intermediate and then the National Diploma...but that first at least six months at art school; I was still wearing grey flannel short trousers as one did then. I hadn't gone into long trousers yet so I would be cycling to school, so I started pretty young. Then by chance I did the intermediate exam, and then did the National Diploma and by that point I wanted to be a painter but they said, "Nobody makes a living from painting, do the commercial art course."

So I did a year of the National Diploma, which was a two year course, tried for the Royal College as a Graphic Designer and Sir Robin Darwin, who was the head of the college was sitting in on this particular viewing of the work, saw the work and said "Perhaps you should show it to the painting school" and the painting school accepted me. So at the age of 21 I'd got in to the Royal College, then did National Service for two years in the RAF so I think when I got in I was probably one of the youngest people ever to get into the Royal College. Then of course it is the three year course and one goes from there. Then I did a year travelling in Europe doing a Leverhulme Scholarship, studying popular art and of course it was very soon after that that we met and made the film.'

Peter has had a prolific career and is still very much in demand and working hard. He then shared with Ken the current projects he was working on.

'I'm asked to do a lot of things. At the moment the main picture I'm working on is a picture that's been commissioned by the Knight Bachelors, which is the category of knight that I am. They've newly got a chapel in St Paul's Cathedral and I've been commissioned to make a four foot square painting to go in the chapel, so it is only the second time that a picture has been commissioned by St Paul's. The first time was *The Light of the World*, by Holman Hunt.

I'm told this, I can't really believe it, but this is only the second time. But in contrast to that, of doing a kind of religious painting, last week there was an opening that I designed three shirts for Fred Perry, you know, the classic button down, the classic polo shirts, and I designed three kind of pop art shirts for them so the work is…I'm doing lots of interesting things at the moment and there are lots of contrasts.'

As the conversation swung back to Ken, Peter asked him how it was working with Oliver Reed with whom Ken had collaborated numerous times.

'And how did it work with two giants like Alan Bates and Oliver?'

Ken: 'They both had their problems and it was a question of sort of delving into them and laying them bare.'

Peter: 'In controlling them I guess. Laying them bare is a good analogy for the naked fight scene, isn't it…How did you handle that?'

Ken: 'Well…'

Peter: 'Were they drunk? Was Oliver Reed drunk at that point?'

Ken: 'I think they'd had a few drinks.'

Peter: 'Actors were different then weren't they? I'm not saying actors now aren't great, that someone like Jude Law isn't a great actor but someone like Oliver Reed or Peter O'Toole, they were great actors and they were hell raisers weren't they?'

Ken: 'Yes, they knew how to pull off a scene.'

Peter: 'Did they rehearse it?'

Oliver Reed and Alan Bates in The Women in Love

Ken: 'They did and…up to a point and then they just let themselves go.'

Peter: 'I would imagine it was a pretty genuine fight by then, or it looks it on film, an amazing scene.'

Ken: 'Yes, it was.'

Peter: 'He's such a larger than life character (Oliver Reed) and you worked with him…I mean I'd still like to know how you handled him.'

Ken: 'Yes, he was a strange bird. He had to be handled with kid gloves. He had a weird way of working. If you could find out the method to his madness you could get a good performance.'

Peter: 'How did you do that?'

Ken: 'More by luck than judgement.'

Smoke, Dope and LSD – Ken asked Peter how he had handled the excess that was notoriously prevalent in Peter's creative world and that era of the sixties.

'Well there were areas within the art world where there was no excess, it went on as

184

before, there were gentlemen painters, it was quite a gentlemanly thing to do but I was with the Robert Fraser Gallery and Robert was a friend of the Stones and a friend of the Beatles and I guess looking back he was supplying their drugs as well so I was surrounded by a drugs scene which I never, ever got involved with.

I think one of the reasons, was having been a child smoker and stopping at age 12, I'd kind of forgotten how to smoke so at the first dinner party where a joint was passed round, it was passed to me and I held it and I didn't want to be embarrassed at smoking it badly so I passed it on in a way that was a moment and from then on I didn't do any drugs at all.

But I guess I drank to excess, I drank a lot but that was simply a matter of getting better in the morning, drinking a lot at night, missing some days and other days being well enough to paint but luckily I didn't get into drugs so I was never in a situation where I might have been destroyed.

I suppose my main links with excess were with the music business rather than the art world. There were nights when they were recording Sgt Pepper, The Beatles, and I was going in every night to see what had happened and the only people in the whole of Abbey Road that weren't stoned were myself and George Martin. The Beatles would be stoned; quite often Mick Jagger was there in the evening.

I remember a nice incident when he was there with Marianne Faithful and Marianne

St. Peppers Lonley Hearts Club Band album cover designed by Sir Peter Blake

disappeared for about an hour and then came back and said, "Oh I've just been down to the other studio and there's a group of little boys making a record and I feel so old, these are children." It transpired it was Pink Floyd who were recording in the other studio. (That would be one of our other contributors, Nick Mason, cropping up as a lad in the early days of Pink Floyd)

But there were nights, there was a night in my painting studio when Robert Fraser was there with Paul McCartney and they both were probably doing their first LSD trip and they were as high as kites, they were seeing colours and saying, "Oh it's wonderful." Paul said, "You've got to do this, you've got to try this, no one should go through life not having done an LSD trip." Again I managed to avoid doing it but there were temptations weren't there? But I did drink a lot.'

For the final chapter of the show, Peter shared how well his daughters were doing also crossing over with careers in the arts, including Rosie who at 24 has just graduated from the Royal College of Art specialising in illustration. Peter also felt he didn't really have any regrets, as in the terms of his professional arena he felt he had realised his goals and ambitions.

As a wonderful ending to the show, and a memory that will stick with me for a long time, Peter asked Ken if he regretted not marrying Glenda (Jackson), and if he still had a crush on her. It was an enjoyable and diverting final question, part 'tongue in cheek' and partly honouring the closeness of Ken and Glenda's professional relationship... Poignantly Ken's final words of the show were.

'Well to my dying day, I'll always have a crush on Glenda.'

The two contributors toasted each other with a glass of absinthe and Peter came to see Ken be driven off in his car, in what turned out to be a prescient goodbye.

Sir Peter Blake and Ken Russell having a toast

Sir Peter Blake and Ken Russell saying their goodbyes

Postscript –

I do feel very lucky to have directed Ken in his final interview...he was certainly very aware of all that was happening and I could tell from early on during filming that although his speech was slow and he found difficulty in keeping up with the narrative vocally, his mind was absorbing everything and his only frustration was his body letting him down.

We had the luxury of a few hours of filming, and also the support of Peter who was marvellous in leading at certain points and nurturing Ken through certain topics as well as weaving his own life story and anecdotes into the show.

Although maybe a slightly controversial view, personally I feel there is no such thing as coincidence and Ken gained from the show too, even if it was to release some old and painful memories (Marion's tragic death) and to recognise again that he had truly contributed to his place in the world.

CHARLES DANCE

Chares Dance OBE is a renowned British actor, screenwriter and director. Charles has been a member of the Royal Shakespeare Company and has appeared in many stage productions. However, he is best known for his screen roles, and he found fame in 1984's lavish TV drama 'The Jewel in the Crown,' as well as on the big screen in films such as 'White Mischief' (1987), 'Alien 3' (1992) and 'The Last Action Hero' (1993). Charles produced, directed and wrote the screenplay for 'Ladies in Lavender' (2004), starring Dame Judi Dench and Dame Maggie Smith.

Paul McGann is the Liverpudlian actor who made his name in the BBC serial 'The Monocled Mutineer' (1986). He is best known for his role in the now cult film 'Withnail and I' (1987) and for portraying the eighth Doctor in the 1996 'Doctor Who' television movie and subsequent tie-in media. Since 1989, Paul has concentrated primarily on television work, but he has also had roles in a number of high-profile American films such as 'Alien 3' (1992), 'The Three Musketeers' (1993) and 'Queen of the Damned' (2002).

PAUL McGANN

11

CHARLES DANCE & PAUL McGANN

The Thespians – It was a return to the fabulous Gore Hotel for the filming of Charles and Paul and a canny piece of set arrangement to offer a different look to previous episodes that had been filmed in the same room. Although Paul and Charles had met and worked on the production of Alien 3 at Pinewood Studios, they had much in common especially their acting and noted roles. We had access to one of the luxury rooms for the pre-filming introduction pieces which went really well and can be seen as an exclusive feature on the 'Living the Life' DVD.

The Beatle Doppelganger – Charles launched into his and Paul's 'Living the Life' conversation by asking Paul to describe growing up in his native Liverpool.

'So my earliest memories of the city, really, mid sixties you know, being with my brothers, and my sister...when the city was actually really crowded, there was a couple of years, you know by then into The Beatles' success when it seemed it was the centre of the world, and I can still remember, thanks mum! You know there was four boys in the family, four lads in the family and she got us these little identical Beatles suits, you know these collarless suits.'

Charles: 'Wow, did you have mop haircuts?'

Paul: 'Yeah we must have had the haircuts. And, you know we'd be down town by

Charles Dance and Paul McGann in their pre-interviews

the Pier Head or whatever, walking around, and I can remember Japanese tourists, you know they'd stop and take your picture and it was exciting, you know. I can still remember the crowds of people, and then it plainly moved on to San Francisco or somewhere else, so there's always a 'world city'…and briefly it was mine!'

Charles: 'I was born in 1946, when I was growing up there were still bomb sites from the war, and there were areas of Liverpool that looked to me as if they were still bomb sites.'

Paul McGann (right) beside his older brother Joseph

The Aspirational Working Class – Charles asked Paul what 'class' he felt he came from, to which he answered 'the aspirational working class' which he took to mean, that his father was a factory worker and his mother a housewife. He continued.

'Classic working class, you know there was one wage and you got paid on a Thursday, you never had a bank account, there was only ever a roll of money in his back pocket, but they were clean as a whistle you know, and everybody else was, these were church goers, everybody kept their houses clean, there were streets full of people, there were neighbourhoods, proper neighbourhoods. I think the aspirational probably refers to that post war idea that your kids, by right, will do better than you did, by dint of your effort, your work...And for most of us that's exactly what happened, you know I went to a grammar school in the end.'

The *Monocled Mutineer* – Charles went on to ask Paul if he had started acting in school, but he felt he was probably performing earlier than that – as he came from a really strong Catholic parish in the centre of the city with choirs and such like, so even from around the ages of 10/11 he was acting in musical plays, as all his brothers, his sister and his parents could sing. This revelation prompted Charles to remember that he had first heard Paul sing when he had watched the *Monocled Mutineer* and thought then he had 'A wonderful singing voice...a really sweet singing voice.'

Bouncing the theme back at Charles, Paul asked him if he sung or played a musical instrument. Charles confirmed he played the guitar, and they both jested back and forth as to whether he played like an actor (knew only a few cords but looked good) or could 'actually' play – Charles was the latter. Considering Paul has starred in so many movies and television productions, he is still recognised and revered all over the world for his famed role in *Withnail and I* which Charles brought up early in the conversation.

'So tell me about *Withnail and I*, because *Withnail* has become a cult movie now, the same you know the way *The Jewel in the Crown* is a cult television show, and I know that people have kind of, '*Withnail* evenings'. I have friends in America who have to see it about six times a year...that particular film kind of came out of left field as it were, because you know with the greatest of respect, neither you nor Richard Grant were bankable commodities.'

Paul: 'No we'd never been in a picture.'

Charles: 'Umm, we all knew who Bruce was but you know your man in the street didn't know, whereas if you were trying to make a movie now, the first question that a potential financier asks is "Who's in it?" And that's what a sales agent asks'

Paul: 'Of course. I take your point. I think in Bruce's case and in Handmade's case, when Bruce made *Withnail*, he was lucky, in that Handmade, Paul Heller particularly, allowed him to do. It was a million quid; I mean a million quid in the eighties was still a million quid, umm...'

Charles: 'Was it his first film as a director?'

Paul McGann (left) and Bruce Robinson on set Withnail and I

Paul: 'It was...and god bless him you know, on the first morning that we were there, cos Bruce had been an actor, he'd done quite a lot of pictures and he'd written the script, and then the first morning we were there, we were in the cottage in the lake district on that set which is a room about the size of the one we're in now. He got all the crew in and he stood on a chair, I could be making that bit up, but he addressed them and he said," You know I've never done this, I've written it, I know exactly how it should go, what it should sound like and what it should look like and everything else but that's in a sense beyond my competence to make that happen, help me out" and they loved him for it.'

It was something that Charles could totally relate too, having been in a similar situation making his film Ladies in Lavender. He gave a fascinating insight into how he brought all the pieces together to get it made.

Charles: 'I made a film four or five years ago and I said more or less the same thing.'

Paul: 'It's such a good thing to do.'

Charles: 'I said "You know there are going to be times when I know exactly what I want to do and I've a fair idea of how to do it and then there are going to be times where I'm not going to have a clue, and please, just tell me." Because if you go in there and try to bullshit a hardened film crew, you're going to be up shit creek without a paddle before very long.

I mean there's a lot that I need to know technically still I've learnt a fair bit as I'm sure you have because you know you spend hours on a film set and you and I have both done a fair amount of hours in front of a film or television camera so you kind of know what's going on with the hardware and the mechanics of it. But because of what I did at art school I did think, well you know there's a fair bit that I do know as well as all the stuff that I don't know.

Anyway, I found this short story called *Ladies in Lavender* and I sat on a set in Budapest and it was a library set so there were loads of books all over the place so I was sat around for hours...and I picked up this book you know, it was a writer I hadn't heard of, William J Locke.

Anyway I read all of these short stories for the three hours that I was sat there and I kept coming back to this one about these two old ladies living in Cornwall and I thought, "Yeah I know how to do that" and I could see it properly and I was brought up In the West Country and I know Cornwall reasonably well and I know this peculiar quality of light and stuff and odd people. And I thought, "But I'm never going to get this made" cos, you know nobody shags anybody, there's no violence, there are no dramatic car crashes or stunts or anything. It was about two old ladies living in Cornwall, one of whom was an emotional and physical virgin at the age of sixty...'

Paul: 'What could possibly go wrong?'

Charles: 'Absolutely! Immediate money-spinner! And I thought the only way I can get this made is if I go to Judi Dench and Maggie Smith, and I thought I might as well start at the top. And so I went to Judi and took her the script and to my astonishment she said, "I'd love to do it darling" and then I went to Maggie and she said, "Is Jude gonna do it?"(An excellent impersonation by Charles) so I said, "She says yes" and she said, "Oh all right then"...and then it was kind of relatively easy.'

Paul: 'You're a man who got his wish list!'

Charles: 'Well you know, once I got them and I kind of cast other people it was on their names that the minimal amount of money was raised but since then I've been trying to get two things off the ground and I don't have Judi Dench and I don't have Maggie Smith and its really really difficult, you know, and the budget has to be half, I mean I think the budget was about three million for *Ladies in Lavender*,'

Charles Dance and Judi Dench on set for the 2004 film Ladies in Lavender

Paul: 'Did you get the light? You said about the light in Cornwall?'

Charles: 'Yeah, well I knew of Peter Biziou's work. Peter is the most wonderful cinematographer, he just lives and breathes and thinks light and we went down to Cornwall and I said, "I want these two women to look better than they've ever looked before, not necessarily flatteringly but really..." and he said "Oh god yes, look at this light, look at this light Chas." you know.'

Paul asked if Charles knew the light because of having lived near there and Charles explained how his father had died when he was only four years old and his mother then married the lodger, who worked in Devon, so they moved there to be together. Charles described how his earliest memory was being at primary school and hearing everyone talking saying, 'the Kings dead' in reference to king George VI dying in, but following directly on in conversation of his father dying was probably linked subconsciously.

Charles then went on to reveal his East End roots, which he described it as such.

'Because I mean, I come from the, you talk about the aspirational working class I come from the aspirational servant class, which is a tricky thing because the servant class is despised by the working class because they think they're, you know, brown tonguing the aristocracy, and patronised by the aristocracy basically, they're nice to them rather like they're nice to their pets and so on. But that's what my mother was, cos she was one of four kids from the East End of London. I only pretend to be aristocratic and I get asked to play toffee nosed people because of the way my face is put together... when I did Gosford Park I said to Robert Altman, I said, "You know Robert, I should be downstairs, not upstairs" and he said "Oh no not with that face Charles."

Charles Dance (second left) in Gosford Park

The Cutting Room Floor – The men shared a bit of banter about Charles being considered the 'Thinking woman's crumpet' and Paul being voted by GQ Magazine as, 'Sexiest man alive' they both laughed off the tags and Paul recalled Sigourney Weaver on the set of *Alien 3* holding a copy of the magazine and looking him up and down.

The Pinewood Factor –

Our Production offices at Back Door are based at Pinewood Studios, and the whole series of 'Living the Life' was edited there too. Paul and Charles filmed *Alien 3* at Pinewood and Charles went on to Direct interior scenes for *Ladies in Lavender* there. Joanna Lumley filmed many movies at the studios, amongst them: *On Her Majesty's Secret Service* and Tim Burton's *Corpse Bride* and also the television series *The New Avengers*.

Leslie Phillips is the last living actor who was based at Pinewood right at the beginning when the studios opened in 1936 Leslie has in fact filmed 36 movies here. At the Pinewoods 75th anniversary in 2011, Leslie spoke at a couple of functions considering his 75 year career ran alongside the studio's 75 years in the business including the filming of his three *'Carry On'* Films.

Britt Ekland also filmed her Bond movie at Pinewood too *(The Man With The Golden Gun)* as Mary Goodnight in 1974, Robin Gibb unveiled the Heritage Foundation Blue memorial plaque for Sir John Mills with his (Sir John Mills) daughters and family. Stephen Fry played 'Smithers' in the Film *Storm Breaker* and is due to film a role for *The Hobbit* this year (2012).

Tim Rice filmed *Joseph* on three separate soundstages in 1999, Ken Russell directed a couple of movies and television at Pinewood including *Prisoner of Honour* in 1991, and Finally Alan Davies filmed a Christmas special of *Jonathon Creek* here in 2008.

Recalling the *Alien 3* Film set, Charles asked Paul how it felt to have most of his role end up on the cutting room floor.

Paul: 'Yeah, most of what I did, although we were there for months weren't we, most of what I did just...'

Charles: 'Freezing our arses off.'

Paul: '...ended up on the floor, umm, was quietly really disappointing...cos you know you wanna be brave and sort of take it on the chin and say you know "Well I'll live and learn" sort of thing but umm, no I was gutted to be honest.'

Paul, during the filming of 'Living the Life', was actually performing in a West End play (*Butley*) and was rushing off after we wrapped to do that nights show, which got Charles and Paul talking about the theatre per se and how much stage acting Paul had done. Paul also mentioned how he had caught a performance of Charles in *Shadowlands* which he absolutely loved, and it triggered Charles into sharing an amazing story of how he stopped mid-acting once, walked off stage and came back on to start it all over again.

'Most of the time it was okay, but there was a night when, I think it was before we came into town that I really quite surprised myself. We were in Richmond and you remember the play starts with a long, its him giving a lecture, and it's about two and a half pages long, and I walked on and I started to speak and thought, "This is crap, this is crap" and all the other actors were standing behind a screen, like kind of statues. Anyways I got six lines in and I thought, "No this is crap" and I said "I'm going to go off and come on again"

Paul: 'Did you do it?'

Charles: 'Yeah! And the stagehands were thinking what the hell's going on! And there was a time where I thought I'd never be able to do that and It surprised me as much as I surprised anybody else, and I thought, "If I ever feel like that again, that's exactly what I'm going to do again, I'm not going to fight my way through an evening if I feel its shit." You know?'

Paul: 'Do you ever get scared?'

Charles: 'Yes! Christ yeah, yeah! I haven't been for a while but there was a period in the middle of that for about ten days and I don't know why cos I don't think anything particularly dramatic was happening in my private life or anything but it just, for about ten days it just, the timing was off it just wasn't quite right.'

The conversation then moved on to how Charles originally got into acting.

Leonard and Martin –

'I went to art school cos my adolescence manifested itself in a stammer. With some people its acne, or its bad behaviour or whatever, for me, for some reason at the age of thirteen I developed a stammer and it stayed with me till I was about eighteen and I couldn't be seen to be a stammerer like stammerers I know now who would just openly st-st-st-stammer, I used to make up the most complicated sentences to get round words I knew I would stammer on. So there was no way that I could ever think about being an actor, cos up to that point I'd done like I'm sure you had done, school plays, I liked showing off you know but I didn't really know how you became an actor.

I thought you had to be the son of John Mills or something I didn't even know drama schools existed until I was about 16. I used to hang out with a guy, he was very good looking, used to have this wonderful voice and he was forever quoting Shakespeare and I said, "What are you gonna do when you leave school?" and he said, "I'm going to RADA", I said, "What's that?", he says, "Royal Academy of Dramatic Art", I said, "Oh really, oh great right drama school". Anyway I went to art school and then this stammer started to go when I was about eighteen.'

Paul: 'Just of its own accord?'

Charles: 'Yeah, so I rang this guy up, because I knew he'd known a couple of old theatrical guys down in Plymouth who coached him for his RADA audition, and I rang him up and said, "Who were those guys you met?" and he said, "Oh right yeah Lenny", I said, "Yeah, will you give me the number?". So I got this number and left, finished at art school and I went back down to Devon where I was living with my mother and I rang this number and this voice said, "Lords Wood 249", I said, "Is that Mr. Bennett?", "Yes who's that?", and I said, "My name's Charles Dance and I want to go into the theatre" and he said, "Oh god!".

We arranged to meet at a pub miles away from anywhere, I walked in and my only experience then of homosexual men were guys who wore chiffon scarves and had limp wrists and frequented bars that you were told not to go into, and there was this guy who looked like Samuel Beckett, hawk like face with tweeds, big guy, with dogs sitting in this pub and he kind of looked at me over his glasses and said, "Charlie Dance, buy me a pint of mild, boy". I went to the bar got him a pint of mild came back and he said, "Drop your jaw boy", now I'm twenty one at the time and I'm quite gauche and there's local people in this pub and I'm sat there and he's said, "Drop your jaw", and I said, "What?!", he said, "Open your bloody mouth". So I'm sat with all these kids looking at me and I could hear people saying, "Leonard's got himself another young man."

Paul: 'Here's another one!'

Charles: 'And he looked at me and he said, "Closed throat boy", and I said "Oh really?", he said, "Yeah it's going to be a long job", and he lived with this guy called Martin who was German and had been a member of the *Berliner Ensemble*, and they lived in this little cottage miles from nowhere and I spent about two years with him and we worked our way through Shakespeare, and Shaw, and Beckett.

So they taught me what I would've learnt had I gone (to drama school) a bit more and also a bit less because I didn't have contemporaries to rub shoulders with and learn from but you know, they taught me a lot, because the old man had died when I was four, and my stepfather was a nice enough guy but he wasn't much of a father figure, and the two years that I spent with these guys, they were just little pearls of wisdom you know, I used to buy Leonard his drink, that was the payment he wanted no money, and Martin who very rarely went out, he stayed in the cottage and did all the cooking I would do the garden for him

Paul McGann (left) and Dominic West in the stage production of Butley

He had the most wonderful voice you know. He'd actually

been, he'd worked in the theatre, he was York rep, where Leslie Phillips who we both know, was, and he knew of Leslie Phillips then, and Leslie probably doesn't remember him but that's where he started. Then he met Martin there, but they were also of that generation and that age when they lived in fear of a dawn raid by the police.'

Paul: 'The play I'm doing in the evening, *Butley* of course, two of the central characters possibly three are gay men...but this is set three or four year after the repeal, once the law had changed.'

Charles: 'After The Wolfenden Report, yes,'

Paul: 'I mean it's sobering to think that these men had to live in as much fear as they did.'

Paul then described how he fell into acting. Initially he had moved to London when he was 17 to join his brother Joseph who lived and worked there and it wasn't until he was 19 when he returned for a visit to his old school (to watch his younger brother Stephen in a school play) that he reconnected with his favourite priest, who had directed Paul himself years earlier in school plays. Paul continued.

'So anyway a few years later, I went to see Steven and the priest said, "What are you doing" so I said, "I'm selling shoes and doing this type of thing", and it was him he told me about RADA, he said, "You should go to RADA", I'd never heard of it, I remember him saying, "Glenda Jackson went there", and at the time Glenda Jackson was the Queen of England. So I was suitably impressed, and it was him that sent away for the forms, the prospectus. He said, "Come up to the priests house" you know, I was getting cold feet by then it all sounded a bit grand.'

Charles: 'Did you go through you audition pieces with him?'

Paul: 'Yes...anyway, me being me, I turned up with three or four days to go, eleventh hour is my middle name, and I was there on the Monday. Anyway in the prospectus it said you had to do a classical piece and a modern piece, clear contrast whatever it said. Because this guy was a classicist anyway and a frustrated actor he said, "You're doing Clarence's speech from *Richard III*" which he knew by heart. The only modern piece, remotely modern book, that this man had on his shelf was the film script not even the play of *My Fair Lady*.'

Charles: 'Wow.'

Paul: 'Yeah. I turned up for RADA, the RADA audition, got through the Clarence and the tower OK, just about remembered it. But then, aged nineteen whatever it was, pretended to be Stanley Holloway, the chimney sweep turning up to ask whoever his name was for a fiver for his daughter, in a cockney accent. Tell you I can still see the faces of this panel. It was the worst thing ever...it was a disaster. I remember running down the street, I just wanted to get out of the room, you know I could see their face saying, "Make it stop". Anyway I got out of the building and legged it, and the young lad, there's always a young lad, you know the kid who shows you in.'

Charles: 'Yes, right.'

Paul: 'I'm outside in Mallet Street heading back to Euston station and I can hear this voice "Paul..." stops me you know. I was just embarrassed, "That was just terrible" he said, "Yeah terrible, shocking, but they've seen something, come back in". And it was really only then that I was into the school which was a real thing you know. I was amazed actually. Then I got the bug I think, it was only then I got ambitious for it...

I was there (RADA) with some fantastic people, Ken Branagh? Mark Rylance? All there at the same time. I remember one day we were in the common room and I can remember Branagh talking about going to the theatre as a kid and Branagh said the same as me, he said he never went, he said its movies. I became an actor because of movie stars, "Jimmy Cagney" he said, another kid would say, "Oh yeah Jack Nicholson" or whoever it was, it was movies, most of them, we were working class kids...so it tended to be movies, that's why we were there, "Sod this theatre lark" I remember Branagh saying jokingly.

RADA for me, cos I'd not been a good student at school, RADA was a kind of finishing school, there was a library there. I got into books but of my own accord, I mean under my own steam, of my own volition. There was a lovely librarian there, Lloyd Trot, and you know they'd put books in front of you. So you know it was an education as well, and it worked out...I was happy, happy there.'

Cultivating The Mystique – Both Paul and Charles agreed that the old thespian style of not being available for too many interviews and keeping back some of the mystery was important to them as actors, compared to the modern trend of media 'whoring' where they associated newsprint (real or online) as indicative of their success. They explained it further and then wrapped up the show with a confession of the insecurities of being an actor.

Charles: '...You see these kids now and I think, learn from the mistakes I made and that other people made. You know, don't, don't do interviews, don't do it, it's much better if people don't know anything about you, because the less they know about you they more they want to know about you.'

Paul: 'I agree with that. Maybe it is slightly old fashioned now but you know I think performers, actors in particularly should cultivate, if they can a certain mystique. You know why should people see you in your own clothes, it's not necessary, I can't prove it but somehow I think it instinctively detracts, you know the next time you go out as a character maybe it's going to lessen the impact as they've just seen you on the sofa with Paula or something, it's just not the same thing.'

Charles: 'But it sells newspapers and it sells magazines.'

Paul: 'But you don't have to tell them the truth.'

Charles: 'No indeed, like Gambon, Micheal Gambon who just lies which I think is great.'

Paul: 'As long as you can lie well, lie elegantly, lie entertainingly, that's fine isn't it?'

Charles: 'Yeah, yeah. More and more, or I find anyway, as you get older work begins to thin out, it's a pyramid you know there's only a certain...'

Paul: 'You lie, you never stopped.'

Charles: 'That's not true Paul, it's not true. You know you have to try and find ways to create your own work, whether it's adapting something or, you know, otherwise we're just in the market place. Those days, thankfully I haven't experienced in a while where weeks go by and the phone doesn't ring you know you think, "Nobody loves me anymore" cos that's one of the reason we're actors, we all have that desire to be loved and anybody that says any different is lying.'

Paul: 'Well, love is maybe taking it too far.'

Charles: 'Liked very much then.'

Paul: 'Affirmed.'

Charles: 'Adored. Yeah.'

Paul: 'Employed...'

Charles: 'All of us, we're all racked with insecurities.'

202

Paul: 'Yeah, but that's how it should be, shouldn't it? What do you want a load of smug actors?'

Charles: 'No but that's going from the sublime to the ridiculous you know, I think we're probably more insecure than people in a normal work of life don't you think?'

Paul: 'I'm often wary that actors get a, I mean actors don't do themselves a lot of favours sometimes, but you know actors get a slightly bad press, you know somehow they're emotionally incontinent or...'

Charles: 'Or talking about how hard it is...they're certainly not as tough as people seem to make out you know I mean, we don't go down coal mines we're not out in Afghanistan or Iraq.'

Paul: 'Yeah you know that's true and when all is said it's not a tough, tough job.'

Charles: 'No and I do get a bit upset when actors start saying, "Well you know it's a very tough life, it's a hard, hard life"

Paul: 'No it aint.'

Charles: 'No it ain't, we're very very lucky.'

Charles, knowing Paul was heading off to the theatre took that as a natural ending and they shook hands and de-mic'd, sealing the show with a very 'luvvie' goodbye, outside the venue with a wonderful and frank insight into both men's lives in the can.

Charles Dance and Paul McGann saying their goodbyes

JEREMY CLARKSON

Jeremy Clarkson began his career as a
fledgling journalist for the Rotherham Advertiser
before moving into specialising in auto
journalism. He is known across the globe for his
role in the phenomenally successful 'Top Gear,'
one of the most popular shows on the BBC, with
an estimated 350 million viewers worldwide
which is due, in no small part, to Jeremy's
dynamism, relationship with his co-hosts and
genuine passion for cars and motoring.

Nick Mason is the drummer for Pink Floyd, the band which helped to create one of the most influential musical movements and sounds of all time. The progressive rock icon is the only constant Pink Floyd member since its formation in 1965 and he has lived an incredible life within the music scene. He is also a prolific collector of classic cars and a qualified pilot.

NICK MASON

Breathy Little Monster – It is always difficult to arrange timings to bring together two high profile personalities at the same time, a combination of schedule checking, practicality and serendipity. Jeremy, for this episode of 'Living the Life', had a very short window of a crisp winter's morning and early afternoon until he flew out to Norway for some *Top Gear* filming later that day. Not only that, with other commitments like finishing off some journalistic writing in the morning, it meant filming at his Holland Park Penthouse apartment and a strict arrival time of 10.00 am and we had to be out (fully) by 2pm.

Consequently, we had our full crew and all necessary equipment (camera, lights, monitors etc) all stacked outside the lift to Jeremy's top floor flat at 9.59 am ready for the off. We were let in and as Jeremy continued to finish off his article at his hallway desk, there was a manic burst of activity deciding on which room to use for the filming before setting everything up. Jeremy wryly observed that he had broken two of the major rules, namely: never allowing a camera crew into your own home and also not being held to a rigid schedule...oops!.

We filmed Jeremy's intro just off the main set in his kitchen, and ever the professional presenter, Jeremy delivered directly down the barrel of the lens, an engaging and witty first take piece, alluding to the class of real rock musicians like Nick who had very much lived the life of a professional musician compared to 'some breathy little monster' winning a television talent show.

In keeping with the 'Living the Life' loosely themed intros, we decided on filming Nick's piece to camera outside the building, with Nick rolling up in his car and answering the standard early questions from there. It is worth mentioning that on the first take

Jeremy Clarkson doing a pre-show piece to camera

I'm asking the cameraman to frame in tight on Nick as he slowly rolls up, thinking we don't want the standard Audi estate car in shot, much to my cameraman and Nick's surprise considering that the so-called car in question was an Audi PS8, one of the fastest, most expensive and high-end estate cars in the world... oops again !. I called for another take, and widened the lens.

With a little mix of humour and mischief, both Jeremy and Nick decided to start their intros with different versions of how they first met – Jeremy opted for the *Goodwood Festival of Speed* and Nick opted for *Le Mans*...whilst it made for a good intro it brought to light an important pointer for future episodes, namely; it is okay for the pair to know each other or to be acquaintances but to be good friends makes for too much familiarity and resistance to fully opening up.

Nick Mason arrives on set in his Audio PS8

Having brought up the discussion of where they first met, Jeremy and Nick opened the show with further investigation of the theme.

Jeremy: 'Where did we first meet; I thought it was at the Goodwood Festival of Speed?'

Nick: 'Yes and I thought it was at Le Mans, with Noel (Edmonds.)'

Jeremy: 'Oh the panel's thing. Well when was that...Welcome to the amnesiacs'

Nick: (shrugged, looking vague)

Jeremy: 'Well when did the Goodwood Festival of Speed start?'

Nick: 'About 15 years ago, it was about 5 years before the revival, and that's been going about 11 years now...what were you doing at the festival?'

Jeremy: 'I went...when they, when Charles March first started the Festival of Speed, we went down there because it was old *Top Gear*, to go and cover this remarkable event, and it was brilliant in that first year, because I remember seeing Rowan Atkinson walking about like a normal person, and then you came out of a tent.'

Nick: 'I wasn't camping there; I know I wasn't camping there.'

Jeremy: 'No it was a tent with Verve Clicquot written on the side of it, don't worry it wasn't actually a little boy scouts one, but then, I'm sure that's where I first met you because I remember being really nervous and thinking, "Oh my God the last time I saw him was at Knebworth" – which is actually the first time we met, although we were separated by 3 1/2 miles, cause I was at the back and you were very much at the front hitting things... Umm so we can't remember where we first met?'

Nick: 'No we can't.'

Jeremy: 'But it would have been something to do with cars rather than music...why don't you talk about music very often?'

Nick: 'Well I do, I do talk about music quite a lot but it tends to be in the context of um sort of interviews, I suppose, so it's probably more interesting to talk about other stuff, like cars.'

Loitering into Fame –

Jeremy explained that now both of them were settled down to chat, not at an event and without a glass of champagne in their hands, he wanted to know how the era of huge rock in the seventies and being part of such whopping success felt. Nick, in a much understated way, said to him it was just normal and with the success of *Dark Side of the Moon* it was five years into their career, so a gradual success in a way. He continued;

Nick: 'Well it was in our case. As someone once said, "Some men strive for fame," in my case I loitered into it...It was sort of fairly accurate in a way, I don't think (pause) I don't know...that sort of intensity, of wanting to be something, umm, I think I more or less did drift into it to some extent.'

Jeremy: 'But you did want to be an architect.'

Nick: 'Well I didn't want to be an architect that badly, I probably wanted to be a racing driver...I think at one point, probably because of my dad I thought I might try and make films. And I think that the idea was that architecture is the most wonderful grounding for almost anything, because there are elements of fine art, there are elements of technology...'

Jeremy: 'But you do have to have a Saab (both laughed) that's the only drawback to architecture...so you did school, and architecture at technical college, but your father, he was Shell wasn't he. He made motor racing films for Shell – Is that where the love of motoring comes from?'

Nick: 'Absolutely, I was brought up in an environment where he raced a vintage Bentley, made films about motor racing, went to watch motor racing, and I had three sisters and I think the special dad time was going off with him to go motor racing...I'd sort of got the bug; I was interested in it, and into vintage cars and vintage racing and so on.

Buoyed by Nick revisiting his childhood, Jeremy asked when he first picked up a pair of drumsticks.

Nick: 'A friend of my parents who was into music, played the piano and said, "You know why don't you play along with a pair of brushes on an African drum"...When I was 12 or 13 something like that, and I thought, "Oh yeah this is good," and then there was this....my first band...was put together on the basis that one of the guys had already got a guitar, the rest of us had nothing, so we all asked for money for Christmas so we all decided to go off and buy the instruments and be a band...I went to a place called

Chazzy Foots, which was in Golden Square but is now in Denman St. 7-12 Shillings and I got a *Gigster* Bass Drum, a Snare Drum , a High Hat, one Symbol.'

Jeremy: 'That was the start, and that was before you'd met Gilmore and Waters?'

Nick Mason (on drums) playing with his first band'

Nick: 'Oh long before, long before this was, I still have the odd picture. In fact I still have an old tape somewhere of the first recording...called The Hotrods.'

Nick returned the focus back to Jeremy and asked him about his early starring roles.

Nick: 'Talking of childhood then, you were a radio star in your youth'.

Jeremy: 'Oh yeah before...no...I wasn't a radio star...I appeared on Saturday afternoons when nobody was listening to the radio, on Radio 4, as a child in the *Jennings* books, that were made for radio.'

Nick: 'And then, was that from then on...show business beckoned.'

Jeremy: 'It was £7 a day you got paid, aged 11, that was huge money, massive...I was able to buy an entire new Hi-Fi, so I could listen to your records on it.'

Nick: 'Were you Jennings himself?'

Jeremy: 'No, I was Atkinson. I was Atkinson, and some other boys were other things... and you just stood around a microphone in Leeds and read things off a piece of paper, and they gave you £7. It was just, I remember I used to see people from *Up North* walking around the studios... it was the most glamorous and exciting thing I'd ever done, so that was. Yeah...obviously no, I didn't think I was going to be an actor...My dad was in rep, Wolverhampton rep, the same time as Leonard Rossitor.'

Nick: 'Ahh!'

Jeremy: 'He liked acting a lot, my mum liked acting...but it seemed a rather precarious way of earning a living and I was told very firmly at school that I would be useless... cause I was once a German soldier in a school production, and I walked out. Every single person in the audience fell about laughing because apparently I was quite unconvincing as a German soldier, and the helmet didn't fit because I've got a massive, massive head and the only...what are those, coalscuttle helmets they had? It was like a drum with a pea on it. This spotty youth and I decided there and then that acting wasn't...wasn't ever going to happen.'

Jeremy attempted once again to elicit some anecdotes from Nick of Pink Floyd's heydays and the huge Stadium concerts. Nick again doesn't so much say it is normal but, that being part of a band, he was very comfortable in that situation and had a lot of support from the other members, and then he laughed humbly that later on they used to incorporate a lot of film and other visuals into the shows and eventually with *The Wall*, they were literally playing lots of it behind a wall – like a chef in a kitchen.

Pink Floyd concert

Jeremy agreed though, that it is like showing off, and describes his take on some of the *Top Gear* adventures.

'It is showing off, I always think when we go off to make films on *Top Gear*, and then you bring them back, and somebody makes them actually into the right length, and then they get shown to the studio audience and it's a bit like...secretly everyone wants to show friends their holiday photographs, you know you can't do that, you know you can't say, "Come over tonight and watch. We've done a video of our holiday." You can't do that obviously, nobody is interested, and yet with *Top Gear* what it actually is,

Top Gear team, Richard Hammond (left), James May (centre) and Jeremy Clarkson (right)

is just the three of us go on holiday and then we make a film and we show it to people and people actually like watching it,.'

Ukrainian Hookers – Laughing at the nuances of fame, Jeremy humorously described the first time he was invited over to Nick's.

Jeremy: 'The first time I came round to stay at your house, and I thought, "My God, I'm actually going to stay with a member of rock aristocracy" and I got down there thinking, "I wonder what kind of debauchery will be involved in this evening with Nick."

Nick: 'It was a wild night.'

Jeremy: 'I just thought, "There'd be Ukrainian hookers for sure, drugs that you can barely imagine," I got down there and we had, I think it was a chicken casserole, you then made some cocoa, put your slippers on and fell fast asleep in front of the Ten O Clock News.'

Nick: 'You should have been there the week before.'

Jeremy: 'It was a bit like New Zealand...I thought it would be leopard skin everywhere, there'd be leopard skin and naked waitresses coming in saying...can I perform any services for you, but it wasn't like that at all...And I actually thought, because I know I've got a reputation for wild living...if anyone could see the two of us now, with little bits of dribble in front of Huw Edwards telling us about some terrible calamity.'

Both of them were laughing at Jeremy's description, and eventually (after a few times of Nick asking) Jeremy described how he 'fell' into journalism, and also gave a fascinating insight into the affluence of motor journalism.

Jeremy: '...but journalism, yes I did go to journalism college because I was thrown out of school, and then I was walking down the village street and the general manager of our local paper, the Doncaster Evening Post, was coming the other way and he said to me, "What are you doing, you should be at school?" And I said "I know, but I've been expelled"...he said "Well you'll have to be a journalist then, because everyone who gets expelled from school ends up as a journalist."

So I thought..."well that's reasonable, so I'll go and do that" and then when I was at journalism college this kid, it was block release so I was on the Rotherham Advertiser and this kid from the *Harrogate Herald* turned up with a brand new Lancia, spanking new. And I said, "How...where did you get that from?" and he said, "I've got this great gig...if you get a little bit of a column in the newspaper and you write about cars, they lend you a car for the week full of fuel and insured, and then you just say. That fantastic Lancia, brilliant in every way and then they take it away and bring another one." I just

Jeremy Clarkson as a young journalist

thought, "Now that's what I call a job." It's a bit like being a food critic; that's still my ideal, I can't understand how people make a living from reviewing food. It's just, well, "Mmm..." '

Nick: 'Well I think probably people feel the same about cars. The interesting thing as I see it...one of the things that you did... you slightly broke the mould of the way motoring journalism was done, because it was unthinkable to be truly critical of a car. In, well you don't call them the old days, but they'd withdraw the cars.'

Jeremy: 'Never mind withdraw the cars. If

you were to say you didn't like the new BMW, Audi or whatever it might be, you weren't invited on the next launch and that was the critical thing that motoring journalists still do...lead a life that Elton John would consider to be extravagant. You'd say nobody can live a life like that...they fly first class, stay in the best hotels, drink the finest wine and they are given amazing gifts to go home with.'

Nick: 'The goodie bag.'

Jeremy: 'Computers, and heavens knows what...and you get back to Heathrow and just board another private jet to another amazing hotel in the South of France to drive another amazing car that isn't yours in the sunshine, that you haven't paid the fuel or the insurance for, you get absolutely pissed out of your mind on the finest *Chateauneuf-du-Pape*, you fly back to Heathrow, you get on another private jet to...somewhere exotic.'

Nick: 'What was the point at which you decided you were strong enough?'

Jeremy: 'No it wasn't that, I simply became too busy to go on car launches and once you're too busy to go then you've got nothing to lose. Then you can start to say 'I don't like this car'. You're not coming on the next launch...and you're like, I can't go anyway, I'm too busy. Anyway, I had children and I didn't want to spend all my life whizzing around the world drinking other people's scotch.'

Nick: 'That would knock you out of being in a band then.'

Lack of Responsibility – Nick then opened up and shared how it felt being part of Pink Floyd and especially the touring.

Nick: 'It is that curious existence, it is the bubble and you exist in the bubble and it tends...it's a great marriage breaker, inevitably.'

Jeremy: 'Why?'

Nick: 'Because you are living a different life, and it's a different world. I think partly you are operating in that world and you are not sharing it with whoever is at home, it's difficult...it's a long time.'

Jeremy: 'How long was your longest tour?'

Nick: 'At least a year.'

Jeremy: 'So you were away from home for at least a year?'

Nick: 'Yeah.'

Jeremy: 'I know to a much smaller extent what you mean, because we get back from tours which only last six weeks but they're quite full on and you do a lot of miles, and you get back and you've led this ridiculous life which is all helicopters and super yachts and then you get home and the bins need emptying.'

Jeremy Clarkson (left) and James May (right) on the 2007 Top Gear Artic Special

Nick: 'You know...know what it's not even the helicopters and the cold buffet in the dressing room; it's the lack of responsibility.'

Jeremy: 'But...well exactly.'

Nick: 'All you have to do is be in the lobby at 4 o'clock, if you can manage that, and there are one or two people who struggle with that.'

Jeremy: 'What, in Pink Floyd?'

Nick: 'Generally...I mean for most bands, that's what you needed to do, just be in the lobby when you're told to be and from there on everything is taken care of. Nobody ever says there's a problem with the dishwasher!'

Jeremy: 'Well exactly, no recycling happens when you are on tour...never happens... no.'

The Grim Reaper – There is sometimes a synergy with 'Living the Life', where the structure of the show allows the time for the contributors to just keep talking and as they move from topic to topic, however conditioned they sometimes are, an emotive theme will just suddenly 'pop out of left field'. One of those moments was with Jeremy and Nick talking Rock n Roll, when Jeremy brings up the subject of death, and shares very openly how much the subject plays on his mind. He starts by casually asking Nick what's next for him, and suddenly death is the topic of conversation.

Jeremy: 'Where do you go now then, what's next for you, apart from death?'

Nick: 'Thanks.'

Jeremy: 'Because I think about that all the time. Don't you...as...where is it going to happen.'

Nick: 'I...err...I try not to think about it too much.'

Jeremy: 'I think about it at least 50 times a day. I wonder where I'll be, I sometimes say to myself The good thing about sitting here now is that I know I'm not going to die in the next 10 seconds. But sometimes, I don't know, if I'm driving a car...how you know that an eagle isn't going to crash through the window and kill you. I spend half my time thinking, "What if it's now? What if it's this second?" I do all that all the time, but then... anyway...ignoring the fact that we are all going to die, possibly in great pain with a tube up our nose, I think it is very important to die in an anecdote. It's no good for your children to say, "Dad died with a tube up his nose...in dreary hospital."

I can remember once being in a plane...a 1950's Russian plane that had been used by the Angolan Air Force before being sold to a two bit airline in Cuba, and it went upside down in a really violent thunderstorm and I thought, "This is it," and I can remember thinking as it was going down, "Still at least this is quite good for the kids. How did your dad die? In a thunderstorm over Cuba in a Russian plane"...it sounds good.'

Nick: 'Yeah, it's enormously worthy to think about your children and how they are going to worry about your death.'

Jeremy: 'I never like being boring particularly...I can't...I don't mind being anything but boring...I always think when I'm driving very fast, "What if the wheel falls off?" I always think that..."What if I die now...is it going to hurt?" That's...honestly its awful...it's awful when you are preoccupied with death to the extent that I am. You've no idea.'

Nick: 'No... I've no idea.

Jeremy: 'Cause...I've got to go to Norway this afternoon and it's already occurred to me. That's not a very good anecdote if the BA jet goes down in the North Sea.'

Jeremy Clarkson and Nick Mason feigning sleep

Jeremy Clarkson and Nick Mason saying their goodbyes

Nick: 'Well there's a really boring possibility of a really boring car crash on the way, there's a possibility of the flight going down, there's the possibility of food poisoning on the flight'

Jeremy: 'Well James May's going to drive me all across Norway in the snow, so we won't be killed at three miles an hour, which is his idea of top speed in inclement weather.'

On a tight filming schedule, the show came to a natural conclusion and finished with an allusion to the cocoa and casserole once more, as both contributors feigned falling asleep for a little afternoon nap.

HOWARD MARKS

Howard Marks, known as 'Mr. Nice,' had a
privileged upbringing and was educated
in Wales before gaining a place at Oxford
University and graduating with a degree in
Physics. He achieved notoriety when he was
uncovered as one of the largest international
suppliers of cannabis and was jailed for 7 years.
The public has been endlessly fascinated with
his life, and his autobiography was a best-seller
and his story has been made into a film with
Rhys Ifans playing Howard.

Peter Stringfellow has spent his life in the nightclub industry and he is the notorious British owner of Stringfellows table-dancing clubs. He has, over the years, booked a host of famous musicians including The Beatles, and his King Mojo Nightclub showcased the likes of Jimi Hendrix and Tina Turner.

PETER STRINGFELLOW

13

HOWARD MARKS & PETER STRINGFELLOW

Angels – No I don't mean the contributors, who although gregarious, polite and good natured, would probably not be considered – or want to be considered – angels. This was the venue for the shoot, Peter's upmarket club on Wardour Street in Soho, London. For the pre-show intro we had the wonderful opportunity, albeit with a little poetic licence, – to take advantage of Peter and Howard's sense of fun. Firstly we filmed Howard coming out of the 'SO HIGH' shop (a cannabis paraphernalia establishment on Broadwick Street), and then had Peter hollering at him from outside his club saying 'no time for that Howard, come on.'

With some canny editing (thanks again, Jamie Munn) it looked as though Howard was just down the street and not a few blocks away on an entirely different road. Although a light hearted intro, it placed Howard in the cannabis psyche for which he is infamous and also placed Peter at his clubs for which he has his own brand of infamy. With Peter beckoning to Howard the way he did, it also set up the pro and anti-drug stance of both contributors.

Back in the club, and on set, Peter had two magnificent throne seats for them both, and with a bottle of club champagne on ice, they relaxed into their conversation which Peter began by welcoming Howard to Angels.

Howard Marks outside So High Soho

Peter Stringfellow (right) with Director Jules Williams outside Angels Club

Peter: 'Howard it's a pleasure to have you in my club. This is Angels. The iconic Stringfellows is further down the road. This is my new club of four and half years. Of course Stringfellows is thirty and I came to London when I was 40 years old. But I started in Sheffield at the beginning of the war, 1940 when I was born. You were born at the end of the war?'

Howard: 'That's right, I mean my parents told me it was the day the war finished which was August the 13th 1945, the World War, not the one with Germany.'

Peter: 'But Sheffield was a tough city. Wales is supposed to be tough as well.'

Howard: 'It's pretty tough, yeah. But I didn't grow up in the city. I grew up in a mining village, you know so, errr, I was terribly inhibited by big cities. I was too scared to go to Cardiff half the time so I was a very mild mannered, shy, nervous little kid, frightened of the city.'

Peter: 'Well that's very weird, because that could be a description of me. Seriously, I'm the oldest of four brothers, but in that era. I had a brother three years after I was born. But I had a peculiar memory of being a kid. Number one there would be a difference between me and you. You're very clever, aren't you? You went to Oxford eventually, is that right?'

Howard: 'Well my cleverness has been exaggerated and documented, yes.'

Peter: 'You did very well educationally wise.'

Peter Stringfellow (left) with his brother Paul (right)

Howard: 'Yeah, yeah.'

Peter compares Howard's education with his own declaring how, by being dyslexic, he found school difficult and struggled. They joked about Howard studying Nuclear Physics which he did, and Howard went on to describe how he handled school.

'At school, although I was clever I suppose and could pass examinations and things, I wasn't a tough guy, okay. So I was subject to bullying you know, for different reasons. But I was subject to bullying because I was a swat like you know. I did too well in examinations to be accepted by my contemporaries.'

Inmates: Peter was aware that Howard had been to prison, and raised the topic by explaining how he went to prison himself as a young man. In the retelling it also became apparent that both the contributors were literally 'smiley' people. Peter even referenced the fact during the show, how they both smiled easily and looked for the fun in the conversation.

'I also went to prison, when I was 20yrs old. I was a flash kid you know. I learnt the only good thing I could do was talk, so I became a salesman.'

Howard: 'Yes.'

Peter: 'A door to door salesman...I worked for a company called Dobson's in Sheffield. Everybody in Sheffield knows about this, of course. And one of the things I had to sell door to door was carpets. So I went to their warehouse to get these carpets and one day they did a check on the stock and I found out I had about ten carpets that I am not supposed to have. So, hey, I sold them. What's wrong with that, five pounds each or something? And I thought, "this is nice", so the next time I went in I accidentally brought some more out with me. So after about eight weeks of this I got arrested. I went to prison for three months.'

Howard: 'They sentenced you to three months in prison?'

Peter: 'Yeah, today they would have given me twenty pounds to help me get back home in a taxi or something. And they'd say we're very sorry we put you in the position you found yourself.'

Howard: 'Yeah.'

Peter: 'And community work, can you go paint somebody's house for a couple of weeks. That's what they would do now, but then it was much more serious and I think that was the best thing that ever happened to me when I was a kid. The judge looked at me and said "you are a different kettle of fish." He says "You're glib." I didn't know what glib was. Glib? I'm glib? Is that good? He then said "You need a sharp lesson, young man." and he was right. He sent me to Armley for two weeks... and Armley's a real prison. That was a real prison.'

Howard: 'Yeah, that still is a real prison.'

Peter: 'Black and white, prison keys, bars, people in the corner. Oh terrible, terrible.'

Howard: 'Yeah.'

Peter: 'And that frightened me to death. The rest of it they sent me to a normal prison which was like a holiday and I came back tanned and it was quite nice. But after that never, ever...'

Howard: 'But what was the lesson you learnt?'

Peter: 'Frightened to death. I was frightened...number one when I came out I was so ashamed because I couldn't get a job, that's why I am here now. I couldn't get a job, no-one would give me a job. I had to go back to selling and then how do you make money? It's a long story but I found myself renting a church hall in Sheffield for three pounds and putting a local band on and eventually, I call it The Black Cat Club Friday Nights.'

The Beatles factor –

Considering no surviving member of The Beatles was involved in the show, it was amazing how often they cropped up in conversations. Stephen Fry, when describing his sugar addiction, told us how he used to buy bubblegum and there would be factoids inside the wrapper, like 'George Harrison eats eggs for breakfast.'

Cilla Black described in great detail her early career singing auditions with the lads, and how they all mingled as friends in the same social circle. Sir Peter Blake described The Beatles smoking pot and Paul McCartney taking LSD at Abbey Road Studios, and Robin Gibb and Bill Wyman referenced their musical achievements.

Paul McGann hilariously described his mother dressing him and his four brothers up in little imitation collarless suits as kids with bowl haircuts and Howard confirmed that he had met Sir Paul but laughed off Peter's suggestion that they had shared a joint, claiming they hadn't.

Howard: 'Was that your first club *The Black Cat*?'

Brian Epstein and The Beatles at the Black Cat Club

Peter: 'That was it yeah; well it was a club church hall Friday nights opposite a cemetery. Then I booked this group called The Beatles.'

Howard: 'I've heard of them.'

Peter: 'And then negotiated with Brian Epstein, their manager, on a pay phone outside the church hall and we agreed £65. I came out sweating, I had paid Screaming Lord Sutch fifty quid but the point is, and the question I was going to ask you is, when you went to prison for the first time did it not...stop you dead in your tracks? Did it not frighten you?'

Howard: 'Yeah, seven years in actually the only federal penitentiary in the United States that has a death row. So like, I was doing my time in the shadow of death row which was just quite heavy you know. But because it was such a heavy place the rules and regulations were quite lax in a sense, because there's no point telling someone who's

Terre Haute (U.S. Penitentiary) where Howard Marks served time

serving seven life sentences to do your shirt up or something like that. There's no point, he's got nothing to lose. And I actually emerged a far better person than when I went in. You know those seven years did make me into a better person. I mean there's quicker ways of improving one's self. But it did make me into a better person.

Death Row – It was an interesting part of the show, with Peter explaining his short sharp shock experience of prison, and then Howard very casually describing his huge sentence in one of the hardest prisons in America.

Peter: 'When you came out the first time, after seven years in real prison, did you not come out going "never again"?'

Howard: 'Part of me was thinking "never again I don't want to go back into that shit. I really don't want to go back there" and then part of me thought "it's God telling me to fuck them one more time, just do it." '

Peter: 'I would have thought after seven years in that serious prison that was a watershed in your life...meaning major change.'

Howard: 'Yes it did make a massive change in me. And in fact after those seven years I didn't revert to drugs smuggling anymore, after the two years I did. After the seven years I straightened out, but only because I was lucky enough to be given an advance to write a book. I think without that I would have definitely gone back to it again...yes I enjoyed doing it and I knew I was good at it and there is some kind of big headed pleasure in carrying on doing what you think you are good at. It was for that, plus I was getting away with so much I felt it was God rewarding me, you know.'

Peter: 'There's nothing in you that says looking at you that you've had a tough time due to drugs. You're in your sixties, you're affluent, are you rich?'

Howard: 'No, this doesn't pay me like the old game.'

Peter: 'No, so it doesn't…would you ever do drugs again?'

Howard: 'Well, umm, I consume them still now at 65.'

The Drug Debate –

Peter: 'Do you say legalise marijuana?'

Howard: 'I mean I would, yes. I'd say legalise it for sure but at the same time I would issue a warning that it certainly doesn't work for everyone. You know it might work for me it might not work for you. I mean it's the same with alcohol, some people behave totally inappropriately no matter what drug they take. So I certainly wouldn't want to force feed anyone drugs or even persuade them to take any, but to some people they keep it together and it enhances their life particular musicians and artists. They find their work improves, their life improves and they enjoy life more, and I think to rob those people, the sort of brilliant people like Paul who you mentioned, of that pleasure and happiness without any rational reason for doing so whatsoever is wrong.'

Peter goes on to share an anecdote about LSD, and discovers that Howard has not only taken that too but taken it every day for a year, by which point he roars with laughter, asking if the programme will ever get shown. Howard then talks Peter through his first forays into cannabis and LSD.

Howard: 'My first recreational drug, my first illegal recreational drug was marijuana which, of course was in pretty short supply in Wales despite the green grass of home there. I didn't try it until I went to Oxford. Just one…I was 19, when I first smoked a joint and thoroughly enjoyed it. I laughed a lot, time seemed to slow down so there was more of it. I enjoyed James Brown's Please Please Me much more than I had ever enjoyed it before. I just liked the entire experience, I knew it was illegal of course but that didn't bother me. I enjoyed it so much I did what I think is a fairly rational reaction and I smoked another, one because I enjoyed it and another one and another one and ended up smoking dope all day and being stoned all day. Then acid came along while it was still legal at the minute I took it every day for a year in 1965. It's not really; it wasn't then a recreational drug, it was almost some kind of cerebral masturbation really.'

Peter: 'I heard it be described as a few things Howard, but that's the first time

Howard Marks running for Parliamentary election

masturbation's come into it.'

Howard: 'Well you're doing it yourself.'

Peter: 'You see we're talking we're laughing, we're happy. This is confusing and frustrating for a lot of people. Here we are, me anti-drugs if you wish only because I used to be frightened of such stuff, and you championing them.'

Howard: 'Always, ever since that first joint really, I felt a law prohibiting people from smoking marijuana was fundamentally wrong and sinister and I still believe that. I believed it all my life and in fact I stood for parliament once in the 1997 general election. I formed a single issue party, just to legalise cannabis.'

Peter: 'Single person single issue. You and one issue.'

Having exhausted the rich vein of drug discussion, Peter referred back to Howard's childhood finding out that Howard's father was a sea captain in the Navy and his mother a school teacher. Peter had to ask something he was struggling with; how with a disciplinarian Merchant Navy father, did the 'lawlessness' develop. Howard (very

Howard Marks, Oxford Graduation

similarly to Joanna Lumley) related how his father may have been strict and 'run a tight ship' at sea but wasn't the corporal punishment type at home. There were rules, he continued, but he never thought about breaking them until he was a teenager. Peter compared it to his experience.

Blame it on Oxford –

Peter: 'I'm trying to equate what have we got similar. I mean you're cleverer than me, you've got a Captain in the Navy through your father, you had quite an affluent upbringing. Mine was all opposite side of that. My father was a very basic guy, very strong, quiet discipline, he never hit me...he took his belt off a couple of times and all that. He'd run up the steps and we'd scream, myself and my brother, because we all lived in the attic. But he never, however mother she slapped us all the time...anyway, how did your father, an ex-captain, with a reputation where he lived for being upfront and honest take the news that his son, little Howard, was doing drugs of all things?'

Howard: 'I think it was balanced by the Oxford bit if you like. Alright he shouldn't be a drugs smuggler but it's something to do with Oxford.'

At this point Peter roars with laughter – 'So Oxford got the blame did it?'

Howard: 'Yeah, yeah, yeah.'

Peter: 'Had you not gone to Oxford you would have been in big trouble.'

My First Hooker –

Howard: 'We haven't even spoken about women yet.'

Peter: 'I know we're in this night club of mine filled with beautiful girls taking their clothes off and somewhat of a reputation internationally of being involved with women but we haven't mentioned any. Is there a reason? Are they that important to you or not?'

Howard: 'Yeah...I mean they're very important to me...and of course one misses them a lot when one's in prison. You know, a great deal, as I'm sure you did in the Merchant Navy.'

Peter: 'No I didn't honestly. I was a fantasy kid at 16, in the Merchant Navy I'd never been anywhere near a women. I mean women didn't come into my life. I mean did you have a first girlfriend?'

Howard: 'Yes but it was a bit of a shambolic affair, I had a first hooker that I remember better...' (They both laugh hysterically)

Peter: 'Oh Howard you are funny at times, you can't remember your first girlfriend but you can remember your first hooker.'

Howard: 'Oh very well because it took place not far from here actually I mean when I was 17 and you'd of been what 20, 22 or something like that. And those five years are very important five years aren't they. A lot happens between the ages of seventeen and twenty two in both our cases I would think. And err, before I got accept for Oxford I was chosen to be interviewed by Kings College. So I had had an interview, an entrance interview with Kings College in London. All I could think was "thank God now I'll be able to go to Soho," which was like I don't know a sort of fairy land for a...Welsh kid.

I'd read about it, read as much as I could, talked to locals who had been up to Soho everything like that and I remember so well looking at the A-Z. You know Oxford Circus, okay, walk down there passed Poland Street, passed this and there's Soho street right. A bit disappointed like when you turn like into the Soho Street, there's not much there... and then there's a bit of a square and I was thinking, where's all the hookers, where's all the strippers, where are they? And then walked down Dean Street a little and on the right St Anne's Court okay.'

Peter: 'So you remember the address. My God.'

Howard: 'I remember everything, like I said I do remember my first hooker and on the right hand side of the first door was the name Lulu okay. "Dare I press this bell, yes." Pressed the bell, and you know and well I won't go into the details but afterwards everything's fine. Okay and I thought, "well this is great you know...you know. I'm not gonna bother trying for Oxford, I'm coming here to London and I can go and see Lulu every day." So I went out and got a bit drunk and thought "I'm gonna have a look see if Lulu's still there" and obviously she didn't recognise me. "Hello, how you doing?", "I'm the guy who came here two hours ago." "I've never seen you before in my life." And I remember standing outside there feeling forlorn and being jealous right because she was shagging other people.'

(Stringfellow claps unable to contain his laughter).

Peter went on to explain how he married his first girlfriend and reiterated a remark that Bill (Wyman) had made in an earlier episode – that you marry the girl up the road. So although Peter had his wonderful daughter from the relationship, the marriage itself didn't last. Another similarity that unfolded during the series was that both Peter and Bill – born only a few years apart had glamorous aunts and both had periods of their life womanising too – 'there's no doubt I put women on pedestals no doubt at all, different creatures. I didn't know how to talk to them, nothing.'

Howard, no slouch in the marriage department, listed his first marriage to a Latvian lady he met at university, a second long term relationship which resulted in a child and a second marriage ending in divorce and three children.

Ravaged by Life – Death, the good old stalwart of conversation that rises unbidden into most episodes was the next topic to surface with Peter and Howard, with Howard asking Peter if he feared death, and then Peter also going on to share an exclusive with the show, that unbeknownst to all but his closest friends and family Peter had suffered a cancer scare and had part of one lung removed.

Howard: 'Do you fear death?'

Peter: 'Good point, no but I don't want to die. How's that for an answer...I'm a going to tell you something now…how's your health?'

Howard: 'Hmm surprisingly good given the amount of abuse my body has taken'

Peter: 'Have you ever had any close calls...health wise, not an accident?'

Howard: 'Yeah...I was A & E'd into a hospital last October with my heart, it stopped... they err stopped it beating very fast and let me go...but I have to take beta-blockers every day...which makes me feel very relaxed and stoned.'

Peter: 'So you have had your touch and you have thought about death then have you?'

Howard: 'Yeah I mean its I...I'm using someone else's name, do you remember Gilbert Harding... '

Peter: 'Of course I do the guy with the glasses.'

Howard: 'He was asked you know a similar question to this you know "do you fear death?" and his answer was I think "No I don't fear death I'm slightly concerned about the process."

Peter: 'I can't imagine me dying. I'm gonna tell you something secretly now which I've not told anybody. Including or…certainly not the press.'

Howard: 'Mmm.'

Peter: 'A couple of years ago I rang my doctor up and said "I'm coming in for a check." he said "What for, have you got symptoms?" This is a new word for me." Have you got symptoms?" "No, I just want to check, just give me a check top to bottom." He said "You can't have it on your private insurance, you're gonna have to pay for it." Couple of hundred quid? No, £2700 or something, I was like that. (Balancing gesture with his hand).

Howard: 'Whether to go through with it, yeah.'

Peter: 'Two grand!! I said "Book me in, I cancelled once and then got to an appointment." Quite a nice story in a funny way, he gave me those new scans from top to bottom... does the lot, does my brain, I have problems up there. I'm crazy, something's wrong. Check everything you know. So this specialist then rang me up and said "We would like to talk to you." So I went in and he brought my chest up, x-ray. Chest, I meant down there. "I don't smoke, what's the chest up for?", "we're not happy about this" and he pointed to a little white spot. He said "Do you smoke?" "No never in my life." Never smoked, half a Woodbine, 12 years old. "My God does that kill me?" He said "Well there's two things you can do here you can wait for six months". I say "What are you trying to tell me?" "Well it might be cancer." So I went and I woke up..."is it alright?" "No it was the big one." I had cancer and they took half my lung away.'

Howard: 'Yeah.'

Peter: 'They went from the back voomp. And I woke up thinking Christ, I'm alive I've been near death. Well...the specialist says "You're a lucky man." Only because I went for a test I didn't need...and he says "Six months later different story, if you had waited."'

Howard: 'I don't particularly want to devote energy into dying healthy. I want my body to die ravaged of life somehow or other.'

Alias – Having explored the emotional relationship they both had with death, Peter asked Howard to share the story of some of the aliases he had used during his drug smuggling career, and some of the 43 odd of which had been immortalised on the Super Furry Animals Album cover. Howard remembered one of his first fake passports he used on a flight from Dublin to Brussels, where he had assumed the name Peter Hughes, and he describes how at Customs the officer stared for what seemed an eternity at the passport and then looked up and said 'Howard,' by which time Howard thought 'Jesus Christ I've been rumbled' only to realize a fraction of a second later that the guard meant, Howard for 'Howard Hughes' the famed American aviator and recluse who had been in the news. I felt this is a perfect example of Howard's subconscious creating a nervous situation to have to deal with because it was his early days of smuggling and he hadn't relaxed into it yet.

Peter found that hilarious and then shared that he soon gave aliases short shrift when back in the 70's on a trip to New York, Peter shared a likeness to Peter Frampton, so milked the attention for all it was worth, blagging entry into Studio 54 and the VIP area. After complimentary champagne and a double vodka, he asked for the bill only to be confronted with a whopping £18,000, by which time the penny dropped that it was Peter Frampton's long outstanding drug bill. Much backtracking and apologies followed and a chastened Peter remained 'Stringfellow' ever since.

Peter Stringfellow and Howard Marks saying their goodbyes

Another episode drew to a close and an honest, frank and entertaining show was in the can, and Peter and Howard parted on genuine terms of friendship.

Peter: 'And I'll say this about you Howard; you haven't given me any major surprises because somehow your book reflects who you are. You're as nice as your book says, I was wondering if there was another you. After the book I thought "he can't be that nice" but you are. Sorry to say you are that nice, and umm, we talked about friends a little earlier, well I think now in my 70th year I've made another good friend.'

Howard: 'Thank you, so have I.'

DES O'CONNOR

Des O'Connor CBE is one of only a handful of legendary show business entertainers. He managed the truly enviable feat of mastering the stage and the screen. During the course of his remarkable career he has recorded 36 albums, selling over 16 million copies, and he has fronted his own mainstream television shows for over 45 years which is a record incomparable anywhere in the world.

Alan Davies is the intelligent acting and comedy
favourite. Much loved for his brilliant turn as
'Jonathan Creek' in the series of the same name,
Davies has delivered both serious acting roles,
hilarious stand up comedy routines and funny
and insightful contributions as a regular panellist
on the television series 'QI' with Stephen Fry.

ALAN DAVIES

14

DES O'CONNOR & ALAN DAVIES

Biscuit Tins and Bowling Pins – The venue for Des and Alan was Shoreditch House, the East End bastion of the Soho House Group. Apart from being a wonderful venue, it was perfect for the filming of these two professionals. We had two private rooms for filming – the Biscuit Tin and the Biscuit Pin (which has its own bowling alley). For those who are acquainted with Shoreditch House, the Biscuit Tin was the room where we had the most depth of field available to us because of the size. To be slightly technical, the plush luxurious sets of some of the previous shows belied a hidden cramptness off camera. In some cases I would be stood almost on the feet of one of our cameramen while the other producers would be squashed into a corner of the room watching the monitor. Oh the selfish availability of space, from our point of view.

What it did mean was that Des and Alan's chairs on the main set were staged well back from the rear wall adding a fantastic depth of field to the overall look of the show.

Intros – We filmed the piece to camera intros for Des and Alan – exclusive on the extras of the 'Living the Life' DVD – in the Biscuit Pin, adjacent to the main set. So if you look closely at Alan perched (soberly) on the bar guiding the viewer through the condensed history of his contact with Des and expectations for the show, you can spot one sneaky pair of bowling shoes that got missed in the set up, and with Des, just out of shot, were the actual bowling lanes themselves.

Des O'Connor in the Bowling Room at Shoreditch House

Alan Davies in the Bowling Room at Shoreditch House

Punctuality –

One thing that always struck me when filming the 'Living the Life' episodes was the punctuality and professionalism of the contributors. Every single person arrived at their allocated venue on time, well presented and mentally aligned to the personal requirements of such a show.

If Seb Coe can race from a top level meeting with Euro sporting dignitaries, and be on time present and eloquent, before racing off to another commitment, and Jeremy Clarkson can finish filming only to fly straight off to Norway, and Paul McGann can leave the set and head straight to the theatre for a night's on stage performance, it leaves little excuses for any of us not to be good with timekeeping.

The adage 'If you want something done, ask a busy person,' certainly held true for the filming of the series.

Des O'Connor with a 70's perm

The Hair Bear Bunch – I talked earlier of the professionalism of the contributors, and Des and Alan were no exception. Des had brought along a photograph of himself in the 70's with (at the time) a fashionable perm, as an ice breaker with Alan for the start of the show. A Des quip about Alan's hair and muting of the word 'perm' and the show was off and running.

We talked earlier in the book about the emotional intelligence of the series and also the thought and serendipity that went into the pairings. As with so many of the other shows, Des and Alan were a perfect combination. Des had actually given Alan exposure on his chat show when Alan's career was in its fledgling stages. Also Des is every bit the old school professional, with a wink and a smile and constant commitment to keeping the viewer happy. For 'Living the Life' though, the beauty of the show is a chance for us to glimpse the man behind the personality and the emotional experiences that have shaped that man. Alan, who was very emotionally literate due to having undertaken counselling did, as the show progressed, not only share the traumas that had triggered certain behaviours and drives in his life, but pushed Des to reveal more of his own experiences. An example was when Des at the beginning of the show explained his difficult childhood.

Rickets, Bombing and an Iron Lung –

'Yeah, I was born in '32. I didn't have the brightest of childhoods, cos I couldn't walk till I was 6...I had Rickets, malnutrition, and I used to wear these things – callipers I think they're called, on the legs and then my dad came in one day and saw me, I'd unbuckled them and I was standing up by the chair and he called my mother and said "listen if he can stand, he's gonna walk one day" so he helped me to walk. And I'd been walking nine months, and I got run over.'

Alan: 'Oh god.'

Des: 'I did, I got run over and dragged up the street for 100 yards. Stuck in the Goldsmith Row Hospital there, in an Iron Lung they used to call it in those days, ventilator these days...for six months.'

Alan: 'Six months...is Rickets something you contract or something that develops?'

Des: 'Well I hate to sound Dickensian but there wasn't a lot of food around as a kid you know.'

Alan: 'Where did you grow up?'

Des: 'In Stepney...in the East End of London and it was pretty rough, as people say there weren't many polo players in Stepney. It was a real rough area in those days. But you know, you get through it and looking back I try, I don't know whether you're like me, but I draw a curtain across anything I don't particularly want, I don't want to say remember but I don't want to dwell on, and I only believe you can live today, you

238

can't even live on tomorrow cos that's gonna be today when it arrives here, you can only live today. So I don't remember that much about those early days other than it was tough. We got bombed, the house was a direct hit and we were dug out of the Anderson shelter, so I can remember those bits but I don't want to dwell on them.'

Alan: 'Who were you with in the Anderson shelter?'

Des: 'My mum and my sister, it was as though she knew that we had to be careful that day, because you know you hear the siren go off and then you hear the airplanes coming over and she said "quick quick quick!", rushed us all down to the shelter and then kind of spread herself over us like a mother hen with the chicks, and the house got a direct hit, and most of it came over on top of the shelter, and they dug us out in about three and a half hours. Those are memories you can't...I remember my father turned up eventually, came down the hill on a bicycle, and I thought, "Dad's borrowed a bicycle". He'd borrowed a bicycle because he'd heard the bombs, and I remember my mum saying, "we've lost everything" and my dad saying "no, I've just counted, everything is still here", that's something you remember you know.'

Alan: 'Yeah, yeah, and he helped you a lot when you had Rickets too?'

Des: 'Helped me to walk...Yeah, I used to get a bit of banana, very rare luxury in those days, a banana...there wasn't any bananas. And a little bit of chocolate, and a bit of Guiness! How on earth that mixture ever got to a 6 year old kid I don't know, or 3 year old kid at that stage. But I used to try and get to it and my dad used to say, "no I'm not throwing it you, you've got to come and get it, things come to you very rarely, you have to go and get it yourself," so, that's another lesson learnt.'

Alan: 'Has that stayed with you always? Because you've had this extraordinary career that's continuing now over fifty years, you must be quite driven. Do you think it came from those childhood experiences of over-coming Rickets?'

Des: 'I think Alan, that...I don't know of any heavyweight boxers and I don't know of any professional comedians that were born with a silver spoon in their mouth. I think you go out and, humour comes of poverty very often, not a lot else you can do but laugh you know, my father could always make me laugh, there was always humour. On my birth certificate guess what it says, cos my dad was a dustman...it says, "fathers occupation – scavenger"...so I'm the son of a scavenger! What was your dad?'

Total Kleptomaniac – After revealing his father was a 'scavenger' Des asked what Alan's father was, and they both laughed at him being an accountant, and a confirmation of the fairly boring tag that the cliché associated with accountants carried.

Alan Davies as a young boy growing up in Loughton

Alan: 'Yeah he's pretty dull. His big passion is sport and he really just loves all sports, so that's how we were brought up, we had a nice house, nothing like your beginning at all, nice suburban. Was born in Chingford, then we moved to Loughton, the three children, my older brother and my younger sister, but then my mum got leukaemia. I was six and we used to go and see her in the hospital but they didn't tell us at all what was going on, we had no idea that it was terminal, that they couldn't treat it, and in fact after she'd died my brother and I were told not to tell my sister.'

Des: 'She was the younger one?'

Alan: 'She was the youngest, she was only three. "Don't tell, don't tell her about it", so she would say "when are we going to see mummy? When are we going to see mummy?" and we would be saying "oh we can't today", it was quite peculiar, and also I think my understanding of it is, that they didn't even tell my mum that she was terminal, because it would worry her about the effect it would have on her three young children. And she had one sister who lived in Australia and they didn't tell her either, so she never got the opportunity to spend time with her only sister and say goodbye really.'

Des: 'Were you always aware that, you know, "I'm on my own now, there's not a mum here", did someone come in and help you?'

Alan: 'My dad would hire people to sit with us in the early evening, so we had a succession of different ladies that would be there when we got in from school and they would make us our tea, and we'd sit and amuse ourselves till my dad came home and then whoever it was would go home again. We had one lady in particular called Jenny who we were all very fond of, but I disgraced myself because I was pilfering money out of her handbag for ages.'

Des: 'Were you really!'

Alan: 'I was a total kleptomaniac and I...'

Des: 'You are serious about this? You were stealing money!'

Alan: 'Yea I would steal from her handbag, steal money. It's one of the things I'm most ashamed of in my life, but couldn't stop myself doing it and I was told later that it may have been connected to the fact I'd lost my mum, and I was becoming a real hoarder because any feeling of loss created huge anxiety, and I'm still the same I've kept virtually everything I've ever owned in my house you know, boxes full of things, my wife tries to help me get rid of it. But yes, I think it was partly to do with that.'

Comedy, Acting and Fainting – Des moved the conversation onto how Alan had started his acting career.

'It was after I left school and went to college and did this new fangled course called Media Studies in the early eighties, that's when I started Drama and that's when I started thinking I could perform, it had never occurred to me until I did that course. The Drama teacher said "oh just come along to a class, see if you enjoy it and just try it for a week, if you don't you can do English or Sociology or one of the other subjects." But I tried it for a week and I loved it, and I still love it, it's showing off really.'

Des: 'It is, I think when we come into the business we show off a little bit don't we.'

Alan: 'I feel like that, and you know you look around all the time and you think "I'm still getting away with it," any minute someone's gonna tap you on the shoulder and say "OK..." '

Des: 'You started off with the comedy though?'

Alan: 'That's what I really wanted to do, comedy.'

Des: 'Never thought about acting at that stage?'

Alan: 'No I was thinking about that, we were doing lots of plays, but when I went to

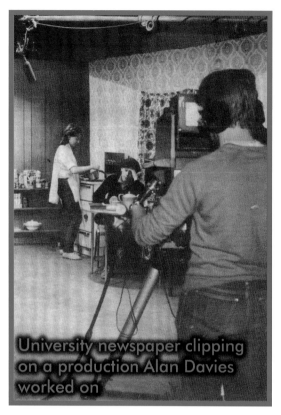

University newspaper clipping on a production Alan Davies worked on

university...I did theatre at university, and when I got there I wanted to do comedy, I was thinking "I'm gonna meet someone and we're gonna collaborate" you know, like all the great...all the comedy performers of that time in the eighties like French and Saunders, or Rick Mayall and Adrian Edmondson. All these up and coming comics that I really admired, they'd all met at college, "this is what's going to happen to me". Then I got there and all the funny people I'd met were really lazy, but stand up presented itself as an option. There were a few stand ups that came to the university and I started to think "well maybe you can just do it by yourself". And you had to generate your own material.'

Des: 'I was gonna say did you write it yourself, or did you pilfer it again?'

Alan: 'Yeah you know, God that was really verboten, that was the one thing really frowned upon. I don't know what it was like for you when you were developing your early act?'

Des: 'Well you just reminded me of Glasgow Empire and things like that, no one told me the national sport of the Scottish people was go to the Empire on a Friday night and wait for the English comic, oh that was just the most brutal...'

Alan: 'Now that's a famous story about you isn't it?'

Des: 'It is, I fainted with fear.'

Alan: 'Did you actually faint or did you take a dive to get the hell out of there?'

Des: 'Well, what had happened, I'll tell you what had happened Alan, prior to that week, there was an act called Dorothy MacKenzie and Reid...Dorothy Reid and Mackenzie that's right. They were accordion players and they would sing Scottish songs, perfect for the Glasgow Empire, but tragically the husband had got knocked down, I think in Sauchiehall Street which is where the Empire is, and got killed the week before hand. She was in all the newspapers obviously but she said "I will go on, he would have wanted me to go on on Monday night", and she got her young nephew so it became

The Glasgow Empire

Dorothy Reed and Mac, and they went on and did it, and I've got to follow them. So when they first went on the audience gave them, well not a standing ovation but a two minute welcome and then she would sing these songs, and I would have to follow. It wasn't the funniest moment of my life.'

Alan: 'They didn't have a little interval or something?'

Des: 'No it was a variety bill, you were the second comic on so you went on and you did it. This particular night on the Thursday night I heard "Oh I can't do it" and silence, she'd run of the stage emotionally torn apart. And they said "Get on, get on!" So I've run on, and trying to do jokes at that moment, I mean I was about as funny as a road crash. I remember the MC's head came over the foot light, cos I'd fainted! I'd thought to myself "I can't be doing with this" you know, and went down in a heap. You can actually hear a silence, it gets louder, when you're expecting a joke the silence gets louder, and I went down in a heap and the musical director pulled himself up and he said "Is this in the act?", and I said "I've fainted, get me off", and they dragged me off through the back of the curtain, they literally dragged me off. Eric Morecombe later said I was the only comic to sell advertising space on the soles of his shoes. So yeah, I think a comic, that's tough.'

Talking of comedy itself, Des made an astute observation; that there is a successful cross-over of comedians that go into acting and do a fine job, but there are no examples of actors that go into stand-up comedy. It was a valid point and both Des and Alan said the actors they had spoken to were horrified at the thought of going on stage as themselves – which reiterates the point Robin Gibb made about Peter Sellers, saying he acted because he didn't know who he was. Peter stood out as a good example of someone who was an actor, and although he acted in comedies, never did actual stand up. Both contributors then shared many stories of life on the road, touring venues and returning to acting. Des thought Alan's subsequent roles had been brilliant and he could see Alan moving into feature films – an idea that Alan was not averse to. Des then posed the question of filming nude scenes.

Des: 'How would you be if your agent or manager rang you up and said something like, "We've got a great part for you but there's a lot of nudity," there's a heavy romantic bedroom scene with, say, Kate Winslet, would you cope?'

Alan: 'Yes, I think I'd cope...but I've never been very happy with my penis, never been happy with it, so I definitely would worry about the nudity.'

Des: 'So you'd have a double in would you?'

Alan: 'I did have to do a scene once, it was a BBC thing and I was lying in a bath and in the scene I was actually under the water and someone came in the flat, it was my wife, my character's wife who I was splitting up with, so he comes out of the water and thinks "Oh my God", she comes in and, anyway to cut a long story short we have an argument in which she chases him round the house.'

Des: 'And you've got to be chased?'

Alan: 'And I was in the nude, dripping wet, and we filmed it in February in this freezing drafty studio. And they gave me quite a large piece of flesh coloured cloth to cover my modesty, but it really needn't have been that, a band-aid would probably have sufficed cos it was so cold, and the make-up girls were very sweet about it, they had to keep coming up and making me wet again for continuity. It was a grim afternoon, it's the practicality of doing those sorts of scenes that becomes half a minute or a minute on the television that took hours to do, any excitement goes out the window even it is Kate Winslet.'

Morecambe and Wise – With all the talk of comedy and acting, it was easy to forget that Des is one of the country's most successful singers – a huge career that has

244

included 36 albums. It is all the more remarkable considering that early on in his career he became a target of Morecambe and Wise's humour, mocking the 'crooning' star. Des showed the fortitude he had exhibited when he was a child, overcoming illness and misfortune to take it in his stride, even choosing to take part in Morecambe and Wise's 1975 Christmas show sketch that mocked him. He explained how he felt around that time.

I Pretend single, Des O'Connor's first number one record

Des: 'My mum always thought I could sing so you can blame my mum. My mum used to say "Yes you can sing never mind what they say". But then it changed my life I mean, when Eric started all those insults, even on official police reports I was mentioned. They found a car upside down in the River Trent and in the official report it said that my album was still playing on the CD going round and round. It did change my life a lot but, no, in a funny kind of way it helped also.'

Alan: 'What, Eric Morecambe constantly teasing you?'

Des: 'Yeah.'

Alan: 'You were the butt of a thousand jokes on his programme.'

Des: 'And about 36 national cartoons, "Send more Des records the Iraqis are retreating!" was one of them I remember, and there was one of them with Neil Kinnock pushing a record player through Maggie Thatcher's window at Number Ten with my record on it and the caption said "Maybe this would get her out". So it was there all the time, I don't mind it, although I did at the time.'

Alan: 'Did you think it stopped you having more hit records though and getting offered

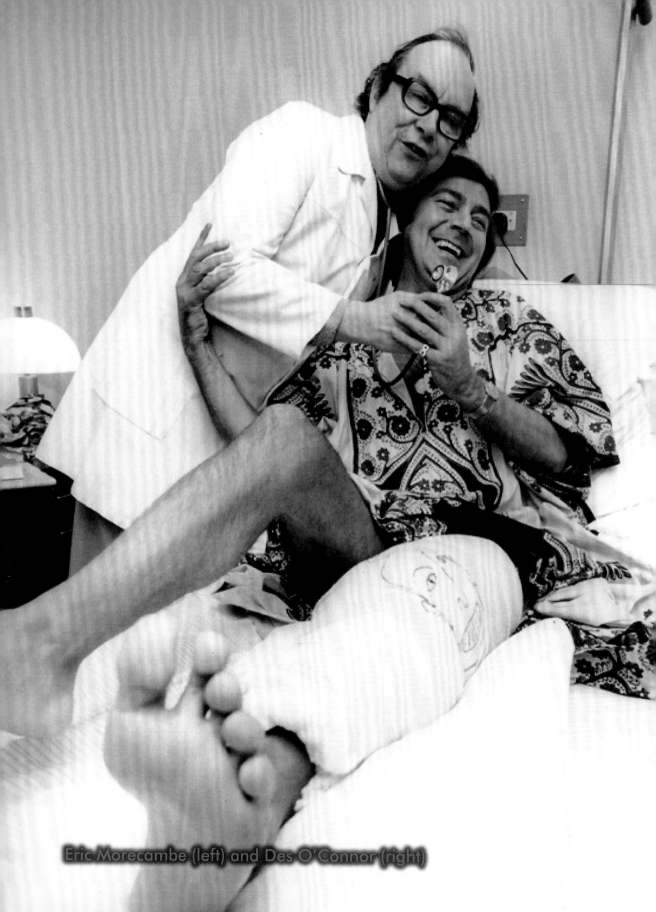

Eric Morecambe (left) and Des O'Connor (right)

good songs and doing more recordings? I mean you've done a lot of recordings goodness me, dozens of albums.'

Des: 'It actually helped in a funny kind of way, because *I Pretend* was the second track that I put out and since then I've done quite a lot of albums, you know, 36.'

Opportunity Knocks – Des, at Alan's prompting, back-tracked slightly in his career to talk about his early marriage and starting off as a Butlin's Redcoat, and in what has proved to be a common theme with most of our contributors, Des showed how he incorporated cunning, hard work, opportunity and a stroke of lady luck to kick start his career.

Alan: 'Is it right Des that you met your first wife at Butlins?'

Des: 'Butlins yes, five pound a week all in and I was at the end of the night, long, long hard day's work. Butlins Redcoat is the best...if there are any young comics watching, potential comics, get a job as a Butlins Redcoat if you can because it's just wonderful.'

Alan: 'Were you a Redcoat when you met your first wife?'

Des: 'No, no I met Phyllis and then they madly invited me back for a second year and I said "this young lady is very talented...", got her an interview and they gave her the job so we went as a married couple which was great. I was 19/20, 20 years of age, something like that but it was a great job being a Butlins Redcoat, I learnt so much.

I cheated actually to get into the Butlins Redcoat show, the guy who was running it, I won't mention his name, I said "Can I come into the show?" cos I'd been an usher at the back, watching the Friday Night Redcoat Review, so he said "what do you do?" so I said "well I sing a little bit, I've got some gags", and then he said "well you're not ready yet", so I said afterwards "What does that producer do?" he said "he sings a little bit and he's got a some gags", there was no chance I was ever going to get in there.'

Alan: 'He didn't want you usurping him.'

Des: 'So one night what I did, cos I'd written off to *The Stage* newspaper, I'd written to twenty two agents saying, I lied, I said I was the Principle Comedian at Butlins Holiday Camp Farley, I was the usher at the back there!'

Alan: 'That's disgraceful.'

Des: 'Disgraceful but I don't believe opportunity knocks, you have to go and get it. So I didn't think anybody would ever answer, and Pete Davies, a Scottish producer, anybody from Scotland would probably know the name, wrote to me saying he was coming to see me, I thought "Oh my lord! I'm not even in the show!" '

Alan: 'You weren't even in the show!'

Des O'Connor as a Butlins Redcoat

Des: 'And he's coming to see me. So I called all the guys sat them down, the other redcoats, cos I knew all their bits cos I was the usher and I knew all their lines. I said "look, my mum and dad are coming to see the show and I've told them I'm in the show and I'm not, do me a favour" I went to one guy and said "I've got £26 in the post office bank" I said "I'll give you £5 if you can go ill that night with food poisoning", he said "let me think about it" so I went to another guy, offered him a fiver, and another, there were four of them, all went ill with food poisoning one night on the show and this producer came to me and said "You, can you still remember some jokes, can you do a spot?", "Yes! I know the sketch" and I went on and I did it. So you know I got my first job at The Palace Newcastle from that fib.'

Alan: 'That's amazing.'

Des: 'I'm not saying people should lie, but sometimes, like you, you're honest you said you used to pilfer when you were young.'

Alan: 'Yeah.'

Des: 'I think you have to make things happen in show business.'

Knowing the strain a show business career can put on families, Alan asked Des how he managed it with a wife and a young child at the start of his career.

Des: 'Yeah it wasn't easy, it's not easy it's tough, that's probably the most difficult thing in show business, if you're married, is to level it off so that you can still work. I mean I had a three-month tour of Australia.'

Alan: 'Do you have any regrets about that?'

Des: 'Oh yeah.'

Alan: 'Did you feel like you put your career first too much? Or at certain times in your life?'

Des: 'I think you're right because I probably did focus too much on my career but at that stage when you start out you've got to pay a mortgage, you've got to provide a home, pay school fees, and someone's got to go and do the job so you know, looking back, I don't know how I could have changed it, and I don't have any advice other than if someone has to travel with a play or on tour then you need an understanding partner, you do need that. So I made that mistake a couple of times, but happily twenty years with the same lady now and I don't see me trotting off on 16 week tours but you know we're away now. I've just done some concerts now so, it's not an easy job to do but would we do another job?'

By way of contrast Alan described his first forays on the stand up circuit and eventually the *Jonathan Creek* series.

'But when I started getting in to that sort of material, as a comic talking about my own life...'

Des: 'That's the best.'

Alan: 'I felt that, that was the thing that gave me a real jump forward, because prior to that it was a very different world, the stand up world I went into, to the variety world where you started, cos it was the alternative comedy circuit, everybody had to do their own material and it was a very political atmosphere and it was certain you couldn't do anything that was deemed to be sexiest or racist or those old fashioned kind of jokes about mother-in-laws and so on, that was all out the window.

We were very self-policing in that regard, the audiences didn't want to hear that sort of old stuff, and so you had to be quite inventive, and quite often you'd turn up and find there had been some politician that had done something daft and every comedian had a line about it, and I thought, "oh I've got a bit about that but so-and-so has already been on so I cant really do it now", and I found that by talking about my own life...it was my own story, and also I found there was a comedian called Bob Boyton, a friend of mine at that time and he said to me "Keep persevering with that stuff about working in the warehouse that's funny that is. You haven't got it yet but it will come, when you're up there, or once you've been up there for a little while the audience will want to know a bit about you, what you're doing now, know who are you, they want to know you personally." '

Des: 'That's right. It's a bit early in your life to ask you this, but do you have any regrets looking back, do you think you made mistakes anywhere? Because you're doing very nicely in your career.'

Alan: 'Most of the things I regret happening in my life I haven't really had any control over cos I was only a kid you know. There was a period in my life after my mum died, the following year my granddad, her dad died, the year after that my dad's mum died, a couple of years after that my dad's dad died, then my mum's mum who was the last grandparent had a nervous breakdown and she emigrated to Australia.

So in that few years while I was growing up everybody went and we as a family slipped a bit, amongst us, we didn't hang together and I don't know if I could have done anything differently at that time but I behaved badly, I was nicking stuff, I wasn't working at school and I was insolent to put it kindly at home with my dad and my older brother and they thought I was a pain in the neck, and they were right you know. So some of those things I would change. In my professional life working as a comic I don't think I would really change any of it.'

Des: 'But you're famous now, how do you deal with fame? Is that something you wear well? Do you like that, people recognising you?'

Alan: 'I'm more used to it now. At the beginning I thought I was going to love it, I really thought being famous was going to be great. I remember going on *Have I Got News For You* the first time, it was a big show in those days with a big audience, and then coming on your show in 1995 on ITV in primetime, you know that was when my dad certainly thought, course there's other shows on channel four or regional cabaret shows or there's little bits and bobs I was doing, that's all fine but it didn't feel like it meant much, but to sit on Des's sofa where all the stars of stage and screen had sat was an accolade and to him it was terrific.

Then I went out the next day imagining everybody I met in the street will have been at home watching Des last night, but of course even with twelve million viewers, still most people they didn't, I mean if they had they didn't really register. So then I was thinking "No I want to be recognised." and then once *Jonathan Creek* came on, and I started doing commercials for a bank and they were on all the time, then I couldn't go out on the street without people shouting, usually they'd shout "It's a perm!" at me, which was a joke from one of the adverts that I'd suggested stupidly. Then I started to panic a little because I thought this is going to ruin my life, because I like going to the pub and I like going to the football and doing the things that I'd always done, and I started to worry that I wouldn't be able to, for a period of time I became quite unhappy with it, but I'm past that now.'

Caroline Quentin (left) and Alan Davies (right) in Jonathan Creek

The Zeitgeist of Celebrity – picking up on the fame factor and also a long running theme that always popped up in the series, Des posed the question whether it was easier to be famous these days. Alan suggested that it depended on what fame actually is, because it's fairly easy to get onto television in itself, but a lot of the 'wannabes' are thrown into things and exploited, and it is creating a generation of children who have the sole aim of being famous.

Alan: 'And they say "I want to be famous" they don't say they want to be an astronaut or a train driver or a nurse or whatever, you know they just want to be famous and actually, well I'm quite comfortable with being recognised these days but it's a bi-product of the work that you do. Famous for what? Just famous. But you have to work hard to develop a talent that's going to get you, as you said, the affection of people who are going to then want to keep seeing you for a long time, you aren't going to get anything lasting just from standing in front of a camera and gurning, you know you've got to be prepared to work. All the people I know, my peers and contemporaries, be it Lee Evans or Eddie Izzard or Jack Dee or Jo Brand all the ones who I was on the circuit with who are really house hold names now, they're the ones who worked the hardest. They were all funny but they worked, Lee is prodigious.

It is a celebrity world at the moment...The word celebrity has become a negative, it's almost as if you feel like saying "he's a celebrity" is something you want to resist "oh I'm not a celebrity", it feels almost like an insult.'

Des: 'Somebody put down celebrity, and I did exactly what you just said, I said "No I'm a...."'

Alan: 'No no no, I'm a comedian, I'm an actor I'm not a celebrity, that's, don't be, that's rude, it feels like its rude. And its odd because the word stems from the word celebrated person, and it feels like it ought to be someone who is celebrated, who's known and celebrated by people but in fact it's become a word for someone who wants to be looked at I suppose.'

Des: 'Well very few things niggle me or get up my nose, and there's plenty of room! But when I see Star of...what's that thing on Four, where they're locked in?'

Des O'Connor and Alan Davies saying their goodbyes

Alan: *'Big Brother.'*

Des: *'Big Brother!* Star of *Big Brother'*

Alan: 'Star of *Big Brother!*'

Des: 'Star of *Big Brother!* You go well hang on a minute. People say "are you watching it?" I say "I'd rather bore a hole in the neighbour's wall and see what they're doing"'

Endings and Goodbyes – It was a wonderful and revealing shoot with Des and Alan. Considering that at the start of the day Des, ever the professional entertainer, came prepared with a whole host of topics and jokes he could segue into the show. When I explained again the nature of a relaxing free flow of conversation based around their emotional journey through their lives and careers, he was ultra-understanding and professional, and I felt he was quite surprised when filming ended that it had gone so well, for not being scripted. We,as a production team, were not surprised as we had two highly successful people who were naturals on camera and had a rich and fulfilling story to share.

Des: 'We've talked about quite a few things.'

Alan: 'Talked about everything, and it's going to stay with me for a while that you came out of the air raid shelter and your house had gone, and you'd only just got over being in callipers and then getting run over and being in an iron lung for six months.'

Des: 'I mean you had a few little...a bad start, losing your mum when you were six.'

Alan: 'Couple of things didn't go the way you wanted them to but, I don't know, in some ways I think it helps you, it helps you in another way maybe.'

Des: 'Nobody gets it all their way.'

Alan: 'No, everyone's got a story.'

Des: 'The hiccups, that's what life is all about. We're getting on a little soapbox now and preaching, but no I've enjoyed it Alan, really.'

Alan: 'I've enjoyed it too Des.'

Des: 'Good luck with your career.'

Alan: 'Always a pleasure.'

CILLA BLACK

Cilla Black OBE famously impressed the likes of The Beatles and many others with her impromptu singing at the Cavern Club and she subsequently signed with Beatles' manager Brian Epstein. After a successful recording career and a brief time as a comedy actress, she became the best paid female presenter in British television history, hosting two of the most popular and long-running evening entertainment shows of the 1980s and 1990s – 'Blind Date' and 'Surprise, Surprise.'

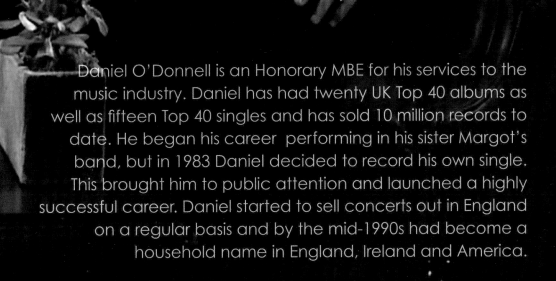

Daniel O'Donnell is an Honorary MBE for his services to the
music industry. Daniel has had twenty UK Top 40 albums as
well as fifteen Top 40 singles and has sold 10 million records to
date. He began his career performing in his sister Margot's
band, but in 1983 Daniel decided to record his own single.
This brought him to public attention and launched a highly
successful career. Daniel started to sell concerts out in England
on a regular basis and by the mid-1990s had become a
household name in England, Ireland and America.

DANIEL O'DONNELL

15

CILLA BLACK & DANIEL O'DONNELL

Very Civilised – It was back to the Gore Hotel for this episode of 'Living the Life', a set of luxury and relaxation befitting 'our Cilla' and the Irish charm of gentleman Daniel O'Donnell. Cilla has enjoyed a huge career both in music and subsequently television presenting – the Queen of Saturday evening TV for much of the eighties, the nineties and into the early 'naughties' as the highest paid female performer on British television. Daniel, we realised had a huge following in Ireland, the UK and America, and with twenty top 40 UK albums under his belt and an Honorary MBE, he was a wonderful match for Cilla on many counts, namely: they are both singers and performers, both have presented television shows and having appeared on Cilla's Surprise Surprise, Daniel and Cilla are good friends and share mutual acquaintances.

The Baby Snatcher – Although one would imagine growing up in the city of Liverpool would be hugely different to the countryside of County Donegal, it was interesting how certain community values and rural habits held true for both contributors. Daniel asked Cilla what it was like growing up in Liverpool and she explained it thus.

'Well very similar because I'm from Irish heritage, and Welsh, and very Celtic actually. So my grandmother, my father was first generation of Irish and so he came over. So I think traditions really live on don't they. Although I come from a city, but with the Irish working class traditions, so therefore you know during…I was a war baby don't all cry… so everything, we had chickens in our backyard where as you had them in probably a

Cilla Black and Daniel O'Donnell in their pre-interviews

garden over there. But the...values were the same.'

Daniel: 'I grew up by the sea; every house was open, was it like that in your street?'

Cilla: 'You never locked the doors, never locked the doors and everybody was friendly with everybody, you know if you went short you went next door. I use to rob children, babies you know and nobody reported them to the police because they said "Ah that's Little Cilla," because my mother was 'Big Cilla'. 'Little Cilla' it will be her you know and rather than have, and I did have, a doll and a pram I'd take the real thing from outside the front door and they never ever bothered because they knew, you know, two hours later I would be back with the baby when it woke up and it was starving, to eat or drink at that time. Yeah it was one of those...it was a very trusting time my childhood but then I go much further back then you, I mean you couldn't do that today.'

Cilla was interested from early on in the show, how Daniel was able to get into show-business, 'stuck out in the wilds of Donegal.'

Daniel: 'I think you know growing up in Ireland there is a song about every crossroads they write songs about the happy occasions, the sad occasions, there is just so much

257

music. I sang in the choir of course, you know, at mass but during lent time they would have concerts and that was my first opportunity to sing. Now my sister Margo was singing again from when I was two, so she started in Ireland around the same time that you would have started here. Even though she was only about twelve when she started singing with a band, which is incredible.'

Cilla Black as a young girl

Cilla: 'Amazing.'

Daniel: 'So we were always aware of music in the house, and even to this day we would have family reunions…you have to fight your way to the Mic, because all my cousins can sing…we didn't have a microphone then, just the…you'd steal the brush, you know, that my sister would have…you'd be stealing the brush, singing you know with the brush looking at yourself to see what you would look like. But that was my initial opportunity, I can't remember not singing. I think I must have bored the tail off people you know that everywhere and every opportunity I was standing you know with my mouth open singing something.'

Cilla: 'It's a very Irish thing I think performing, don't you think?'

Daniel: 'Absolutely and you know going on from, I suppose, that singing and the concerts I didn't actually think that I would be a singer. And I suppose Margaret my sister or 'Margo', her singing gave me a sort of, kind of inside peek at what it was like, I mean it was hard work I thought, she would go away singing, she was still at school obviously when she started and then you know she would go away and be singing late at night and back for school and then obviously the singing took over and she became successful.

I suppose I thought from seeing her that it would be a hard life, I thought I would do teaching. But I loved the music; I loved the opportunity to sing. I remember one night we used to go to the local hotel in Dungloe and there was a group called Las Scala, they were the Murray family they played every weekend. And they used to invite everybody to sing that would be able to sing so I always got the chance to get up and sing with them. And I suppose maybe I was about 15 or 16 by this time and I remember I got up and sang and people would be dancing, it wasn't very big, the floor was small and I remember very vividly, I was singing whatever, maybe Irish ballads or Irish waltzes or whatever. And I was really enjoying it and I was looking at the people and I could see them smiling and singing along and I remember thinking that at that very minute that If I could have my life doing this I could be happy and people would be happy and I would think wouldn't that be a wonderful way to spend your life.'

So many of the contributors fought for what they wanted through passion and a hand from lady luck. Cilla was no different, she told Daniel of the family not having any money when she was a child – her father was a docker and mother sold second hand clothes in the market.

Cilla Black and her mother

Cilla's mother was a wonderful singer though, and was always singing and listening to the wireless, so her childhood was rich in music. Everyone in her household played a musical instrument and they would sing for the rest of the family and friends when they came back from the pub...it was obviously in Cilla's blood as even when she went to secretarial college (Anfield Commercial College) the rest of the girls on her course used to get her to sing in their lunch hour. Cilla then went onto to describe how a friend of hers asked her to come to club and sing and serendipity took its course.

'One day a girl called Pauline said to me would I go down and join her at The Iron Door, a club, it was after school. And I said "what would I want to go to The Iron Door for" and she said "my boyfriend is singing there" and when I get there low and behold it was The Beatles singing and her boyfriend was the late and great George Harrison. So the girls that I went with said 'Give Cilla a go, give Cilla a go!' and it was John Lennon that said to me 'OK Cyril, let's see what you can do'. And he called me Cyril from that day, well if he would have been here he still would call me Cyril, but that's how it happened for me.'

Cilla Black and Paul McCartney (left) and John Lennon (centre)

Amazing Grace –

Daniel: 'My start then came you know through Margaret really, I joined Margo with her band in 1983. I mean your start obviously when you are able to say that you were there when The Beatles were but they were all starting I mean nobody knew...they didn't know what everything was going to lead to you know no matter where you start you know growing up in Donegal when people come to where I live even today they think how do you get out of here to get a start in music. I mean it's the same, you brought up on Scotland Road how do you get the opportunity and yet it's the lucky break...I think that lucky break is so important.'

Cilla: 'It is.'

Daniel: 'It's the girl asking you to come to the club, it's the girl shouting 'Let Cilla have a go', it's these things that give you the opportunity.'

Cilla: 'But I…maybe I was very big headed at the time because I thought "Yeah I'm going to be the biggest star ever," I really did. I think you have to have that ambition, I think you have to have that ego and boy did I have an ego. And I loved it all…I loved being on stage…it's the most fantastic feeling in the world actually, that adrenalin rush when everybody goes "Oh my god, she or he is here." Now tell me what was the very first pop record that you bought?'

Daniel O'Donnell (back row second from right) with Margo's band

Daniel: 'Well now it was a pop record at the time it was The Guards that played *Amazing Grace*. It probably wasn't the hippest pop record ever…'

Cilla: 'No it wasn't actually Daniel.'

Daniel: 'But I have to tell you the truth, I can't tell you a lie after us talking about the good Catholics we were starting out. That was the first thing that I remember…but anyway it went on, I did go on from that. I believed I mean I chose music that I started in the 80's so I should have been singing pop; Duran Duran, Boy George, you know that's what was going when I was starting but I loved Irish ballads and country music, I loved that type of music.

Sometimes people say would you ever want to break out and do something that people don't expect. That was not what I should of sang, I went away from my peers and all the people that grew up in my year, they thought I had two heads wanting to sing this music. Plus, the fact that you know people in the music business thought that there was no market for that anyway, it was a bygone era. I loved it, I must have been determined, I felt that if I loved it there must be of been other people that wanted to hear that.'

Cilla: 'Tell me it would be different for you, because you're a guy, but when I was singing in and around the clubs in Liverpool, you know my parents checked up on me especially me Mam. And I remember dancing the said same place, The Iron Door; everybody remembers The Cavern but The Iron Door was really a big club as well in Liverpool. And I was jiving with Ringo one night, it was two o'clock, I was doing an all night session so it started at eight o'clock in the evening and finished at eight o'clock the following morning…'

Daniel: 'Oh my god.'

Cilla: 'but I was only 15-16 and I was having a jive in between sessions with Ringo, and he said to me "Look at those two old women over there they are great Jivers"…and I looked over and it was my mam and my aunty Vera and I thought that I could of died. I could have died.'

Cilla certainly gave an insight into performers earning that opportunity in a bygone era. Eight o'clock at night until eight o'clock in the morning, at fifteen years of age…I think the 'breathy little monsters' Jeremy Clarkson refers to in the series would struggle with a fraction of that. Cilla went on to describe how she was singing with several bands in Liverpool at 16, and then picks up the story of an audition with Ringo Star.

'I remember when I was working in the office one day and Ringo turned up and he said he was going to, not with The Beatles, he was with 'Rory Storm and the Hurricanes' then and they were going to a place in Hamburg at The Top Ten Club, and he came to ask would I join the band because they needed to have a girl singer. And I said "Oh I'm so thrilled" and he said "well we didn't want you we just have to do what's in the contract." '

Anyway I went home to my father and my father, you know I was just 16 years of age going on 17, and my father he just wouldn't allow me to go, because he realised that I wouldn't come back the same little girl. And it was the beginning of the whole new phase of the northern Rock'n'Roll because it was not long after that that Brain Epstein came on the scene and Brian, God bless him, came down to The Cavern and saw a lunch time session of The Beatles playing there and then signed them up. And that's, it was a knock-on situation, it really…I did my audition with the Beatles for Brian and it wasn't even at The Cavern it was over the water in the Majestic Ballroom in Birkenhead, and well not a lot of people know this, not a lot of laymen know this if you're watching, but you know girls sing in a different key to guys. So I sang Sam Cooke's version of *Summer Time* you know from *Porgy and Bess* and I sounded terrible.

Anyway, I walked straight off stage back on the ferry and I just knew I was dreadful, and I never heard from Brian until I was singing a year after, that's why I came a year after The Beatles. And I was singing in a club called The Blue Angel and I'd sing anything and I was singing jazz, a song *Bye Bye Black Bird* it was, and then I didn't know that Brian was in the audience. He came up to me and said "Why didn't you sing like that at Birkenhead?", and I said "Because I'm singing in my key with proper musicians," because The Beatles couldn't read music…so…that's when he signed me, which was unbelievable…'

Daniel: 'That's amazing, yeah.'

Cilla: 'Unbelievable.'

Daniel: 'Was there actually a point or a defining moment when you thought you know "I'm going to make it" or this is it?'

Cilla: 'Oh yeah, when I got paid…I got money, I actually was earning money by singing, by doing the thing that I loved. I didn't like London at all and when Brian Epstein said I've got you a season at the London Palladium, and my reply to that was "why couldn't you have got me the Liverpool Empire"…you know what am I doing…I mean you know the London Palladium is the most famous theatre in the world, and he said "don't worry it's only going to run for four weeks." And he'd signed for the run of the contract and nine months later I was still there. And I had two number one hit records while I was there on three hundred and fifty pounds a week. I could have killed him. I could have killed him.'

Both Cilla and Daniel have reputations for being talented and professional, which may sound obvious but one of the themes that became apparent from the series was that professionalism was hewn on the playground of dogged persistence, drive and a little piece of luck. Most people within our production crew knew of Daniel, his music and his career success but didn't realise how doggedly he pursued his dream. He told Cilla a great story about how he saved to cut his own album and hawked the 1000 copies around the country to shift them and raise his profile.

'Well I suppose I found it difficult (success). I went with my sister and her band for two years in 1981 and in 83 I made a record, a first record.'

Cilla: 'Bet that cost you a few bob?'

Daniel: 'Well I saved up, I couldn't get anyone interested in me but I think this is where the determination comes, I believed, so I had saved up enough money to go in a studio.'

Cilla: 'What do you call enough money?'

Daniel: 'Well it wasn't Abbey Road, but It cost me £600 to record four songs, which was on a budget, and I was able to get a thousand singles – the 45's – for another £600. So I had a thousand records for £1200 and I sold them then for £1.50, if you were a friend of mine you got it for £1 but I had very few friends.

I sold them everywhere Cilla I even went on a bus, I don't know if you know Knock Shrine, where our lady appeared back in the 18 hundreds, and we used to go every year on the bus trip to Knock and I went to Knock with all the older people and I sang on the bus and I sold them my record, most of them didn't even have a record player but they bought my record because I was…imagine, this is how I started.

So then I made…I think one of the things that was very important there was a big Irish festival in Round Wood Park in London, it went for years and in 1984 I got the opportunity to come and sing at this festival in Round Wood Park and there would be anything up to 60,000 people. Now we were on at midday so there wouldn't of been 60,000 at twelve in the day, it went on until six in the evening or eight or whatever, but I got on at 12'o'clock that day and Mick Clerkin who owned Ritz Records at the time, he was there and somebody had told him that I was coming on and that he should look out for me. And that then…the next year I was there at three in the afternoon and in 1986 I was on at six, the best time.'

Cilla: 'Wow!'

Daniel: 'I think that period of uncertainty and difficult to get people to see me, it gave me an opportunity to better myself you know, stand on the stage and you're singing to a small crowd you know if you did something...oh I shouldn't do that again or I should do that again, so you're learning it's very difficult to be thrust into the...you know, the middle of it all without any preparation. But I remember in 1986 we went to this place called the Rutherford Inn and the dressing room was below the stage and we were down stairs getting ready and somebody came down and I said "Is there many here?" and they said "The place is packed" and all of a sudden I could hear slow clapping and

Daniel and Majella O'Donnell wedding

"Dan-iel, Dan-iel", I got frightened and I didn't want to come up from downstairs...'

Cilla: 'How fabulous.'

Daniel: 'So it was even though I had waited so many years, three years, it was instant and that night I thought this must be, this must be it. And from there on in you know one thing led to another, and again even though the success had started there was lucky things that happened and I'm sure you will say even after two number one records and all of the top forty hits that you had and then you moved into the television there's lucky things that bring you from one thing to the other.'

Daniel went on to regale Cilla with how he had met and fallen in love with Majella in Tenerife, but because she had been married and because of his catholic beliefs he didn't know how they could be together. However once he realised he didn't want to be without her they found a way, and eventually Majella was given an annulment from her first marriage and they were then able to have their own ceremony.

Talk of Majella prompted Daniel to ask Cilla to describe how she had met Bobby – her husband, who sadly died in October 1999,

Love of My Life –

'**Daniel:** 'I mean you met Bobby very early in your life.'

Cilla: 'I was but a child, I was…I guess I was 16 going on 17 as the song goes and I was working in a coffee bar in The Zodiac Club in Duke Street actually in Liverpool, and I saw this blonde guy, I thought he looked Steve McQueenish and he had a sun tan and nobody in Liverpool had sun tans so I assumed either he must have money or he was off one of the boats you know…because it was a big port at the time. I thought he, I thought Bobby was probably Swedish so I went over to chat him up because I thought he'd be a soft touch, and I was so disappointed when he told me that he came from Anfield, you know…because I thought…the reason why I had thought he had money was because he'd gone on a £48 two week trip to Lloret De Mar in Spain.'

Daniel: 'So this is where the tan came from?'

Cilla: 'That's where the tan came from, yeah. But we started seeing each other occasionally, he wasn't with me from the age of 17 as a lot of people think, because we had rows and everything, for instance he never came to my 18th birthday party, all The Beatles and everybody else did, but I'd fallen out with him by then. I was doing a TV show for the BBC and actually having a row…Bobby used to take everyone out to Lorenzo's every week, which is a very chic, still is, in Beauchamp Place, and I was having a row with him I don't know what it was over. And Peter Brown a dear friend, he's still a dear friend today, said to me "You know you two sound like an old married couple why don't you get married?" And Bobby said "well you fix it up and we will" and that was my proposal…and then that was it I've never had down on one knee, I don't know how you did it with Majella, no ring or whatsoever, no romance and that the way it happened.'

Daniel: 'And yet he was the love of your life.'

Cilla: 'Love of my life, yeah I'm still madly in love with Bobby, I don't think you get over that.'

Daniel: 'No, but you have to…I think you'll maybe agree or disagree, but you have to love because that's what the one that's gone would want you to do.'

Bobby Willis and Cilla Black

Cilla: 'No he wouldn't, no not Bobby, no I mean I remember when the kids were quite small and we were all in the living room and he said, he was a bit of a devil Bobby, and he said to the boys "Now, you know when I'm gone I want your mother, I want your mother to be happy," and the kids were going "aww, aww dad." "No, no I want your mother to be happy, I want your mother to be happy, but if she brings a fellow home here I want you three to knock seven kinds of…" and its unrepeatable what he said "out of this guy." But he did…no I know for a fact, he's sitting up there now, yet mind you, he's sent some dogs for me to go out with, I mean oh my God…and that's how I know, that's how I know…and not one of them has had a working prostate, so you know, I'm a never say never girl but I know in my heart of hearts I don't think I will ever get married again.'

The Rudest Red Riding Hood – Every episode of 'Living the Life' has drawn up the topic of excess – handling the culture of drugs and the Rock n Roll lifestyle – and with Daniel and Cilla it was no different. Daniel was interested to know how Cilla had stayed grounded around the heady days of 60's excess.

Cilla: 'Oh my mam would have killed me, but I did try, I did try smoking cannabis, I'm not a smoker anyway, never have been, I was invited to all the parties and yeah they did smoke cannabis, but…I did try it one day, I did try it but a lot of the, the thing about the boys, in the early days they used to go into the bathroom and smoke and I remember there was a guy, Tony King, and I was rehearsing for my very first pantomime at Wimbledon Theatre, doing *Little Red Riding Hood*, I tell you, and I went in my own bathroom and I smoked, he brought round this funny cigarette and I smoked it and I tell you when I was rehearsing I was the rudest *Little Red Riding Hood* you've ever heard at rehearsals. So I did try it yeah, I did try it but I didn't like it, it just made me swear and I don't swear. I didn't like the experience. You know LSD was quite big at the time, I've never done…never even been tempted, I've always been frightened of it actually, and no I don't like the idea of drugs.'

Daniel: 'I was never one that drank alcohol, I've nothing against people drinking alcohol I mean you know I enjoy the fun, or the Craic as we say, in the pubs. But I just never, you know, bothered. I tried drinking, you know, but I just got sick.'

Kangaroo Testicles – I mentioned the zeitgeist of celebrity earlier in the book, and part of that piece was driven by Cilla's reaction to it. The way she described it was echoed by nearly every contributor, and what was probably as topical as the 'famous for five minutes for doing nothing' argument was the Celebrity Jungle show (*I'm a Celebrity Get Me Outta Here*). Cilla was one of the most animated and it was worth hearing it in her own words.

'What I can't stand about people or 'token celebrities today'...I hate that term you know 'Stars' I like, but you can't call them stars. I hate being called a celebrity myself, I am not a celebrity, I've worked my...I've paid my dues for goodness sake. Don't put me in the same boat as someone who's been on *Big Brother*. Please don't put me in that boat. I can't stand these so called celebrities who go to all these places, who court all these press people and then all of a sudden when they are famous for five minutes, "Oh leave me alone I don't want to be photographed".

Daniel: 'Isn't it amazing how in recent times that, that culture has come to the fore, that people are famous because of reality TV, it's, it's...amazing, I find it amazing. I mean *Big Brother* I know is finished now, but so many people are famous because of that or you know going on the jungle, you know, or different things like that.'

Cilla: 'I love that jungle thing.'

Daniel: 'Don't tell me you would go on it?'

Cilla: 'No I would never go on it. I said if you ever see me going on the jungle...

Daniel and Cilla – (At the same time) – 'shoot me.'

Cilla: 'Yes...no I would never, ever do a program but I love watching it though. I love these so called celebrities trying to rejuvenate their career by going in there and being made to do these dreadful things. I go "Bring it on, shove another slug and kangaroo testicle down their gob" I love all that, I do...I love it only for the fact, to see the celebs suffer.'

268

Cilla Black and Daniel O'Donnell saying their goodbyes

Cilla and Daniel wrapped up the show reminiscing about their achievements and looking forward to the future, having had a laugh they agreed they were naturals and after a 'well known' couple's TV job.

Cilla: 'We are naturals; somebody should put us on the tele.'

Daniel: 'We may be the next Richard and Judy, you never know.'

Cilla: 'We could do.'

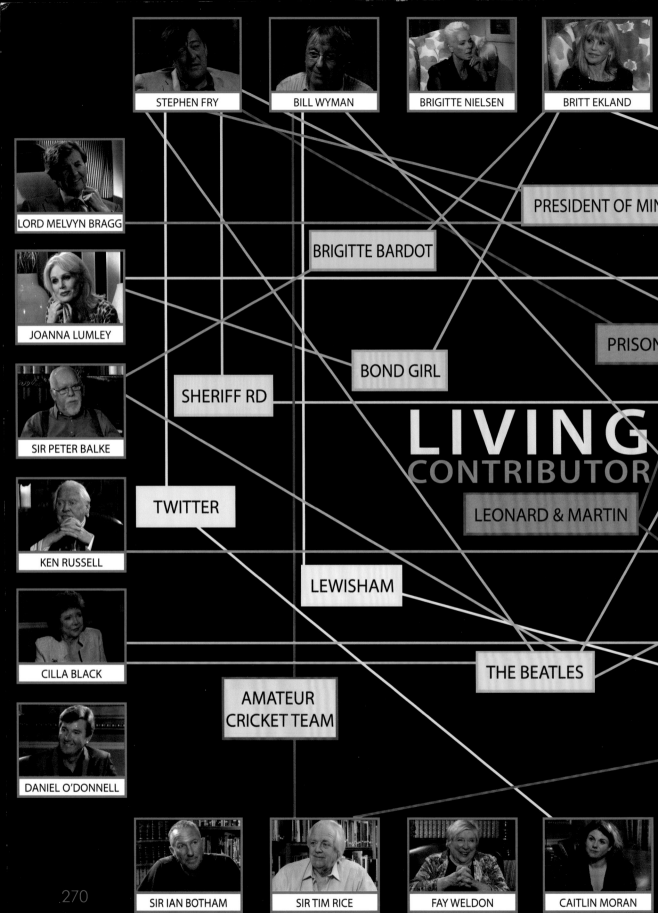

STEPHEN FRY

BILL WYMAN

BRIGITTE NIELSEN

BRITT EKLAND

LORD MELVYN BRAGG

JOANNA LUMLEY

SIR PETER BALKE

KEN RUSSELL

CILLA BLACK

DANIEL O'DONNELL

PRESIDENT OF MIN

BRIGITTE BARDOT

PRISON

BOND GIRL

SHERIFF RD

LIVING
CONTRIBUTOR

TWITTER

LEONARD & MARTIN

LEWISHAM

THE BEATLES

AMATEUR
CRICKET TEAM

SIR IAN BOTHAM

SIR TIM RICE

FAY WELDON

CAITLIN MORAN

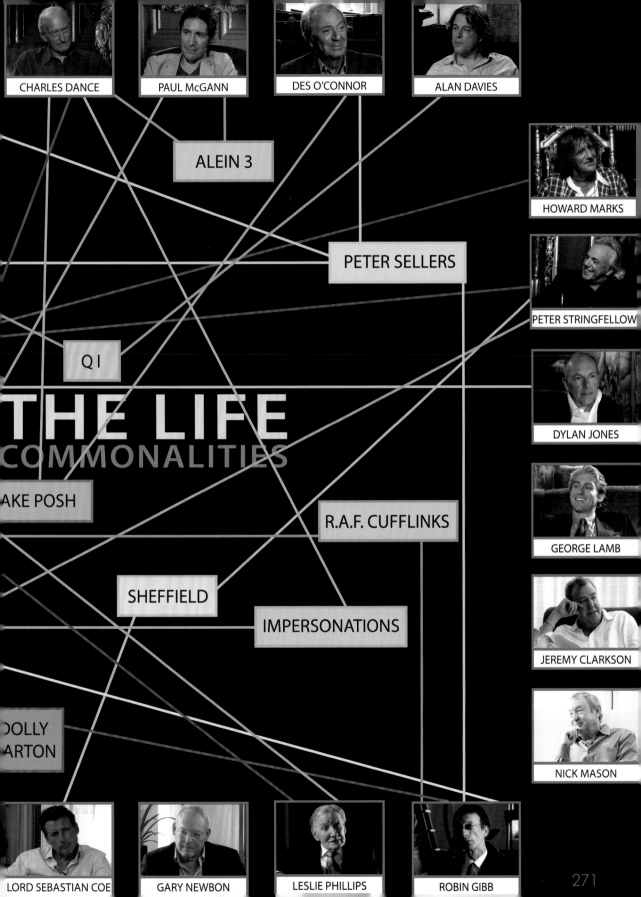

CHARLES DANCE

PAUL McGANN

DES O'CONNOR

ALAN DAVIES

ALEIN 3

HOWARD MARKS

PETER SELLERS

PETER STRINGFELLOW

Q1

DYLAN JONES

THE LIFE
COMMONALITIES

AKE POSH

R.A.F. CUFFLINKS

GEORGE LAMB

SHEFFIELD

IMPERSONATIONS

JEREMY CLARKSON

DOLLY
ARTON

NICK MASON

LORD SEBASTIAN COE

GARY NEWBON

LESLIE PHILLIPS

ROBIN GIBB

271

LIVING THE LIFE BY THE NUMBERS

Map of where contributors where born

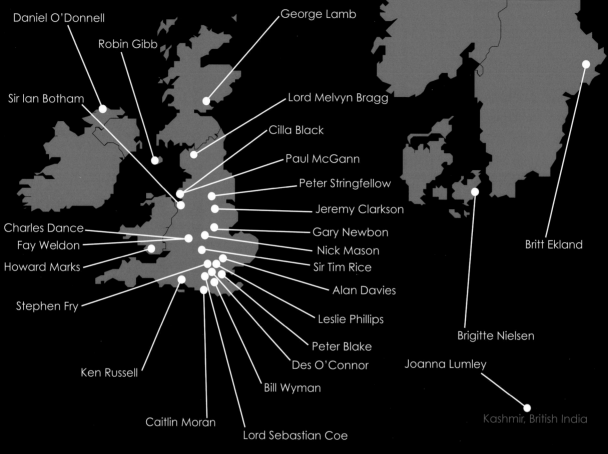

Daniel O'Donnell

Robin Gibb

George Lamb

Sir Ian Botham

Lord Melvyn Bragg

Cilla Black

Paul McGann

Peter Stringfellow

Jeremy Clarkson

Charles Dance

Fay Weldon

Gary Newbon

Nick Mason

Howard Marks

Sir Tim Rice

Alan Davies

Stephen Fry

Leslie Phillips

Peter Blake

Des O'Connor

Ken Russell

Bill Wyman

Caitlin Moran

Lord Sebastian Coe

Britt Ekland

Brigitte Nielsen

Joanna Lumley

Kashmir, British India

Bar Graphic for the decade contributors where born

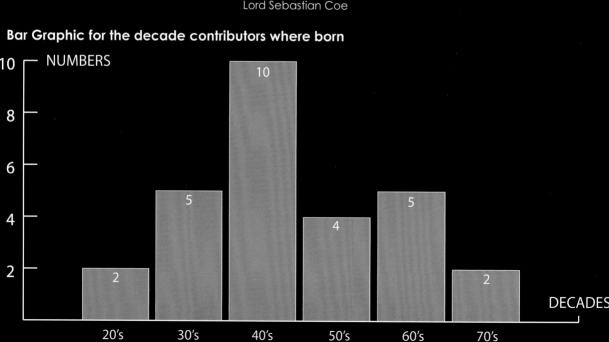

NUMBERS

20's	30's	40's	50's	60's	70's
2	5	10	4	5	2

DECADES

Contributors astrological star signs

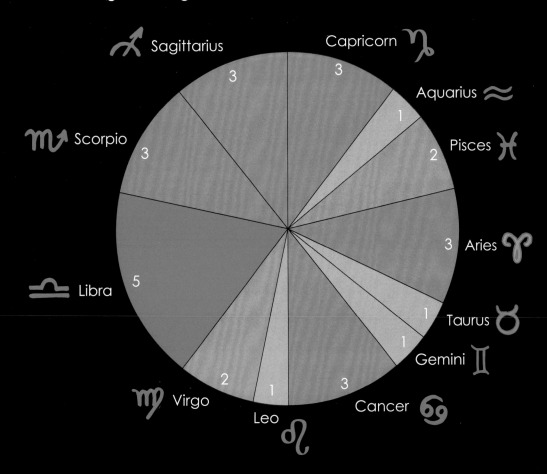

LIVING THE LIFE ON TWITTER

Tweets, Twittering, and Twittersnappers

Twitter is the form of social networking that has defined the revolution of instant communication. Love it or loathe it, it has nonetheless firmly nailed its intention at the door of comment.

With regards to 'Living the Life' its influence was tangible and an excellent example of a new kind of interaction between, viewer, performer and broadcaster. We had the stalwarts and so called 'twitterati' in Stephen Fry and Caitlin Moran through all levels of participation to newly ensconced @lesliephillips_.

Stephen kept his followers updated during the days filming, Caitlin confessed to feeling much more comfortable behind her laptop and the verbal sparring of twitter compared to being in front of the camera, and Leslie Phillips garnered 20,000 followers over lunch and trended a new phrase #twittersnappers.

Many of our other contributors and the production team got involved and their tweets fed comment out into the digital ether of certain episodes and also viewers feedback. Below is a small representation of some of the threads that were generated in the name of @_LivingTheLife_.

@missbrittekland
Britt Ekland

Living the life: Britt Ekland meets Brigitte Nielsen-watch a preview of the show now http://t.co/sp17bmil @brigittenielsen @missbrittekland

09/12/2011 via Twitter

@lesliephillips_
Leslie Phillips

@GameOfThrones: Game of Thrones is out... Charles Dance Paul MCGann discuss" Living The Life"22nd Jan Sky Arts 8pm Captivating x

27/11/2011 via Twitter for iPad

 **@skyarts**
Sky Arts 1 HD / 2 HD

Cricket icon Sir Ian Botham and musical impresario Sir Tim Rice chat about life in the spotlight tonight: http://t.co/ywlvmovb

15/12/2011 via Twitter

@lumleynews
Joanna Lumley

Joanna will appear on the Sky Arts programme "Living the Life" on the 13th of November! Make sure you don't miss it: http://t.co/bwp1bhgq

07/11/2011 via Twitter

@juleslifeforce
Jules Williams

Dylan Jones meets George Lamb for Sky's Living the Life - http://t.co/afqnq7ui (uk) http://t.co/bmcep8c via @gqrecommends

27/11/2011 via Twitter for iPhone

@_livingthelife_
Living The Life

"@MissBrittEkland: Tequilla still sleeping http://t.co/affa1vg4" Darling he is just resting until his debut in "living the life" tonight X

11/12/2011 via Twitter

@caitlinmoran
Caitlin Moran

I'm all OVER the place like a TV rash: at 8pm, me and Fay Weldon in converstaion in Sky Arts "Living The Life". We get quite tiddly.

04/12/2011 via Twitter

@lesliephillips_
Leslie Phillips

Just setting down, fire and slippers with two darling ladies (watching Living The Life with the wonderful @caitlinmoran and Fay Weldon) DD

04/12/2011 via Twitter for iPad

@gqrecomends
GQ Recommends

TV Pick: Watch @_LivingTheLife_ this weekend with @DylanJonesGQ and @GeorgeLambShow http://t.co/kj3tqe6m

25/11/2011 via Twitter for iPad

@mcgannlibrary
mcgannlibrary

Watch Paul McGann and Charles Dance in an episode of @_LivingTheLife_ 22 Jan on Sky Arts http://t.co/gyql04gr

02/11/2011 via Twitter

JACK REED

'Runner' and assistant to Leslie Phillips

Jack, the Jack Russell with a penchant for sets, filming and crew nibbles. A much loved member of the family he liked to arrive on set early and oversee the setting up of equipment and revel in his role as chief sniffer as and when newcomers turned up to film.

He has recently recovered from 'collar envy' when Tequila arrived on set with a theatrical flourish matching Brit Eklands dress. Some of his finer moments have been captured below.

JACK x

279